MANKIND'S OEDIPAL DESTINY

MANKIND'S OEDIPAL DESTINY:

LIBIDINAL AND AGGRESSIVE ASPECTS OF SEXUALITY

Peter Hartocollis, M.D., Ph.D., Editor

INTERNATIONAL UNIVERSITIES PRESS, INC.
Madison Connecticut

Library of Congress Cataloging-in-Publication Data

Mankind's oedipal destiny : libidinal and aggressive aspects of sexuality / Peter Hartocollis, editor.

p. cm.

Includes bibliographical references and indexes.

ISBN 0-8236-3097-8

1. Oedipus complex—Congresses. 2. Sex (Psychology)—Congresses. 3. Psychoanalysis—Congresses. I. Hartocollis, Peter.

BF175.5.033 M26 2000

155.3—dc21

00-057222

Manufactured in the United States of America

CONTENTS

Contributors vii

Preface: An Overview of the Fourth International Psychoanalytic Symposium at Delphi
Peter Hartocollis ix

Chapter 1:
Sexuality in Nonneurotic Structures: Yesterday and Today
André Green 1

Chapter 2:
New Perspectives on the Oedipus Complex
Hanna Segal 25

Chapter 3:
Experiencing the Phallus as Extraneous: Women's Twofold Oedipus Complex
Julia Kristeva 37

Chapter 4:
From Oedipal Problems to Phallic Universe
Pentti Ikonen 55

Chapter 5:
Moral Masochism and the Affect of Resentment
Friedrich-Wilhelm Eickhoff 77

Chapter 6:
The Concept of Libido in the Light of Contemporary Psychoanalytic Theorizing
Otto F. Kernberg 95

Chapter 7:
The Oedipus Complex and Male Homosexuality
Richard C. Friedman & Jennifer I. Downey 113

Chapter 8:
On Homosexual Dread and Homosexual Desire
Charles W. Socarides 139
Chapter 9:
The Oedipus Complex and the "Third Position"
Judy Gammelgaard 171
Chapter 10:
Oedipus and the Search for Reality
Charles Hanly 187
Chapter 11:
Matricide and the Oedipus Complex
Harold P. Blum 209
Chapter 12:
The Oedipus Complex as a Lifelong Developmental Process: A Psychoanalytic Reading of Sophocles' *Trachiniae*
Michael Parsons 229
Chapter 13:
Prohibition and Transience
Osamu Kitayama 251

Name Index 271
Subject Index 275

CONTRIBUTORS

Harold P. Blum, M.D. Member of the American and Vice President of the International Psychoanalytic Association; Honorary Member of the Hellenic Psychoanalytic Society; Training and Supervising Analyst, New York Psychoanalytic Society; Director of the Sigmund Freud Archives.

Jennifer I. Downey, M.D. Associate Clinical Professor of Psychiatry, Department of Physicians and Surgeons, Columbia University, New York City.

Friedrich-Wilhelm Eickhoff, M.D. Member of both the German and International Psychoanalytic Association; Editor, *Jahrbuch der Psychoanalyse;* Training and Supervising Analyst of the German Psychoanalytic Association; Vice President, Archiv zur Geschichte der Psychoanalyse e.V.

Richard C. Friedman, M.D. Member of both the American and the International Psychoanalytic Association; Clinical Professor of Psychiatry, Cornell University Medical Center; Research Professor of Psychology, Derner Institute, Adelphi University, Garden City, New York.

Judy Gammelgaard, Ph.D. Member of the Danish Psychoanalytic Society and of the International Psychoanalytic Association; Assistant Professor, Department of Psychology, University of Copenhagen.

André Green, M.D. Member of the Paris Psychoanalytic Society and of the International Psychoanalytic Association; Training and Supervising Analyst, Paris Psychoanalytic Society.

Charles Hanly, Ph.D. Member of the Canadian Psychoanalytic Society (Toronto Branch), and Vice President of the International Psychoanalytic Society; Training and Supervising Analyst of the Canadian Psychoanalytic Society; Professor Emeritus of Philosophy, University of Toronto; Honorary member, Institute for Psychoanalytic Training and Research, New York.

Peter Hartocollis, M.D., Ph.D. Member of both the American and the International Psychoanalytic Association; Training and Supervising Analyst of the Hellenic Psychoanalytic Society; Professor Emeritus of Psychiatry, University of Patras, Greece.

Pentti Ikonen, Phil. Mag. Member of the Finnish Psychoanalytic Society and of the International Psychoanalytic Association; Training and Supervising Analyst, Finnish Psychoanalytic Society.

Otto F. Kernberg, M.D. Member of the American and President of the International Psychoanalytic Association; Professor of Psychiatry, Cornell University Medical College; Director, Personality Disorders Institute, New York Hospital, Westchester Division; Training and Supervising Analyst, Columbia University Center for Psychoanalytic Training and Research.

Osamu Kitayama, M.D. Member of the Psychoanalytic Society of Japan and of the International Psychoanalytic Association; Professor of Psychoanalysis, Graduate School of Human-Environment Studies, Kyushu University, Japan.

Julia Kristeva, Ph.D. Member of the Paris Psychoanalytic Society and of the International Psychoanalytic Association; Director, Ecole Doctorale, Langues, Litteratures et Civilisations, University of Paris.

Michael Parsons, M.A., M.R.C.P., M.R.C.Psych. Member of the British Psychoanalytic Society and of the International Psychoanalytic Association; Training and Supervising Analyst of the British Psychoanalytic Society.

Hanna Segal, M.B., Ch.B., F.R.C.Psych. Member of the British Psychoanalytic Society and of the International Psychoanalytic Association.

Charles W. Socarides, M.D., F.A.C., P.S.A. Member of both the American and the International Psychoanalytic Association; President, National Association for Psychoanalytic Research and Therapy of Homosexuality.

PREFACE: An Overview of the Fourth International Psychoanalytic Symposium at Delphi

When Freud discovered that the roots or, rather, the "nucleus," as he called it, of his adult sexuality and neurosis was grounded in his sexual attraction to the mother of childhood and his rivalry (hatred and fear) toward the father of childhood, he recalled a Greek drama he had read in high school, Sophocles' *Oedipus Rex.* The recollection, whether sudden or insidious we don't know, gave him the idea that his childhood fantasy was more than a private, idiosyncratic affair; that it was, indeed, inherent in human nature, an oedipal destiny fraught with conflictual libidinal and aggressive wishes that determine an individual's personality development. An irreverent commentator might say that the Oedipus story, as enacted in Sophocles' play, impressed Freud's adolescent imagination so much that, years later, he read it into his own case—a spurious argument, a psychoanalyst would say, for young Freud would not be so impressed unless the myth resonated with his own oedipal conflict.

Be that as it may, few analysts then or now would dispute the existence of the Oedipus complex (Kohut just ignored it). And yet, many new clinical findings and concepts have been discovered since Freud's time, not to speak of extra-analytic observations and research findings, to warrant the question whether the nuclear concept of psychoanalysis remains at the center of our theory. To begin with, there is Freud's own reference to preoedipal determinants of human personality, studied systematically by his followers in Europe and somewhat belatedly in the United States, along with a controversy that has surrounded the concept, especially in the United States, with regard to female sexuality and, more recently, with regard to sexual orientation or preference. So the question became the theme of the Fourth International Psychoanalytic Symposium at Delphi (a scientific and cultural enterprise carried out jointly by a small group of Greek and Canadian psychoanalysts since the early 1980s), when the editor of the present volume undertook to organize it in the summer of 1996, as always in Delphi.

What better place than Delphi to discuss the Oedipus complex! The gathering included psychoanalysts and mental health professionals with a psychoanalytic frame of mind from around the world. Those who led the discussion were selected not because they had written before about the subject, but because they knew the theory well and could conceptualize in an original way, yet represented current points of view nationally and internationally—object relations theory and psychoanalytic ego psychology; Kleinian and French psychoanalysis as influenced by Winnicott and Lacan; Central European and Scandinavian points of view; and, from the other side of the world, Japanese. My assignment to them was to reexamine the theme of the Oedipus complex in the context of psychosexual development and evaluate its importance in the formation of adult sexuality, whether or not the Oedipus complex was an obligatory determinant of mature sexuality, be it heterosexual, bisexual, or homosexual.

Curiously enough, though not surprisingly in retrospect, few were willing to comply literally with my instructions, especially when it came to speaking about object choice as a major aspect of adult sexuality. Some chose to focus their discourse on hitherto ignored or undervalued aspects of the Oedipus complex implicit in Greek mythology and the tragic poets, in particular the Oedipus myth.

The symposium papers that make up the thirteen chapters of the present volume were arranged so that they were relevant to the theme of adult sexuality and its relationship to the Oedipus complex as I had in mind when I invited their authors to the Symposium, those dealing with the theme only tangentially (in my view rather than theirs), being placed later in the book. As the theme of sexuality is ubiquitous in psychoanalysis, I placed papers using a particular subtheme or paradigm, like phallicism or the myth of Oedipus, together. In other words, there was no intention to rank the papers according to their presumed significance or to please their authors, with one exception: my placing André Green's contribution first was a sentimental gesture, as it took me back to the time I was editing the proceedings of the *Borderline Personality Disorders* (Hartocollis, 1977) conference in Topeka, when I had placed his paper after that of Bion; and as Bion was no longer with us, I gave Green his place in the new book. Besides, it so happened that the theme of the Symposium was suggested by him at the end of the previous Delphi Symposium.

According to Green, the main thing that happened to the Oedipus complex and our approach to sexuality since Freud's time has been a shift of emphasis from the classical neuroses (Oedipus), to the preoedipal pathology of the borderline personality disorders (Narcissus), already implied in Freud's case of the Wolf Man with its archaic sexuality ("primary anality") and psychoticlike mentality.

The emphasis on archaic sexuality and a pregenital phase of the Oedipus complex are Melanie Klein's contributions to the theory, as Hanna Segal reminds us in the second chapter of the book. According to Segal, perhaps the most authoritative Kleinian thinker of our time, the child begins "coming to terms" with the Oedipus complex while working through the depressive position, in what she describes as a "third area" of developmental space. Drawing our attention to Bion's pair of basic concepts, "the container" and "the contained," she discusses their role in the development of the mental apparatus, the capacity to symbolize and to think, together with the development of self-awareness, which she sees as a function of the early Oedipus complex and the experience of the observing part of the child in the primal scene.

Julia Kristeva, the maverick Parisian analyst with a literary bent, who neither hides nor touts her reliance on Lacan, believes (with Freud) that psychic bisexuality is more pronounced in women, being related to a preoccupation with the phallus ("phallicism"). The infantile illusion that there is only one sex, identified with the possession of a penis, conditions the Oedipus complex, dominating the unconscious of both genders. The illusory character of the phallus in women gives rise to passivity and the desire to have a penis—penis envy being a variant of phallicism—leading to masculine protest or, "more naturally," to the desire for a child and motherhood.

Phallicism as a defense against the problems of the Oedipus complex for both women and men is the theme of another European analyst, Pentti Ikonen of Finland. The infant's inadequacy as a sexual partner to adults, emerging in primal scene fantasies and relived later on within the oedipal situation, is experienced as humiliation or offense to the child's narcissism, irrespective of gender. Whether as a stage of psychosexual development or as a defensive organization against oedipal disappointments and narcissistic insults, the phallic organization denies the mutuality that characterizes human sexual relations to the effect that sexuality becomes gradually phallicized—invested with phallicism. Phallicism and the idea of forcible penetration inherent in it molds our image of power and, socially encouraged, breeds a culture of exhibitionism and violence.

German analyst Friedrich-Wilhelm Eickhoff approaches the theme of the Oedipus complex in its relationship to moral masochism, reviewing critically the Freudian, Kleinian, and French (in particular Bela Grunberger's) point of view along with its sociocultural implications.

Indebted to French analysts, in particular Laplanche, one of the most influential thinkers in contemporary American psychoanalysis, Otto Kernberg, presents an "updated attempt" to link dual drive theory (formerly referred to by himself as ego psychology) with object relations theory. Kernberg's central formulation is encompassed in the following phrase: "Under conditions of peak positive or negative affect states, highly intense experiences of the infant in his relationship with mother generate primary, all pleasurable and gratifying, and all painful and frightening units of self and object representations." Of crucial importance for this development is the affect of sexual excitement ("a central aspect of libido") and the affect of hatred ("a central aspect of the death drive"). Their integration with object relations results in the manifestations of unconscious erotic desire, while fantasies involving the primal scene, the oedipal seduction, and concomitant castration anxiety are part-and-parcel of the fantasied object relations that emerge in the psychoanalytic situation. Serious pathology of internalized object relations, as in severe personality disorders, may affect adversely the nature of gender identity or result in the extinction of the erotic response.

Is homosexuality the manifestation of an incomplete psychosexual development indicating an arrested or inverted oedipal phase, an unresolved Oedipus complex, as Freud and mainstream psychoanalysis would have it? Is it a treatable mental disorder or sexual perversion with its own preoedipal and oedipal dynamics? Not so, according to Richard Friedman, extra-analytic researcher and psychoanalytic clinician from New York. He, together with like-minded colleague Jennifer Downey, argues that psychodynamic formulations regarding homosexuality are of dubious validity as they derive from patients seeking treatment for neurotic or borderline personality disorders; and that successful analysis may result in conflict resolution and symptom relief but no change in sexual orientation. Friedman and Downey point out that childhood sexuality viewed from the position of adulthood, as in analysis, is subject to retrospective distortion. Although the onset of sexuality occurs during childhood, it is in the form of elements of sexual activity that do not become fully integrated until puberty or adolescence. Erotic object choice is usually not the outcome of unresolved preoedipal or oedipal conflicts. Hormonal considerations are important in this respect. Friedman and Downey imply that most of our cherished formulations about the Oedipus complex and sexuality are fanciful constructions unsupported by unbiased clinical experience and biopsychological research.

Charles Socarides, also from New York, stands on the other side of the argument. He makes his point by examining the syndrome of "homosexual dread" that afflicts some heterosexual individuals who entertain homosexual fantasies and the fear that they may be homosexual. He maintains that "homosexual dread" is not a defensive reaction against the enactment of repressed true homosexuality, but a defense against regression of the ego to an undifferentiated state with the revival of early oral and anal incorporative fantasies. Such patients unconsciously wish to incorporate the paternal phallus in order to ensure a masculine identity (an idea echoing Grumberger's and, for that matter, Segal's dynamics of normal male sexuality) and to make up for early childhood deprivations and the sense of abandonment and despair.

A number of speakers chose to build their view of sexuality using the Oedipus myth as a frame of reference.

The shift of emphasis to a pregenital stage of development is what Judy Gammelgaard of Denmark underscores in a chapter colored by her background in philosophy. Contending that Sophocles' two plays, *Oedipus Rex* and *Oedipus at Colonus,* have more in common than the name of the tragic hero, she argues that only by abandoning the oedipal triangle and developing a clearer awareness of oneself can one dissolve the guilt associated with the Oedipus complex. Adopting Ronald Britton's (1985) Kleinian concept of the "third position" (equivalent to Segal's "third area") regarding the Oedipus complex and the child's experience as an observer in the "triangular space" of the oedipal situation, she pays particular attention to the emergence of self-consciousness, which she associates with the consciousness of time, supporting her arguments with insights from existential philosophers, as continental analysts explicitly or implicitly do, particularly in France.

Charles Hanly of Toronto, another psychoanalyst who is also a philosopher, refers to the Oedipus complex myth in the context of Sophocles' first Oedipus tragedy. Pointing out that narrative truth is "potentially more profound" than historical truth, he sees the play of Sophocles as reflecting the struggle of the ancient Greeks with the "evolving awareness" of their Oedipus complex, which he connects with the capacity for self-awareness and objectivity. The triangulation of the preoedipal and oedipal situation provides the child with the ability to experience himself in the relationship with one parent as being observed by the other—the ability to be subjective—while the resolution of the Oedipus complex allows for the emergence of rationality and the establishment of the ability to be objective. On the paradigm of *Oedipus Rex,* Hanly examines the relationship of the Oedipus complex with the concepts of psychic determinism and personal responsibility, to conclude that "Mature sexuality [and the sense of responsibility] may owe little to the Oedipus complex, but it owes everything to its resolution."

Harold Blum, a prominent American analyst and scholar, explores a hitherto neglected aspect of the Oedipus myth, matricide, emphasizing its importance for an understanding of the Oedipus complex, which, according to Blum, contains "symmetrical" unconscious murderous wishes involving both parents. Matricidal fantasies are more apparent in borderline patients, clinical evidence pointing to preoedipal disturbances in their mother–child relationship. Matricide is frequently depicted in myth and literature, the prototypical matricidal hero being Orestes, prompted by his sister Electra. It is an often overlooked component of oedipal fantasy, invested with preoedipal aggression and hatred against mother, but difficult to clarify and reconstruct in analysis because a matricidal transference tends to be displaced onto parricidal fantasies and identification with father.

Another Sophoclean tragedy, far less well known than *Oedipus Rex, The Women of Trachis,* is the paradigm for British analyst Michael Parsons in his treatment of sexuality. He thinks that, in spite of their dissimilarities, both plays are motivated by the playwright's Oedipus complex. Like practically everyone else in the Symposium, Parsons emphasized the significance of triangularity in the child's relationship with his parents. The action in the particular play is driven by sex and aggression. Alongside the oedipal triangle, the play enacts an inverted (generational) oedipal conflict, the father's competitive desire for a woman the age of his son, leading to the destruction of the oedipal triangle with the parents' demise and then to restoration (reparation) by the dying father's bequest of his youthful mistress to his awe-stricken son.

A Japanese view of sexuality and the Oedipus complex is offered by Osamu Kitayama with the visual aid of ancestral mythology and folktales. Built around the concept of transience, ubiquitous in Japan's traditional culture and everyday mentality, he traces adult sexuality to the maternal prohibition of looking at the sexual act performed by the parents in the baby's presence. The prohibition is eventually broken with awesome consequences for the maternal image with the generation of guilt and reparation in the young boy.

As I explained at the beginning of this introductory chapter, I do not think it is my task to evaluate the contents of the present volume. Others can certainly do it more objectively than I can. But I may be able to comment on the state of the theory regarding sexuality and the Oedipus complex as it looks from the perspective of the Fourth Delphi Symposium. For one thing, there is little doubt that the preoedipal situation has gained in importance, giving added impetus or credibility to Kleinian theory. In fact, there was little argument among psychoanalysts of different persuations when it came to talking about preoedipal dynamics. Kleinian concepts, whether consonant with Freud's ideas or not—the triangular nature of the primal scene and the importance of the father figure or the phallus long before the establishment of the Oedipus complex, the schizoid and in particular the depressive position, and the significance of its working through for the emergence of the sense of guilt—were used freely by practically everyone.

Another trend that was apparent in the thinking of the analysts who took part in the Delphi Symposium, some of whom have chapters in this volume, was an interest in phenomenological concepts such as self-awareness or self-consciousness, subjectivity and objectivity, also affects, along with a readiness to refer to unconscious fantasy, another Kleinian emphasis that at times gave the impression of an easy resort to a safe area for concepts that might sound paradoxical or arbitrary.

A paradigm that came easy with some presenters as a frame of reference or justification for concepts related to the Oedipus complex was the Oedipus myth itself or other Greek myths and tragedies. In my estimation, this is a dubious practice considering the fact that there are many and often contradictory versions of the same myth, while a particular tragedy may reflect the playwright's conscious or unconscious motivation and inventiveness rather than universal dynamics.

The interest in phenomenology or existential concepts may be tied to French psychoanalysis, either directly through Lacan or indirectly through Green, Laplanche, and others, who, besides their reference to concepts deriving from philosophy (Hegel, Peirce, Heidegger, Cassirer, Sartre), shy away from Freud's structural theory ("deuxième topique"), insisting on the economic point of view while espousing his (and Melanie Klein's) controversial concept of the death instinct or drive. Narcissism, implicit in borderline pathology, was often mentioned, particularly by André Green and Otto Kernberg, while the issue of homosexuality, except in the case of "specialists" like Friedman and Socarides, was handled with diffidence, viewed implicitly in the Freudian tradition as a perversion of preoedipal origin.

In closing this overview of the Symposium's presentations, I would like to express my gratitude to those who, next to the speakers, helped make it successful, beginning with the members of the Greek Organizing Committee, nearly all of them members of the Hellenic Provisional Psychoanalytic Society: Costas Bazaridis, Stavroula Beratis, Calliopi Hartocollis, Sotiris Manolopoulos, Olga Panopoulou-Maratou, Manos Sotiriadis, Nicolas Tzavaras, and the Committee's administrative secretary Eleni Vouga, whose tireless, competent, and personable performance helped everybody find his way, starting with me, before and during the Symposium.

My thanks also go to the members of the Canadian Organizing Committee, Ian Graham (scientific cochairman), Georgie and John Babatzanis; to the members of the International Advisory Committee: Jacqueline Amati-Mehler (Italy), Konstantinos Arvanitakis (Canada), Christopher Bollas (U.K.), Fidias R. Cesio (Argentina), Henk J. Dalewijk (Netherlands), Terttu Eskelinen de Folch (Spain), Luis Feder (Mexico), Alain Gibeault (France), Ilse Grubrich-Simitis (Germany), Max Hernandez (Peru), Alex Holder (Germany), Jose A. Infante (Chile), James Innes-Smith (Belgium), Tetsuya Iwasaki (Japan), Reimer Jensen (Denmark), Sudhir Kakar (India), Paulina Kernberg (U.S.A.), Bo Larsson (Sweden), Eva Lester (Canada), Andre Lussier (Canada), Nicos Nicolaidis (Switzerland), Jose Rallo-Romero (Spain), Arlene Kramer Richards (U.S.A.), Guy Rosolato (France), Simo Salonen (Finland), Anne-Marie Sandler (U.K.), Janice de Saussure (Switzerland), Lore Schacht (Germany), Ron Spielman (Australia), Carlo Vittorio Todesco (Italy), Robert S. Wallerstein (U.S.A.); and to the President of the European Cultural Center of Delphi, Professor Vasilis Karasmanis along with his staff in Athens and in Delphi.

Finally, I would like to express my special appreciation to Ioannis Stamoulis, Governor at that time of the District of Boetia, and his staff at the prefecture of Levadia who, along with the codirectors of the National Museum of Delphi, Rozina Kolonia and Despina Skorda, helped me materialize a youthful dream of mine, the erection of a memorial at the crossroads, the meeting place of roads from Delphi going north to Davlia and west to Thebes, the Split Road (Schisti Odos), as it was known in ancient times, where the young prince Oedipus, trying to evade his human destiny as revealed to him by Apollo's oracle at Delphi, killed a man who happened to be the king of Thebes and his own father; and, going on to the city of Thebes, took as his wife the king's widow, who happened to be his own mother. I may add that, until the erection of the Oedipus monument, most of the modern inhabitants of the area ignored (or, to be more charitable, had repressed) the name of their tragic ancestor and, of course, the oedipal legend itself, identifying the place with the monument of Megas, a white marble cross on the top of a rocky hill overlooking the crossroads from Delphi to Davlia and to Thebes commemorating the killing of an army officer by that name by a notorious 19th century bandit named Davelis. After all, didn't the ancient Thebans believe, until Oedipus' search brought to light the awful truth, that their king Laïus had been murdered by a bandit?

The new memorial, inaugurated on July 27, 1996, by Otto Kernberg, President Elect of the International Psychoanalytic Association at that time, and myself, President of the Hellenic Psychoanalytic Association, carries a gray marble plaque on which the following lines from Sophocles' *Oedipus Rex* are engraved:

ΟΙΔΙΠΟΥΣ ΕΔΟΞ ΑΚΟΥΣΑΙ ΣΟΥ ΤΟΔ ΩΣ Ο ΛΑΙΟΣ
ΚΑΤΑΣΦΑΓΕΙΣ ΠΡΟΣ ΤΡΙΠΛΑΙΣ ΑΜΑΞΙΤΟΙΣ
ΙΟΚΑΣΤΗ ΗΥΔΑΤΟ ΓΑΡ ΤΑΥΤ ΟΥΔΕ ΠΩ ΛΗΞΑΝΤ ΕΧΕΙ
ΟΙΔΙΠΟΥΣ ΚΑΙ ΠΟΥ ΣΘ Ο ΧΩΡΟΣ ΟΥΤΟΣ ΟΥ ΤΟΔ ΗΝ ΠΑΘΟΣ
ΙΟΚΑΣΤΗ ΦΩΚΙΣ ΜΕΝ Η ΓΗ ΚΛΗΙΖΕΤΑΙ ΣΧΙΣΤΗ Δ ΟΔΟΣ
ΕΣ ΤΑΥΤΟ ΔΕΛΦΩΝ ΚΑΠΟ ΔΑΥΛΙΑΣ ΑΦΕΙ[1]

OEDIPUS I thought I heard you say that Laius
was murdered at the crossing of three roads.
JOCASTA That's what they said and they still say it now.
OEDIPUS And where is that land where the murder took place?
JOCASTA Phokis is the name of the land, a split road
leads there from Delphi and Davlia [Translation of Sophocles' verses].

References

Britton, R. S. (1985), The Oedipus complex and the depressive position. *Sigmund Freud House Bull.*, Vienna, 9:7–12.

Hartocollis, P., Ed. (1977), *Borderline Personality Disorders.* New York: International Universities Press.

1

Sexuality in Nonneurotic Structures: Yesterday and Today

ANDRÉ GREEN, M.D.

In the last few decades the central topic of interest in clinical psychoanalysis has shifted from the so-called classical neuroses to the borderline personality disorders. This change has been associated with a corresponding shift from sexuality to ego functioning or to object relationships. In fact, neither ego disturbances nor regressive object relationships should be separated from sexuality and its vicissitudes.

To understand the present situation, one must go back to the firm basis of Freud's psychoanalysis. The relationship between sexuality and the neuroses has implications for an understanding of the coherence of Freud's point of view. If we consider Freud's work as a whole, we can detect a turning point: the analysis of the Wolf Man. Freud (1918) presents in that work some views which are new. He describes hitherto unheard of defense mechanisms: splitting and foreclosure (even if he does not name them specifically). It is now agreed that the case of the Wolf Man opens the way for the study of borderline states. Later on, archaic sexuality will become a topic of major interest not only in the emphasis of pregenital fixation, but also because of its association with primitive ego defenses. Defensive genitalization of conflicts of a different nature (pregenital or narcissistic) are frequently met with in contemporary psychoanalysis. The field of analysis has been extended to face relationships which deserve to be called analytic as well, because of the type of work which takes place in a modified setting. Our views about sexuality are thus changed. It would not be correct to argue that the role of sexuality in these (pregenital or narcissistic) structures is less important than in the neuroses. It would be more appropriate to say that it is different. Finally, in view of all these changes, we will have to ask ourselves what is the meaning of sexuality.

Sexuality and the Neuroses

The relationship between sexuality and the neuroses is so close in Freud's psychoanalysis that each of the two terms irresistibly evokes the other. Nevertheless such a link also calls for certain distinctions. The nosographical differences Freud established from the start between transference psychoneurosis, actual neurosis, and narcissistic neurosis imply that libido undergoes different transformations in each instance. Briefly, actual neurosis results from a lack of elaboration of the libido and leads to direct discharge of tensions in the soma; in contemporary psychoanalysis, Freud's conceptualization of the actual neuroses has proven useful for the understanding of psychosomatic disorders, as formulated by the Paris Psychosomatic School of Pierre Marty. Narcissistic neuroses are supposed to show a lack of possibilities to transfer libido from one individual to another, because of the withdrawal of libido and its imprisonment in the ego. This observation is discussed later. It is still true that psychotic "transferences" are of a very different kind. From these remarks we can observe that two parameters are implicit here: the *soma,* differing from the body and its libido, and the *Other,* the other person to whom the infantile conflicts can be reprojected and analyzed. Even though this conception of psychosis is questioned today, we cannot ignore the severe narcissistic regressions of advanced psychotic states, with their massive withdrawal from reality. It is easy to deduce that the transference psychoneuroses deserved their name from two parameters: (1) an intrapsychic one, with its sexual determinations, implying that we are dealing here less with biological sex and more with psychosexuality and its internal vicissitudes; (2) a transference, which was supposed to be twofold: transference from the somatic to the psychic, with its focus either on the body or on the intellect (as in hysteria and obsessional neurosis); and transference from the past to the present whereby the primary conflict with the parental figures could be displaced later on other figures of adulthood and then to their representative in the analysis: the analyst. Moreover, it was assumed that there was a very close relationship linking the infantile neurosis, which occurred in childhood, the psychoneurosis of adulthood, symptoms of which force the patient to seek treatment, and the transference neurosis, an artificial illness produced by the treatment, which was easier to analyze and therefore to dissolve, allowing the reconstruction of the repressed infantile neurosis, while the treatment relieved the patient of his adult transference psychoneurosis.

This is, of course, only a schematic conception of what was supposed to happen in the patient and how psychoanalysis cured him. After a certain time, this elegant but rather ideal scheme was contradicted by clinical experience. Its triangulation was valid essentially with patients whose personality structure presented a positive oedipal organization. It was far from convincing when the patients presented negative Oedipus complex fixations and even less when there were predominant pregenital fixations. A challenge to this scheme materialized in 1914 with the analysis of a famous, maybe too famous, patient.

The Turning Point: The Analysis of the Wolf Man

The Wolf Man case was probably the turning point when Freud's earlier (1918) model was questioned. We know that this case was written to meet Jung's objections against the importance Freud attached to the past. The title of Freud's study is, "From the History of an Infantile Neurosis," which raises the question: What about the patient's adult neurosis? Nothing is said about the diagnosis of the patient's actual illness. The vast majority of analysts today have not the slightest doubt about the diagnosis of the Wolf Man, who can hardly be diagnosed as neurotic. It is interesting that Freud neither says what kind of neurosis his Russian patient suffered from nor presents any diagnostic alternative. It seems certain that Freud would not have liked the idea that his patient was psychotic. Sergei Pankejeff could not be classified in the same category of illness as Daniel Paul Shreber. And the concept of borderline personality disorder or disorders was not available to Freud at that time. When we read today about the Wolf Man's second analysis with Ruth Mack Brunswick, or those other analysts (W. Solms, Kurt Eissler, and M. Gardiner) who attempted to treat him later (Gardiner, 1971),[1] we get a strong conviction that the patient really belongs to this category. The document most revealing about the personality structure of the patient is the book containing his interviews with the journalist Karin Obholzer (1981). The book has not been welcomed by analysts, because its author was not a professional, and also because she succeeded in by-passing the opposition of the official healers of Sergei Pankejeff to meet him regularly. But even if we leave the last word to the patient himself, his autobiographical *Memories* (Gardiner, 1970) unveils his hidden personality structure when one reads between the lines. Apart from the testimony of those who had direct contact with the patient, the literature on the Wolf Man is abundant, varied, and multifaceted. Is there any major author of psychoanalytic literature who has resisted giving his or her own interpretation of the case? These comments express as many different points of view as one might expect in the spectrum from Klein to Lacan. In spite of my interest in analyzing this chapter of analytic history, I would rather go back for a while to Freud's work, for his description of the case under question is unique.

So far as sexuality is concerned, one notable fact in Freud's writing is the importance of anal eroticism. Let us compare the Rat Man and the Wolf Man because both deal with that central issue. What stands out concretely is the anal component of each case. The Rat Man was an obsessional neurotic in his adulthood.

[1]This book includes Freud's original essay "On the History of an Infantile Neurosis," editor R. Mack Brunswick's "Supplement," "The Memories of the Wolf Man," and other contributions.

The Wolf Man's adult clinical picture was preceded by the obsessional neurosis of a child. Patrick Mahony (1984) rightly suggests that the title of Freud's work should have been: "From the History of an Infantile Psychosis." We are already familiar with the sophisticated procedures of obsessional thought since the Rat Man. But with the Wolf Man, it is an entirely different situation. The anal fixations of the Russian were reflected in his constipation and the regular practice of relieving his bowels by producing a constant excitation of his anus and rectum with the enemas given by other men. These disturbances were associated with various psychical symptoms related to his mismanagement of his wealth, fear of death (through dysenteria), fantasies of childbirth; stools symbolized as small animals were equated with babies[2]; homosexual fantasies were related to feminine identification with his mother and so on. But all this cannot account for the specificity of the patient's personality structure. Freud is aware (even more than any of the other psychoanalysts who treated the Wolf Man) of the patient's peculiar mental condition. Having to decide between two versions of the sexual act (through the vagina or through the anus), Sergei Pankejeff could not come to a conclusion. "The two points of view remained separated from each other by a stage of repression" (Freud, 1918, p. 80). This can be considered as a preliminary intuition of splitting, which was to be described only thirteen years later by Freud's (1917) in his 1927 paper "Fetishism." I have extended this observation, proposing to call the Wolf Man's thinking "biological" (Green, 1982). I am not going to give here the details of the idea. I will only define it as the paradoxical coexistence of a double contradictory opinion on points of major importance for psychological development. One can immediately grasp its relationship to splitting, but what I am alluding to is different. Freud (1918) observed the peculiarities of the attitude of the Wolf Man toward castration. "First he resisted and then he yielded; but the second reaction did not *do away with* the first" (p. 85). Hence the difference with the neurotic process: repression, return of the repressed,

[2]One should remember that Freud's paper "On Transformation of Instinct as Exemplified in Anal Eroticism" was written in 1917 and refers at many points to the case of the Wolf Man.

resistance, interpretation, insight, recognition. Instead, we have a coexistence of currents: one abominating castration, the second accepting it, but at the expense of the penis being replaced by the anus as a source of pleasure, conducive to feminine identification. In recapitulating the case, Freud (1918) again raised the question of the peculiarities of the patient's "mentality," revealed by the psychoanalytic treatment: "tenacity of fixation . . . extraordinary propensity to ambivalence, and (as a third trait in a constitution which deserves the name of archaic) his power of maintaining simultaneously the most various and contradictory libidinal cathexes, all of them capable of functioning side by side" (pp. 118–119). Freud considered that "third trait" as normally belonging to the unconscious, which in the Wolf Man's case persisted in consciousness. I am quoting Freud's statements in order to show how in this neurotic structure the fixation of sexuality on a pregenital level is regularly associated with a disorder in the patient's "mentality." In other words, the sexual sphere is affecting ego functioning, the ability to make judgments. Allow me to use once more a quotation from Freud, which I find important, from the celebrated paper, "Neurosis and Psychosis" (Freud, 1924).

> [In some cases, neither neurotic nor openly psychotic], it will be possible for the ego to avoid a rupture in any direction by deforming itself, by submitting to encroachments on its own unity and even perhaps by effecting a cleavage or division of itself. In this way the inconsistencies, eccentricities and follies of men would appear in a similar light to their sexual perversions, through the acceptance of which they spare themselves repressions [pp. 152–153].

The above sentence draws a parallel between sexual perversions and the results of splitting in the ego. There are very few instances in Freud's work of such a relationship so clearly delineated.

Lacan has already observed the presence in Freud's text of a new variety of repression: *Verwerfung* (foreclosure), a kind of radical rejection. Here again, I must apologize for not being able to discuss the matter in detail. Let me only quote Freud's (1918) comment on the process:

> We are already acquainted with the attitude which our patient first adopted to the problem of castration. He rejected castration, and held to his theory of intercourse by the anus. When I speak of his having rejected it, the first meaning of the phrase is that *he would have nothing to do with it,* in the sense of having repressed it. *This really involved no judgement upon the question of its existence, but it was the same as if it did not exist* [p. 84; emphasis added].

Freud's descriptions of the thought disturbances of the patient are striking when one remembers that they were written in 1914. Moreover, we can see that the Wolf Man stands just in between the Rat Man and *Senats präsident* Schreber. Their common link is through anality, which shows the debasement not only of genitality, but also of the highest paternal values, through the association of God with shit. We can here combine the elements of a structure present in neurosis: (1) predominance of positive Oedipus complex on the negative one; (2) predominance of repression on splitting; (3) predominance of judgment of existence and reality principle on pleasure–unpleasure principle.[3]

The paradox is about the "reality" of castration. Of course, castration is not "real." Freud is condensing his views here. What we wish to underline is the importance of the recognition of the absence of a penis on the mother's body through perception and representation. Castration, therefore, is in fact a fantasy, a "sexual theory," but the absence of a penis on the mother's body is the reality which has to be acknowledged. The castration fantasy is important because it refers to a fantasized action performed by the father (even if the threat toward the child may come from a woman). This contributes to the conception of the father as the castrator—even in the case of an inverted complex. Winnicott (1951) considered castration anxiety as a blessing for the child since it could show him the way to get out of unbearable dead-end agonies related to the dual relationship with the mother.

Another strange statement comes from Freud's pen. As we have seen, he describes a variety of denial of castration, implying that

[3]Freud related the judgment of attribution (good or bad) to the pleasure–unpleasure principle and the judgment of existence (real or imaginary) to the reality principle in his paper on "Negation" (1925).

the rejection asserts its nonexistence. On the other hand, he describes the idea of two currents, one abominating the idea of castration and another accepting it, finding consolation in femininity as a compensation through anal pleasure. We can summarize this state of affairs as follows:

First phase: nonexistence of castration (denial). Second phase: splitting between two contradictory currents, castration as abomination coupled with its acceptance, compensating its outcome in a consolidation with femininity (anality). This may also be stated in the following manner: First phase, there is no vagina, therefore no castration; there is only one hole, the anus, and one organ to penetrate it, the penis. Second phase, castration exists, impossible to deny it anymore, therefore one can lose one's penis, but one can still enjoy sexuality even without a penis by means of anal excitation. In any one of these cases, the vagina is still denied as the sex organ of the mother-woman.

In all instances the problem of the presence or the absence of the penis, the conflict between phallic pleasure and anal pleasure, are closely linked with an intense thinking activity, anticipating some of Bion's conceptions. Freud's demonstration of castration through the hallucination of the cut finger is memorable. I have shown elsewhere (Green, 1993a) that, alongside the positive hallucinations experienced with dread, some clues (the blood is unseen, the pain is not felt) indicate negative hallucinations.[4]

In my opinion, the chapter on anal eroticism in the Wolf Man offers probably Freud's deepest insight into the case. It may be read as foreshadowing the developments to come on borderline personality disorders. Unfortunately, most of what has been written on these nonneurotic personality structures understate the role of sexuality. Destruction comes to the fore, which is partly justified; the ego is the focus of the investigation, which is necessary but incomplete; object relationships almost entirely replace drive theory without reason; and, finally, the return of puritanism has triumphed over the centrality of sexuality. The dysfunctioning of the ego—sometimes viewed in the perspective of object relationships—has severed itself from its corresponding figures in the area of sexuality.

[4]The discussion of this hallucination is developed in *Le travail du negatif* (Green, 1993a).

Considering the global issue of sexuality in nonneurotic personality structures, I will propose two main alternatives, which can be considered as extreme polarities with several intermediary constellations: (1) genitalization of pregenital fixations, in which case there is a compulsive attempt to express genitally features related to pregenitality displaying oral and anal fixations; (2) pregenital expressions masking the genital fixations with all kinds of defenses, from repression to splitting, protecting the hidden genital conflict.

After Freud: Archaic Sexuality

Pregenital fixations soon became the new focus of psychoanalysis. It all started with Melanie Klein in the thirties and developed until the present period, becoming finally a topic of common interest. In France, Bouvet (1967) devoted a great part of his work differentiating between genital and pregenital structures. This preceded the shift of interest in favor of borderline personality disorders which has taken place since then. It is about time to ask ourselves about the meaning of sexuality in this new context. A task of major importance has been accomplished with the work of Stoller (1979), who opened new ways of understanding sexuality, first through his investigation of transvestism and transsexualism, then in widening the perspective on the nature of erotic excitement and its deviations in contemporary society. Recently, McDougall (1995) has described the manifestations of archaic sexuality: addictive sexuality, neoneeds, the importance of very early fixations with pathogenic traumas. The classical concept of a castration complex associated with the phallic phase is no longer the valid reference here. On the other hand, the potentially traumatic nature of *all* sexuality is shown convincingly. According to various authors, the fixations can be traced to as early a period as the oral phase of the developmental line, as Melanie Klein suggests, or the oral and anal phases. But, as we have seen with Freud, it is not quite accurate to "date" all observable disturbances within one period, however early this may be. We should consider the coexistence of different points of fixation, with their corresponding features related to sexuality and to ego functioning as well, with modes of defense different from repression. In such cases, we find expressions of different levels coexisting side by side. We are surprised to see some patients act out diverse polymorphous perversions with neither constant nor exclusive pervert organization. A plurality of perversions can coexist and take the upper hand, according to circumstances, with no rigid fixations of a single type. Patients go from one partner to another at such a rapid rate that the analyst has no way of remembering the names of their sexual mates. It is not so much a question of addictive behavior but a need for change or for getting rid of the object at the first disappointment or at the feeling of any possible menace. In fact, the object is felt deeply as dangerous, threatening when any relation of closeness is established. The following case material will clearly illustrate what I mean.

Case Material: The Analysis of a "Pseudopsychopath"

Arnold asked for analysis when he was 37 years old. He wanted an end to a long period of psychopathic existence having led to extremes, realizing that his relationship to women was problematic, not conducive to his marrying and having a family. For reasons of confidentiality, I shall not linger on the disturbance of his early childhood or on his recent past in adulthood, which were very heavily disturbed. I will only mention that, though he was not responsible for what happened to him in early childhood, there were reasons to suspect a major sense of guilt, which was preventing him from having a satisfactory adult life. Neither will I give very significant details about his mother's pathological sexual behavior, again for reasons of discretion.

Arnold complained of an instability in his sexual potency and a tendency to unfaithfulness in his relationships with women. He had a central masturbation fantasy of falling asleep on the breast of a prostitute after having made love to her, a fantasy that was very closely connected with his relationship to his mother. Analysis showed very powerful homosexual trends. However, he never had any overt homosexual activity, except once, which he renounced fearing the possibility of becoming homosexual and taking pleasure in it. After the analysis started, he would split his sexual and emotional life in two parts. He would experiment with all kinds of sexual part objects, using the receivers of pink telephones to reach orgasm by conversing with anonymous women, looking for sexual partnerships with transsexuals and occasionally transvestites. But it never occurred to him to organize an exclusive perverse scenario or to establish a fixed single type of sexual relationship. His perverse sexual relationships were not exclusive, but alternated with sexual relationships with women which meant more to him. And there was a splitting of affect; for instance, between the need to have a spanking session with an indifferent woman who enjoyed the game, after he was angry with his girl friend, making no connection between the two affects.

For rather long periods he would go without having any sex. In his emotionally significant relationships with women, he was rather shy, extremely cautious about getting involved in the relationship, needing to be sure that the woman he chose would want him as much as he wanted her, as much but neither more nor less. He was scared that the woman could be attached to him more than he wished, imprisoning him with her affection. He was alert to the possibility that her behavior might be indicating the slightest sign of castration and, even more, indicating that she could become dependent on him. On the other hand, he would expect extreme attention to what he was saying to her, being hurt if she appeared to be thinking about anything else than what he was saying. His sexual freedom increased during his analysis, but not his ability to accept the otherness of his partner and the search for a deeper emotional involvement. He would stop a relationship abruptly when he perceived a warning sign of danger that he interpreted as of either rejection or deeper involvement. Underlying his behavior I could see traces of a paranoid character; or, rather, an alternative succession of paranoid and depressive periods. But, considering his childhood, he had ample reason to be marked by psychopathological trends.

The clinical material showed intense anxiety about a seductive, captivating, possessive, maddening mother imago. In the transference, I was seen as a very moralistic and repressive person, as a father substitute, invested with contradictory feelings. I was seen as "a pain in the ass," but also as a protective, admired, and helpful figure. On my side, he raised in me affectionate feelings.

In spite of his past psychopathic behavior, I had absolute trust in him.

Discussion

This case cannot be considered as belonging to either a neurotic or a psychotic diagnosis of personality structure. The presence of psychopathic or perverse trends does not allow labeling him under these categories either. The splitting I have shown between his partial sexuality and his love life cannot be described separately, they cannot be dissociated, as each aspect is revealing of the other. The patient gives us an excellent opportunity to grasp the complementarity that exists between drive theory and object relations theory. We have seen how the acting out of drive manifestations expressed clearly the repressed features, which belonged also to the object relationship. In fact, we can see here the manifestation of a dual functioning: one related to part objects (with part drives), the other to total objects (with a more complete sexuality) in conflict with love.

During analysis, at the height of some transference activation, the patient could express moments of a delusional relationship. For instance, the homosexual transference would take the form of an intrusion of the analyst's words in his brain. If transference is the best opportunity to discover psychic intimacy, one can say that sexuality is the sharpest "analyzer" of the relationship to the other, considering also the relationship of sexuality and love. In psychoanalysis, meaning cannot entirely by dissociated from love. In some instances, the occasional practice of perversion appears as a challenge and provocation to the superego. It is supported by a denial of anxiety, which reappears within relationships of closeness with the object, even outside any sexual context. Love is the most feared issue because of possible rejection, betrayal, or abandonment by the object or because of the threat of the object's unavailability, failure, and dependence on the subject.

Pregenital fixations are uncovered in analysis. A set of correspondences between neurosis and borderline conditions can be discerned. If with neurotic patients analysts are aware of castration anxiety (in men) and penetration anxiety (in women), they may understand what is even more conspicuous in borderline patients: separation anxiety (related to castration), intrusion anxiety (related to penetration). In extreme forms this pair of nonneurotic affects leads to abandonment anxiety (related to separation) and total submission (related to intrusion).

Defensive sexualization (or, better, genitalization) can demonstrate the preeminence given to the drive, with no object other than one attached to the drive. The implicit model, whatever may be the sexual practices, is the autoerotic masturbatory pattern. As for the total object, one can frequently witness primary identification mechanisms, self and object confusion. In fact, in ordinary daily relationships, the subject lives less in a partnership with the object than aside from him or her, coexisting rather than sharing. This may be reflected in the transference relationship.

Where violence overwhelms sexuality, neither desire nor pleasure are experienced. Affects are replaced by emergency needs or peremptory urges. The state of mind is filled with revenge, domination, mastery, desire to annihilate the other's independent will. We are here truly "beyond the pleasure principle." Whether or not we can consider these manifestations under the heading of a "death drive" is open to question. It is undeniable, however, that destruction is here in the forefront, self-destruction as much as destruction of the other, and that we have to consider in detail the "work of the negative" (Green, 1993a). As far as the object is concerned, we may recall a statement by Freud characterizing some psychic structures as witnessing a strong fixation and a weak cathexis of the object.

Some Alternative Issues

In the instances I am going to describe next, the issue is an extinction of genitality and the development of considerable pregenital fixations. I am thinking of several patients who, under conflictual circumstances, can develop a total loss of genital excitability, a disinterest, in fact a phobic avoidance of any situation which could be conducive to a sexual relation. In Bob's case, the patient could go for nearly two years without having any sexual exchange with the woman he shared his life with. He could only see her as a little girl he had to take in his arms. During the analysis, he explained that she reminded him so much of his mother that she inhibited him sexually. In fact, this man was obsessed with the idea that he could have committed incest in his childhood with his very disturbed mother. On the other hand, he felt that his bond to his mother could never be undone. From time to time, he experienced pseudohallucinations, having the impression that wherever he was, at home or walking in the street (especially on his way to his sessions), his mother was calling him. In fact, she lived seven hundred miles away. Before analysis began, his relationships with women never lasted for more than three months. When eventually, thanks to the work in analysis, he fell in love with a woman (to whom he is now married and with whom he has had a son), anal–sadistic traits with the compulsive need to dominate her came to the fore. After more than ten years of analysis with me as his second analyst, he is now able to enjoy sex with her. Oddly enough, even though we had analyzed his Oedipus complex at length, with an acceptance of my interpretations, he was blind and deaf to the early oedipal manifestations of childhood. He was able to detect (and to worry about) his son's strong attachment as a baby to his mother, but he could not admit that at a certain age his son could have experienced him as a rival, wishing to reject him in order to gain possession of his mother when she was alone with her husband.

My two other cases are women. Cecily is the sister of a patient diagnosed as schizophrenic. She has massive anal fixations linked to dramatic toilet training in infancy. She is an illustration of what I have called primary anality (Green, 1993b) in order to differentiate it from the normal characteristics of anal eroticism—which I think should be labeled "secondary anality." Again, the description here is no more than an abbreviation of a case. The narcissistic impairment is predominant. The patient's emotional and sexual life is nonexistent. Her relationship to me can be considered as representing the essence, if not the quasi-totality, of her external object relationships. There is a massive displacement on her work as a researcher, meant to realize a narcissistic reparation of her self-image. But as her work is massively conflictual, the considerable erotization of her cathexis leads to endless corrections of her writing. It took her more than

18 months to write the 25-page conclusion for a book with many authors under her editorship. When she finally ended the work, she decided to take some rest. She went to the swimming pool and felt considerable anxiety seeing the other women in bathing suits relaxed in the sunshine. She felt that they were not decent, exhibiting their flesh or "meat": "It made me think of rotting and decay; it made me think of death," she said. To some extent, it seemed that naked bodies reminded her of feces. To do the same as these women was to lose the pure, idealized body—the spiritual body—of intellectual work. She realized under the circumstances how panicked she was when a man addressed her in a very banal way in ordinary conversation and she was unable to say anything in response, becoming aware, however, that she intensely longed for this to happen. She was obsessed with the idea that any word she might say would finally drive her to bed with him, a situation she could only think of as a constraint. A rape fantasy was obvious.

Diana had also a total absence of sexual relationships, replaced by very intense fixations of an oral nature. She had been divorced years ago, and had several lovers. One of them committed suicide unexpectedly, raising intense guilt in her. Since her divorce, she had made numerous suicidal attempts, some of them very serious, with prolonged comas. After an abortion, very much linked to her family history (her birth was preceded by a stillborn brother), she lived in great solitude, keeping contact mostly with women, some of whom were homosexual or without having any sexual life, or with aged bachelors. When not at work, she had fits of bulimia or drinking excessive amounts of red wine or Champagne. She was also addicted to drugs, mainly tranquillizers and antidepressants. She would spend all her free time reclusively (for instance weekends) in bed, taking sleeping pills, waiting for Monday morning to go back to work. These pregenital fixations, which of course included poor object relationships, were associated to a transference process of a peculiar kind. On the one hand, she never expressed any erotic feeling toward me as her analyst, never making a personal remark, concerning me. On the other hand, it was pretty obvious that I was very important to her and that she was deeply attached to my person. One day, during an emergency telephone call, she told me in a state of acute anxiety: "I love you." In the last session before the summer break, for the first time she said: "I am going to miss you. How am I going to go without you?" On my part, this was the first time that I did not worry about her, knowing that she would be able to bear the separation. In the transference, it appeared that all this behavior—sleeping, overeating, overdrinking—had one single purpose: to enable her to have a blank mind. She complained of being unable to have thoughts, that is, to be able to associate, and, if this ever happened, to be able to draw any conclusion from her mental activity. She complained: "I don't know how to think."

In the above three cases we can see how pregenital fixations are associated with corresponding types of mental functioning: the regressions of sexuality going hand in hand with strange ego functioning. I shall repeat here what I have already said in a recent article (Green, 1996): I consider that the sexual features associated with genitality do not represent the superficial layers of libido development but the heart of the matter, the secret deeply hidden in the core of psychic activity. But genitality here is not the same as what is observed usually; it goes with imperative demands, ceaseless exactingness, inability to accept the slightest frustration, feelings of resentment, narcissistic injury, torturous jealousy, the need for exclusive attention. In other words, as Freud said, sexuality does not appear at a certain stage, it is there from the beginning in a way and with a style far different from the forms it takes with the organization of the Oedipus complex. Dual relationships are seen as a dead end. Triangular ones allow some openness and a range of choices, which permit the individual to escape mutual imprisonment. Fathers are still needed, even nowadays.

Clinical Deductions

Freud's overall intuition of the central role played by sexuality in psychic life has always been mitigated for him with the idea of the differences of its expression and consequences for the mind. He saw sexuality as raw, unsorted out, and ruled by direct modes of discharge in the actual neuroses, just as he saw it as hardly workable when it was withdrawn in the ego in the narcissistic neuroses. Moreover, as I have observed, if roughly the first part of Freud's work is based on the comparison between neurosis and perversion (neurosis as the negative of perversion), it can be said that the second half (approximately after *The Ego and the Id* [Freud, 1923]) shows a change of paradigm: more and more explicitly neurosis is compared to psychosis. Hence the importance of mechanisms such as splitting that indicate ego-altered functioning responsible for what are considered as its bizarre features. So, even in Freud's time, there was an awareness that in some clinical configurations the disturbances of the ego had to be closely scrutinized alongside the fixations of sexuality and in connection with them. Therefore, I consider untrue the commonly expressed view that contemporary psychoanalysis has demonstrated that sexuality could be of less importance than in the past and in favor of supposedly earlier mechanisms devoid of sexual meaning. On the other hand, many so-called perversions are seen as presenting signs related to ego functioning, which makes one suspect some underlying psychotic mechanisms. One may consider that the united front against sexuality, from Klein to Kohut, corresponds to a return of puritanism, an attempt, once more, to undervalue sexuality and, if possible, to get rid of it more or less definitely.

Clinically, we have to consider the problem from various angles. It is impossible to give only one categorical description. We know that we will have to understand the clinical features as a combination of factors belonging to different metapsychological entities. I shall try to describe the main axes of my understanding.

We shall distinguish between direct manifestations of sexuality and repressive or displaced fixations from which sexuality is conspicuously absent. Again, this means that we have to struggle against our tendency to regress to a conception of pre-Freudian sexuality. The manifestations of direct sexuality are those which are immediate regressive fixations. Since "Instincts and Their Vicissitudes," Freud (1915) has beautifully shown how sadism and masochism or voyeurism and exhibitionism are the results of a dismantlement. Sadomasochism is the transformation of an excessive careless contact between two partners exchanged for the sake of genital pleasure toward a mutation which gives the upper hand to aggression with the aim to master, to inflict suffering, to dominate and humiliate the object. Voyeurism and exhibitionism are, on the contrary, issues of distant contact in which some of the preceding aims can be present in other forms, infliction of fear, mastery, contactless introjection, and so on. On the other hand, displaced indirect manifestations of infantile sexuality do not content themselves to infiltrate sexuality with aggression or to transform its aims in this view; they completely overshadow phallic or genital sexuality. Abstinence from any direct sexual gratification is a neglected issue. It can be observed in women with great frequency. But in such cases, oral fixations (drinking or eating disorders, oversleeping, and the like) soon display their regressive nature as a flight from the genital. It means that an attempt is sought to be freed from the bond with a separate object. This, in my view, is less the result of a fixation than the covering up of sexual desires. In anal fixations, the displacement toward desexualized activities (addiction to work or to mental rumination) shows the same attempts to be freed from the vicissitudes of the relationship with a separate object. It can be seen as associated with the feeling of the sexual act as an imposition by the partner (rape fantasies) and the denial of its inner connections with fantasy.

Acting out is usually understood as a defense bypassing the vicissitudes of the internal world to discharge in the external world an anxiety raising conflict. This conception is true but incomplete. To my view "acting" (out) is a transformation, I may even say a conversion, a leap in the acting, of a conflictual issue, most of the time traumatic in essence. Acting out succeeds in giving an expression which indicates a *transition to activity* of inner psychical contents related to more or less overwhelming situations which have been experienced during childhood, as the child was in a state of passivity, expectation, and dependence. Therefore, there is a need to repeat the unresolved and intensely pressuring posttraumatic experiences in a more tolerable context (i.e., by way of initiating it actively). Another subject must be chosen as a substitute for the original self or another situation analogous to the original one, which will enable the subject to mask it with its own seal, to imprint its own signature on it actively.

Of course, all performances can be automatic, with no deliberation or clear conception of the purpose of the acting. Nevertheless, it serves the same aim. Sometimes also, acting out is the result of an anticipation of danger. Anticipation is a process which is prominent in nonneurotic structures. The inability to suspend action necessary to thought gives way to precipitation (Bion, 1967). Too often, it is observed that anticipation leads to an immersion right in the middle of the dangerous and most feared situations, which appear paradoxical in the analysis of transference.

The above remarks lead us to consider the object relationship. In most cases, the projections and introjections coming from internal objects have multiple effects: the respective role of part and total objects, the function of narcissistic, preoedipal, and oedipal objects. Particular importance should be given to the oedipal ones as representing the objects of the double difference of the sexes and of the generations. The structure of meaning is here more accomplished than anywhere else.

Drives and objects cannot be considered out of the balance of love and life drives, on the one hand, and destructive drives, on the other. The nuclear issue is open to enormous variations, which find their origin in the environment, hence the importance of the transitional area described by Winnicott (1953).

It is through these parameters that we can evaluate what I will call "the measure for work of the Ego in relationship to the Other." The Other is not an object, though it is grounded in it. The Other is a correlate of the subject as there is a subject only for another subject. The Other forms a pair with the subject. It finds its expression in the evaluation of the pair ego-superego, as there is no society which escapes the necessity of establishing rules for sexuality. The prohibition of incest has been characterized as "the rule of rules," forming the borderline between nature and culture.

The Meaning of Sexuality

Is it possible to draw a basic model for the understanding of sexuality? I would suggest the following: The core of the sexual situation is the relationship between a drive or a group of drives seeking satisfaction in their close contact (physical and psychical) with a chosen object through which they can be satisfied. Both members of this elementary pair communicate with each other through an ego; that is, a differentiated and complex structure which helps the realization of satisfaction but has also to protect its own organization and other functions. The streams are oscillating from the drive to the object and from the object to the drive. Many factors can stand against the search for pleasure which strengthens the ego: anxiety, overwhelming destruction, fear of disorganization, if not of collapse. It becomes necessary to hypothesize the existence of a psychic structure born from the cultural pressures which rise in society. Such is the role of the superego, whose demands can be as raw, as crude, as imperative, as the demands of the drives.

I can think that other components may have escaped my attention. I cannot think that any of the ones I have considered might be spared.

In neurotic structures, the balance between the different elements of the model do not involve important regressions of the ego. In nonneurotic structures not only the ego is involved in the regression, but sexuality in itself undergoes parallel regression to pregenital fixations. Disorders of thought are the result of such a combination (Bion, 1967). Even in such cases, it is my belief that the oedipal and genital relationship is mute in order to keep secret the most important achievements, which are fantasized and are those of any human being: love in the encounter with the other, sexual enjoyment, closeness and affective intimacy, sharing in a mutually extraordinary experience.

The examination of sexuality in nonneurotic structures presents an excellent opportunity for questioning the meaning of sexuality. I shall, in some closing remarks, propose a schematic view of how we can understand this aspect of the human condition. Sexuality, biologically rooted, is an inner force which is directed outwards. The aim of procreation in animals is, needless to say, pushed aside and replaced by the search for pleasure. We are subjects driven by pleasure seeking through objects for the best and for the worst. This can lead us to sublimation or to darkness. Sexuality is a double oriented force: from inside to inside and from inside to outside and vice versa. This double articulation between the intrapsychic and the intersubjective is the specificity of psychoanalysis. The relationships of sexuality and love are very complex. I assume that both are intermingled in the beginning, needless to say in a very different way from that of an adult. In the course of development, very early on, a dissociation separates sexuality and love. One can think here of Winnicott's stage of concern or Melanie Klein's (1940) and Bion's (1962) depressive positions. The importance is to emphasize the temporarily independent paths of sexuality and love, favored by the defenses—repression, splitting, and so on. This "work of the negative" is a normal process of structuralization but can lead to extreme expressions of negativism, with a more or less total banishment of sexual gratifications. Let us recall Jones's "aphanisis" (1927), an unjustly forgotten concept.

The integration of sex and love is one of the most difficult achievements of human beings' relationships with their mates. Love and hate are at the core of ambivalence; sometimes entirely split off in a sexual life dominated by part objects and partial erotogenic zones, or otherwise, in a religious sublimation which tries to keep sex out of the mind as far as can be. (Though judging from the cases of Saint Theresa and Saint John of the Cross, there is not even a shadow of doubt of the penetration of sex into the most sacred, highly spiritual, achievements; suffering for the love of the object is an essential dimension of godhead.

It may be difficult to admit that the nature of sexuality is such that "natural sex" as simple, self-evident, complete, full and mutually satisfying, with an entirely and ever trustful object, is an idealization or, at best, an illusion. To ease the conditions of a free exercise of sexuality is far from solving all problems. The more sexuality has a free hand, the more it becomes a highly complex and fragile endeavor.

Theorists of biology say that the two great inventions of evolution are sexuality and death. Biologically the sexual function is a very complex one, composed of different stages, from birth to puberty. Psychologically, we find a corresponding, though differently organized, staged structure with its two periods: infantile and adult, separated by a latency period. Drive theory, which was

Freud's creation, has been unduly opposed to object relationships. The two conceptions do not antagonize, they complement each other. In fact, Freud's last theory of drives, with the life and love drives, involves the existence of the object. Drive theory has an irreplaceable quality, it accounts for the force which animates us and pushes us forward. This is not granted once and for all. Withdrawal, depression, or schizoid decathexis show us that it can be neutralized, more or less temporarily lost or severely impaired, more or less definitely. Remember: "Love or life" drives, wrote Freud. The love of life is our most precious gift. The work of the analyst fights on this side.

It is sad to realize that analysts have to rediscover sexuality out of any puritanism or bigotry. Sexuality is the only function in human existence that needs an object as other same object (*autre semblable*). The newborn needs air, temperature, food supplies, drinking. In all this, he is not very different from any other mammal. But he needs the other as same to establish the foundations of the joy of living, the sharing of love, and the premises of meaning. Love and meaning are maybe one and the same thing in man. Love without sex on the eve of life is love that will never be rooted in the body. The spirituality of sublimation is at the end of a long path; today scholars who study the sacred have no doubt that it is strongly linked to eroticism. We shall leave the last word to Freud. In *Group Psychology and the Analysis of the Ego* (1921) he writes, "Eros, which holds together everything in the world" (p. 92).

References

Bion, W. R. (1962), *Elements of Psychoanalysis.* London: Heinemann.

——— (1967), *Second Thoughts.* London: Heinemann.

Bouvet, M. (1967), *Oeuvres psychanalytiques,* Vol. 1. *La relations d'objet.* Paris: Payot, pp. 161–226.

Brunswick Mack, R. (1928), A supplement to Freud's "History of an infantile neurosis." *Internat. J. Psycho-Anal.,* 9:439–476.

Freud, S. (1915), Instincts and their vicissitudes. *Standard Edition,* 14:109–140. London: Hogarth Press, 1957.

——— (1917), On transformations of instinct as exemplified in anal erotism. *Standard Edition,* 17:125–133. London: Hogarth Press, 1955.

——— (1918), From the History of an Infantile Neurosis. *Standard Edition,* 17:1–125. London: Hogarth Press, 1955.
——— (1921), Group Psychology and the Analysis of the Ego. *Standard Edition,* 18:65–143. London: Hogarth Press, 1955.
——— (1923), The Ego and the Id. *Standard Edition,* 19:1–59. London: Hogarth Press, 1961.
——— (1924), Neurosis and psychosis. *Standard Edition,* 19:147–153. London: Hogarth Press, 1961.
——— (1925), Negation. *Standard Edition,* 19:233–239. London: Hogarth Press, 1961.
Gardiner, M. (1971), *The Wolf Man by the Wolf Man.* New York: Basic Books.
Green, A. (1982), Travail psychique et travail de la pensée (communication sur rapport de J. et F. Begoin). *Revue Française de Psychanalyse,* 46(No 2 special):419–429.
——— (1993a), *Le Travail du negatif.* Paris: Minuit.
——— (1993b), L'analité primaire dans la relation anale. In: *La névrose obsessionnelle,* Monographs of *Revue Française de Psychanalyse,* pp. 61–86.
——— (1996), Has sexuality anything to do with psychoanalysis? *Internat. J. Psycho-Anal.,* 76:871–885.
Jones, E. (1927), Early development of female sexuality. In: *Papers on Psycho-Analysis.* London: Bailliere.
Klein, M. (1940), Mourning and its relation to manic-depressive states. In: *Contributions to Psychoanalysis, 1921–1945.* London: Hogarth Press, 1948, pp. 311–338.
Mahony, P. (1984), *Cries of the Wolf Man.* New York: International Universities Press.
McDougall, J. (1995), *The Many Faces of Eros. A Psychodynamic Exploration of Human Sexuality.* New York: W. W. Norton.
Obholzer, K. (1981), *Gespräche mit dem Wolfsman, eine Psychoanalyse und die Folgen.* Reinbek bei Hamburg, Germany: Rowahlt Verlag.
Stoller, R. J. (1979), *Sexual Excitement. Dynamics of Erotic Life.* New York: Pantheon.
Winnicott, D. W. (1951), *Collected Papers.* New York: Basic Books.
——— (1953), Transitional objects and transitional phenomena. In: *Playing and Reality.* London: Tavistock, pp. 1–25.

2

New Perspectives on the Oedipus Complex

HANNA SEGAL, M.D.

The Oedipus Complex Before the Depressive Position

It is implicit in Klein's (1950) description of the depressive position that the Oedipus complex is unavoidably part and parcel of working through that particular phase of development. According to Klein it is during the depressive position that the infant begins to relate to mother as a whole person. That means that the infant perceives his mother more as she is in reality, that is, not split into a good and a bad one, not as a part object, like the breast, in the infant's possession, not saturated by projective identification, but as a separate person, having a personality and a life of her own. That "life of her own" principally includes the father as a sexual partner.

In the depressive position, the infant increasingly relates to an external reality and differentiates it from his internal reality, the reality of his impulses and fantasies. Coming to terms with this

This chapter was previously published as chapter 7 in *Psychoanalysis, Literature and War,* published by New Library of Psychoanalysis.

reality, inner and outer, involves coming to terms with the Oedipus complex.

Klein assumed that because of these developments one could say that the Oedipus complex starts during the depressive position. Nevertheless, triangular relationships exist before the depressive position and some of them can be seen as preoedipal or else as the most primitive roots of the Oedipus complex.

The triangular situation sets in as a result of splitting processes. There is an early split between the good or idealized aspect of the breast and the bad breast, so that the infant is confronted with two objects: the object of desire and the object of hatred and fear.

In my introduction to Melanie Klein's work (Segal, 1964), writing about the paranoid–schizoid position, I described what I called the "third area." I described there two patients, one borderline schizoid and one psychotic, who could relate to me only by splitting off hateful aspects of both themselves and me into a third area, described by one of the patients as "bloody mish-mash," repeating a situation in which the infant can only relate to and feed from the breast, provided he can split off hatred and persecution and locate them in this third area. Such a third area or third object, which contains the unwanted aspects of the self and object, is inherent in the paranoid–schizoid position. This triangular situation is the background of a predepressive oedipal constellation, because it gives a readiness for a perception of a third object. The father's penis is a ready recipient of such split-off projections.

A patient, whom I will call R and refer to again, had a hallucination that a motorcycle was riding into his head. The rider had a kind of mask on, which made his head look like a gorilla. R felt terrified and thought his head would explode. Then he looked at his own index finger and got frightened, because he thought his finger looked like a gorilla. He had a number of associations to this event, but the two central ones were to the image of a gorilla, which reminded him of a psychotic boy; and to his own finger, which reminded him of anal masturbation, about which we had spoken previously in his analysis. Anal masturbation was for him always associated with unconscious fantasies of violent intrusion into the anus of the analyst-mother. We understood that the motorcycle represented his own intrusive self, identified with his finger and penis, and projected into an external object, the motorcycle he had heard outside my window the previous day.

When this early split and projection are maintained in later development, it often gives rise to a situation which appears to be oedipal: one parent idealized and desired; the other hated and persecuting. But if one looks closely at the material, this is not a true oedipal situation, but a continuation of a part object relationship with an excessive split into an ideal object and a persecutory object.

I remember reading years ago the report of a clinic in a training institute about the choice of patients for candidates. It was decided then to choose only truly oedipal patients. One of the patients chosen was a young woman in love with her boss. She was considered to be having a truly oedipal pathology. But when her analysis was started, it became soon clear that she was a severely splitting, schizoid person, quite unsuitable for a candidate.

This kind of part object relationship may also characterize the early perception of the mother as a whole body. Anatomically, so to speak, she is seen as a whole object, but the emotional relation can continue very much on a part object level. The mother's body is seen as containing both riches and horrors, and among them the father's penis, seen as a part object and possession of mother's, sometimes idealized and desired and sometimes very persecutory.

I have come to be wary of women patients who, on consultation, say that their main reason for psychoanalysis is that they wish to be married. On the face of it, it looks like a very reasonable aim. But very often it turns out that these women come to analysis, particularly to a woman analyst, to get out of her a penis or to get out of her mind some secret knowledge about how to acquire a penis. It is called a husband or lover, but very often these women have no idea of a man who would be a person. So, again, what appears as an oedipal situation, that is, rivaling mother for father, is, in fact, a very primitive situation, having more to do with envy of mother, than with oedipal jealousy, and the wish to rob mother of her possessions.

Recognizing father or, to begin with, often on the part object level, a penis, as not being a split-off good or bad aspect of the breast and not being saturated by the infant's own projection, but as an object in its own right, with its own characteristics, and its own functions different from those of the infant or the mother, is an important step in development. The father can then be seen as protecting the mother and the child from a stream of mutual projective identifications, in fantasy and in reality, which is an important factor in establishing the mother's right to separateness. He can also be perceived as a provider of goodness for mother, of the kind that the infant cannot provide, which establishes early on the differentiation between both generations and sexes, essential for healthy development.

I shall illustrate this by some further material from later on in the analysis of my patient R.

One day he told me that, as he was going past my consulting room door to the waiting room, he became very anxious as the thought occurred to him that there was no guard at the door and nothing to stop him from getting into the consulting room and interfering with the analytic session still in process. Then he added, "Come to think of it there is nothing to stop me doing what I want on the couch. For instance, if I wanted to, I could lie upside down." Then he giggled, feeling embarrassed as he realized that upside down in the bed is the position he was in during some loveplay with his girl friend the night before. So, apparently, the situation was as follows: There is no guard at the door, no husband. He could have intercourse with me as with his girl friend and have our positions upside down; that is, with him dominating me—apparently, a plain oedipal situation. He went on to tell me a dream. He said, "I had a dream in which I was explaining to M (his girl friend) about my hallucinations. I was telling her, 'Look, I dream up a car and there it is.' And the car appeared." He got into the front seat. But there was no partition between front and back—no pole to lean against. He started falling backwards, feeling an utmost panic. He woke up with severe anxiety.

My understanding of his associations preceding the telling of the dream and of the dream itself was as follows: The pole is a phallic symbol. But also, I am of Polish origin, and he knows that my husband's name is Paul. In the absence of the pole, the father or the penis in the vagina, there is nothing to stop him from having intercourse with his mother on a genital level, but there is nothing to stop him from unrestrained projective identification with her, leading to the loss of boundaries, confusion, and panic. What he seems to explain to his girl friend in the dream is that when he projects himself into his mother, what used to be his thoughts, "what he dreamed up," is felt by him as a reality in the external world. But the whole process, instead of hallucination at that point, gave rise to a dream. Some time later in his analysis, we noticed that his hallucinations disappeared from the time we analyzed that dream.

Several years later, after considerable change and improvement, the patient was getting married. Before his wedding, for which he was missing a few days of his analysis, he showed considerable ambivalence to myself representing the father. When he came back from his honeymoon, he said that he had never been so moved in his life as he was at the actual wedding ceremony. He decided to marry in church in deference to his dead father, though he himself was not religious. He asked for his father's favorite hymn—"The Lord Is My Shepherd"—to be sung at the wedding ceremony. He said that he had never in his life been so happy and so unhappy at one and the same time. He did not know if at that moment he was regaining his father or losing him. He was so aware of his father's presence in his thoughts, and so acutely aware of his real absence from the wedding. He then told me a dream he had had the night before in which a fisherman was to take him out to teach him how to fish. The fisherman's hands were bandaged because they had cuts on them. But the fisherman assured him that he could still keep his promise.

In the last session before the break, I had occasion to point out to him that he was "very cutting" to me. In the dream I was the fisherman-father with the bandaged hand.

One can see that the first dream is what I would call *pseudo*-oedipal. On the face of it, his first associations to that dream are of an oedipal nature, wanting to make love to the mother-analyst. But what the dream reveals is something quite different. What the patient wants is to project himself into the analyst in a way which results in confusion and panic. In the second dream, on the contrary, the father is seen as a separate person with a truly oedipal ambivalence, the experience of loss and guilt. This can lead to an introjection of a positive identification with his father's masculine qualities.

There is also a difference in the patient's mental functioning. The first dream explains his propensity to hallucinate, a failure of adequate symbolization—what he thinks *is*. In the second dream the external and the internal situations are clearly distinguished. He is aware of his father's real absence, since the father is dead, and at the same time his father's presence in his own mind. His thought is not a hallucination, but the memory of an experience.

The Oedipus Complex and the Mental Apparatus

In recent years, we have been paying increasing attention to the relationship between the early oedipal situation and processes of symbolization and thinking. I have contended that adequate symbolization can only be established with the working through of the depressive position and the differentiation between external and internal realities. I have become increasingly convinced that accepting the reality of the father and the oedipal couple is essential in this process. Attacks on the parental couple, and the links between the parents, unavoidably disrupt processes of thinking. Hatred of the parental coupling becomes a hatred of thinking. Ronald Britton (1989) describes a patient who, whenever she thought he was thoughtful, would scream at him. "Stop this fucking thinking!" (p. 88).

A session of a patient of mine, C, illustrates such a disturbance. She started the session by telling me that she had two very tiny fragments of a dream. In one, she saw me surrounded by middle-aged, stupid, altogether despicable men. Of the second fragment she could remember only that it had something to do with African land and African people. The first dream seemed to both of us pretty obvious, with an impending long weekend. But the hardly remembered fragment of a dream brought up surprisingly rich associations. To begin with, the patient expressed again her horror of racial prejudices she could not free herself from, and which she detested in herself. That seemed to provide a link between the second dream of men I may spend my weekend with and the first about the Africans. But her other associations were more unexpected and illuminating. The patient was a grade school teacher and she started speaking about a particular child's difficulty in learning any grammar, particularly foreign grammar. She thought Africa might represent what this girl felt about foreign grammar as totally exotic and incomprehensible. This child, she said, was quite clever, but very disjointed, unable to make certain connections, and this seemed particularly obvious in the child's total inability to grasp the rules of grammar. After all, grammar, with the sort of patterns it describes, should come more naturally. Then she laughed and said, "Maybe to her, grammar is so foreign and exotic—just like parents in intercourse must appear to the child—beyond reach, incomprehensible, exotic, foreign." This patient was often preoccupied and disturbed by very primitive fantasies of the primal scene. In the first dream intercourse is attacked and derided. She had a prejudice against it, like a prejudice against Africans. And her associations to it suggested that she was aware how her thinking was dislocated by her attack on those natural patterns of relationships.[1]

The Oedipus Complex and Bion's Elements of Mental Space

I would like now to proceed with another aspect of the problem, namely the Oedipus complex, and Bion's (1967) ideas of the relationship between the container and the contained as the basis of the mental apparatus and the capacity to symbolize and think. Klein (1950) contends that the infant deals with disturbing feelings and experiences by projecting them outside, a projection which gives rise to fantasies of a bad breast, and attaches itself to the realities of bad experiences. Bion introduced the idea that such primitive projections are also the infant's first means of communication. The mother receives the infant's projections and modifies them by her reactions, like taking away his hunger, his fear, or his pain. In his pain, the infant gets rid of what Bion calls "beta elements," inchoate, concrete feelings, experienced

[1]It is interesting that this patient, who had no acquaintance with Chomsky's work, assumed, as he does, that we have an inborn sense of grammar.

as things which can be pushed out. If the mother's response alleviates these experiences, the baby can take them back inside, modified by understanding, and they become elements which Bion calls "alpha." But the infant also introjects the breast that can contain and modify the projections, and it becomes that part of himself that can transform "beta" into "alpha" elements.

Bion speaks of the relationship between the container and the contained and the introjection of the container. I do not know if he ever referred to it as "mental space." I see it as also providing mental space, in which feelings and thoughts can be contained and worked on.

Bion's "container and contained" is basically a two-body relationship. But he does say that when the relation between the two is good it produces a third, which is benevolent to all three; and when it is bad, it produces a third, which is disruptive. Britton (1989) has suggested that a mental space at the beginning of the Oedipus complex becomes a triangular space, with three apexes: father, mother, and child. In that space there is an elasticity of relations: there is a relation like that between the three lines linking the vertices; there is a relation between the mother and the child; one between the father and the child; and one between the father and the mother, of which the child is the observer. The third, excluded, can be hostile or disruptive, whether it is the child or one of the parents, or the child's fantasy of one of the parents, as was the case with my patient and his motorcycle intrusion. But if the third, excluded is benevolent, it becomes an important part of the mental apparatus serving as a reflective part in the patient's mind, with which he can observe himself and have fantasies about the parents. And it is also the part capable of benevolent or neutral curiosity about the external world.

When the parental relationship is unbearable to the child, there is an attack on the link between the parents, or the self and the parents, that leads to the destruction of the triangular mental space. This is illustrated by my patient, D, who was tormented by recurring panic. Though intelligent, when in a state of panic, whether conscious or unconscious, she would lose her concentration and all ability to think. In one of the sessions she described acute anxiety about a hole in a wall. Some building work had to be done in her house and she could not imagine it being done without a big hole in the wall. She thought she or her children could fall through the hole, and anyway, the thought of this big black hole put her in a panic. It was fairly clear in the session that she had no idea in her mind that the builder might know what he was doing. The transference implications were obvious. When this was interrupted, she told me that she had another panic attack which assailed her on the way to the session: she had lost her diary that contained confidential information about herself and the work in her office involving other people, and the loss could be catastrophic. It slowly emerged that the loss of the diary had to do with her having read a poster of a lecture I was giving jointly with a man. She did not intend to attend it, but she also wanted to forget the date of the event, not to be troubled by it. The indiscretion referred to what she felt was the indecency of my exhibiting myself on a platform with a man.

The next session was very difficult and analytic work was hardly possible, because of the patient's determination to break all links. Two themes seem to have emerged: one of an internal tormentor, which eventually led to a fantasy of a hand cruelly squeezing out a breast that was filled with a boil. The second theme referred to sexuality. She felt that I and others were trying to impose on her a view of sexual intercourse as something pleasurable and nondestructive, which was a denial and idealization, since "I thought everybody knew that sex was always sadomasochistic." Another view the patient had about sex was of two people coming together in intercourse causing cruel pain to a third person in front of whom they were exhibiting themselves, inflicting on this third person unbearable feelings of exclusion, inferiority, and jealousy. Some links could be established, for instance, the parents-myself cruelly exhibiting to the child and the resulting destruction of her relationship to the breast. But the patient remained on the whole disconnected from me, angry, and very anxious.

In the third session, as she was speaking of the hole, some music from the neighboring flat could just be heard in the consulting room. She drew my attention to it, saying that it made her think of people dancing. She did not feel disturbed or persecuted by it. Eventually, we could establish that the terrible hole in her mind was the missing space in which she could perceive her parents, represented by me, dancing together. Later in the session, she started speaking about her difficulties in preparing a report that she had to do at work, but in a much quieter and more understanding way. This patient had an idealizing relationship to the breast, but this relationship was very fragile, only to be maintained by a splitting off of ambivalence. The appearance of a third object turned everything into torment. Not only was she tormented by fantasies of sexuality infused with cruelty, but the original relation to the breast was destroyed by this intrusion and also turned into torment. When this intrusion took place her mind became itself disjointed and fragmented, and she was filled with intense paranoid and hypochondriacal fantasies. At those points, her capacity for understanding and symbolization got lost. My talking to others was experienced as my forcing her to witness an actual sexual intercourse. The bad feelings about me became a tormented and tormenting poisonous breast inside her, experienced as physical symptoms. She could get rid of the resulting persecution by making a hole in her mind instead of a space accommodating the dancing parents, though later, in the third session, she showed how the containment and understanding provided by the analytic situation led to a transformation of "beta" into "alpha" elements.

The Oedipus Complex and Self-Awareness

The importance of the role of the observing part of the parental intercourse is shown in the following material. Two dreams of a patient in an advanced stage of her analysis illustrate some features of this triangular space. The first dream follows an event in the transference. I asked the patient, K, if she could come ten minutes earlier for her session. She gave me apparently good reasons for not being able to change her time. As I had unavoidably to leave my consulting room at the earlier time, I told her that I was sorry, but I would have to cut her session ten minutes short. It soon transpired that in such a case she could think of ways of coming ten minutes early. The next days she had the following dream.

> She was walking down a lovely road bordered by leafy trees. She came to the end of the road and there was no way to go on. She retraced her steps, and on the way she saw a clearing. And in that clearing she saw a couple having a very vigorous sexual intercourse. The intercourse was not only physical. The man seemed to have been telling the woman how passionately he loved her. She observed this scene with great interest.

Her first association was to tell me that there was nothing voyeuristic or exhibitionistic about the scene. The couple were making love in a clearing in a forest. They were concerned with one another, not exhibiting. She felt no voyeuristic excitement. She did not seek to see them, unlike in some other dreams, she was just interested, not excited. She associated the end of the road to my firmly telling her that I wished to end the session ten minutes early.

I think that the leafy road which she enjoyed so much represents her phantasy of being inside me, controlling me, a very common psychic stance in her. The frustration about the end of the session shows her that this has come to an end. She sometimes uses the expression, "No way!" "No way" can she maintain the phantasy of being inside and controlling me. When she gives up that fantasy, she is confronted by another space which opens a clearing in which the parental intercourse happens. And in the dream it is unspoilt by voyeuristic projections.

Further work, of course, led to the recognition of repressed feelings of jealousy and rage, and she had to make room in her mind for those feelings as well. But it is important that she could be also an objective and appreciative observer.

Some time later she had a similar dream, bringing another aspect of the new space and a new way of relating. In this dream, she was in the kitchen with me, washing-up. We were talking about marriage, and I was telling her that I married a Pole because Poles are so passionate. In that dream her relation to me in terms of feeding and washing up is not spoilt, and is even enriched by her knowledge of me as part of the couple. Similarly, her relation to me as mother does not disturb her own appreciation of father.

The primitive Oedipus complex is a part object relationship dominated by splits and projection. The mature genital Oedipus complex necessitates the recognition of parents as separate, complete persons in a relationship with one another, including a sexual relationship. The acceptance of this configuration is very painful. Unlike the relationship between the container and the contained as a two-body relationship wholly beneficial to the child, this is a situation in which the child is the third, excluded, with all that this implies of jealousy, envy, rage, and depression. Patient K, whose two nice dreams about the parental intercourse I have reported, had another dream later on, after a successful holiday. In the dream, she called me to mend a light in her room. I came in, but accompanied by my husband. She was in an absolute rage. All weekend she was surprised at her rage, since we did mend her light, feeling rather ashamed about it. But the point was, she did not really like the light being mended, since it showed me as a couple and brought the awareness that I depended on my husband for help, not on her. The working through of this oedipal ambivalence and the mobilization of the reparative impulses, resulted in establishing an inner world with a creative sexual couple as the central internal object and model. The oedipal scenario was always with us, but it evolved from the most primitive perceptions to mature ones.

References

Bion, W. R. (1967), *Seven Thoughts.* London: Heinemann.

Britton, R. (1989), The missing link: Parental sexuality in the inner world and the therapeutic situation. In: *The Oedipus Complex Today: Clinical Implications,* ed. F. Britton. London: Karnac Books, pp. 83–101.

Klein, M. (1950), *Contributions to Psychoanalysis 1921–1945.* London: Hogarth Press.

Segal, H. (1964), *An Introduction to the Work of Melanie Klein.* London: Heinemann.

3

Experiencing the Phallus as Extraneous: Women's Twofold Oedipus Complex

JULIA KRISTEVA

"[B]isexuality . . . comes to the fore much more clearly in women than in men"
[Freud, 1931, p. 374].

The Phallic Kairos

At a time when many practitioners and theorists view psychoanalysis as a transaction of organs and drives, while others make of it a mathematical formula of the signifier or a theory of "mind," or yet again a cognition, it seems to me necessary to uphold the viewpoint that the originality of Freud's discovery lies in discerning a *copresence* between the development of thought and that of language. It is an attentiveness to this twofold expression (thought-language) of speaking-being that forms the very core of the analytical experience and which, therefore, far from representing human essence in biological terms, centers the study of the psychical apparatus, its operations, and its blockages, on the biunivocal dependence of thought-language/language-thought. Such an interaction takes place within language and, accordingly, it is in this medium that Freud was to explore that "other scene," the unconscious, whose contents (representatives of the drive) and logic (primary process) nevertheless fundamentally differ from conscious linguistic communication. In defining my psychoanalytical approach and practice as the study of the copresence between language-*and*-thought, my aim is not simply to dissociate myself from the two trends currently in favor, the cognitivist and the phantasmatic-organicist approaches. I wish also to indicate at the outset of my discourse the basis on which I view female psychical bisexuality from the perspective of the relationship of women to the phallus.

The question to which I shall therefore address myself is that of the relationship of the female subject to the phallus. As a certain "phallic monism" is constantly drawn to our attention in clinical experience, I would first of all like to present a couple of particularly acute examples of the kind of adherence to the phallus that characterizes certain women: an adherence that effectively structures them, but at the price of often traumatic suffering.

Mystery and the Unbearable

Armelle occupies a high-ranking post in an international organization. Mother, wife, mistress, and author, she would seem to lack nothing, unless it be a personal satisfaction which, she insists, is not of a sexual nature: "I am not frigid," she specifies. This dissatisfaction is accompanied by the feeling of being like a little girl whom no one takes seriously and who never realizes her true capacities. Additionally, Armelle is led to take on all sorts of tasks and chores, even the most tiring and thankless, as though setting for herself superhuman goals. A veritable martyr, Armelle has made for herself a bed of nails upon which to lie and impale the flesh of her back and stomach. The martyrology of saints that her family background has handed down to her is superimposed here upon the structural *jouissance* or complex pleasure of the Freudian fantasy, "A child is being beaten": Armelle is being beaten, Armelle beats Armelle, Armelle pierces Armelle till the blood flows; her entire body is a phallus-penis finding its pleasure in sadomasochism by way of punishment for clitoral pleasure and to avoid recognition as a pierced-castrated body. Armelle is fixated at the pivotal point situated *between* what I term *Oedipus-1* and *Oedipus-2* (I shall come back to these terms later on). Her professional success, her phallicism in the symbolic order, has been acquired at the price of denying her bisexuality: she aspires to be all phallus. Her perverse pleasure is at the expense of the physical and mental exhaustion of the "superwoman."

Dominique is characterized by a slender, boyish body and by a way of talking, marked by allusion, secrecy, and omission. It is with difficulty that I find out that she has sexual relationships with women, but that the relationship to which she gives most importance is with a man, with whom she adopts a masochistic role. Much later, Dominique will reveal that this man is her immediate superior at her place of work and, even later yet, that he is black. Dominique had greatly admired her brother who was a year older than herself and with whom she had lived a mirror-relationship, as though doubles or twins, before the arrival of a baby sister, born five years after Dominique. The idyll lived by Dominique in her role as boy-double came to an end at adolescence, when her brother was killed by a car. "I don't believe women have a sex. When my brother died, it became apparent to me that the area between my legs was smooth, like a plastic doll." Without a penis, without a clitoris, without a vagina, Dominique lives the failure of her psychical bisexuality by offering her anus as a hollowed-out penis to her sadistic partner. Another variant of phallic monism.

I shall come back later to what these examples have shown us of phallicism's unbearable nature for women. For the moment, I would like to insist upon the universality of the phallic reference, which makes its appearance in both sexes, although in a somewhat different way, well before the phallic phase and the Oedipus complex that this phase announces. As a result of language, of the paternal function, and of the mother's desire for the father (for her own as well as for that of her child), the *trace* of the phallus, what Lacan (1991) terms "a phallus without incarnation" always-already organizes the subject's psychosexuality. Primary identification, narcissism, sublimation, idealization, the setting up of the ego ideal and of the superego, are but some of the well-known stages that mark this organization.

It is necessary to underline the importance of what Freud calls the phallic phase, which, structurally, plays the major role in organizing, in both sexes, the copresence of sexuality-thought of which I have spoken. Many authors have called attention to the particular characteristics that determine the *penis* being cathected (or invested libidinally) by the two sexes and becoming the *phallus,* that signifier of lack—of lack-in-being—or of desire, and, in consequence, signifier of the symbolic law. Its visibility and ability to become erect, the narcissistic gratification and erotogenic sensations that it offers, as well as its "detachability" and, therefore, "severability," all permit the penis to become the mark of difference, functioning as the pivot of the binary distinction, 0/1, upon which all meaning is based, and, in this sense, operate as the organic (i.e., real and imaginary) element of our psychosexual computer. The greek term *Kairos* ("propitious moment or encounter")[1] might well seem a fitting designation to give to this eminently subtle and, in this sense, mysterious encounter of meaning and desire that, effectuated during the phallic phase—all in being prepared for in advance—therein shapes the destiny of the human being qua speaking cum desiring being. The subject—whether anatomically male or female—is formed by this *phallic Kairos:* such is the revelation that psychoanalysis, long after the Greek mysteries, announces. Our psychical destiny is, essentially, to bear the consequences—that can aptly be qualified as tragic—of this mystery.

A veiled mystery, indeed. For, given its very structure and under the threat of castration, the phallicism of both sexes succumbs to repression and is succeeded by the latency period. Phallic primacy is for this reason the hallmark of *infantile* genital organization; it is precisely the factor differentiating *infantile* genitality from *adult* genitality, which in principle recognizes the existence of two sexes (Freud, 1923). And yet, phallic monism—with its recognition of one sex alone, the penis, of one libido alone, the masculine, and of a sole symbol for the activity of thought, the phallus—remains, for the two sexes, a fundamental datum of the unconscious. As such, phallic monism can be understood as an infantile illusion that subsists as an unconscious reality serving to structure the psyche. The transformation of an illusion into an unconscious

[1]More specifically, this term signifies what comes at the right moment or touches its goal; that which is timely, advantageous, or appropriate; the dangerous critical point. In modern Greek, it means "time" or "epoch." While its etymology is uncertain, it is thought to derive from "encounter" or "to cut."

reality: is this not a case of an illusion destined to a fine future? Indeed, we are confronted here with the basis of what Freud (1927), in one of his later works, would name "The Future of an Illusion," inasmuch as every religion truly draws upon the cult of the phallus.

That phallic monism is a residue of the infantile phallocentrism conditioning the Oedipus complex is an aspect of the Freudian theory of sexuality that has received insufficient attention. Similarly, it has not been sufficiently grasped that, as a consequence of the repression of this phallicism into the unconscious, the unconscious as such is phallic. This means that the unconscious lacks "genitality" in the sense of an acknowledgment of sexual differences, Or, to put it more bluntly, there is no unconscious psychical genitality: while one can speak of a biological instinct of procreation and of the advent, at puberty, of a desire for the other sex, nothing in Freudian theory indicates that there exists an unconscious psychical representative of the other sex as such.

To these first two aspects of phallic primacy, that is, its central role in the organization of the unconscious and its character as an infantile illusion, in the case of male sexual development, a third one must be added, namely the Oedipus complex. Determined by the phallic *Kairos,* it is subject to a veritable catastrophe, which takes the form of the boy's turning away from incest and murder, and culminates in the institution of conscience and morality, in which Freud saw "a victory of the race over the individual." Through the mechanisms of desexualization and sublimation, the early object cathexes are replaced by the agencies of the psychical apparatus, the id, the ego, and the superego, and neurosis alone betrays a "struggle" on behalf of the ego against "the demands of the sexual function." One might well wonder here as to that other form of "struggle" represented by the subject's creative use of thought or language, which, even though showing a proximity to neurosis or, indeed, to psychosis, cannot nevertheless be reduced to these two. Our examination of bisexuality may allow us a certain insight into this form of "struggle" that Freud, for his part, did not query in these terms.

As is well known, phallic primacy was to be taken up and invested with a particular value by Lacan (1991) in his rehabilitation of the function of the father and of language in speaking-being (*parlêtre*: which can also be translated as the "subject of speech"). Attributing to the phallus the values of "seeming" and "evanescence," Lacan positions it as the locus of lack and source of anxiety, and it is for this very reason that it can function as the primary symbol determining the process of sexual identification. "The man is not without having it, the woman is without having it" (p. 274). It seems to me interesting to compare this formula with Winnicott's (1971) proposition concerning the maternal element, which, as he moreover specifies, has nothing to do with the drives: the maternal element simply *is* (the self is the breast, the breast is the self) and does not *do* anything (the breast is a symbol of being, not of doing). Being, having, doing—are the distinctions really as clear-cut as Winnicott would like us to believe? The remarks that follow may be understood as both an elaboration and an inflection of Lacan's and Winnicott's propositions on the matter.

The Sensible versus the Signifier: The Extraneousness of the Phallus, the Illusory

In girls, the *Kairos*—that decisive encounter between the mastery of signs and genital excitation that forges the subject as a speaking-cum-desiring being—takes a particular form: it is the clitoris that assumes the phallic function. This function is simultaneously real (experienced), imaginary (fantasized in the oscillation of activity-passivity), and symbolic (as regards the cathexis and development of thought processes). Infantile masturbation and incestuous desire for the mother characterize this first phase of the Oedipus complex (*Oedipus-1*), by which girls (as much as boys) are structurally defined before they reach a second phase (*Oedipus-2*), which causes them to change object, with the father taking the place that was previously mother's. But, even in this first structuring of the subject (*Oedipus-1*), there are differences between the phallicism of girls and that of boys, which perhaps have not been sufficiently noticed.

The attention given to the role played by language in organizing psychical life, however judicious it may be, has too often prevented us from appreciating the importance of the role played by sensuous, that is, prelinguistic or translinguistic, experience. And yet, it is precisely the girl's sensuousness, so strongly stimulated by the symbiotic bond with the mother during the preoedipal phase (phase of primary homosexuality), that enables her to evaluate as much the different capacities of the boy's sexual organ as the excessive narcissistic cathexes of which the boy is the object. Indeed, whatever may be the degree of organic satisfaction and paternal valorization experienced by the girl (for nothing prevents the girl from being just as satisfied and valorized as the boy), her phallicism must be understood as displaying a structural dissociation between the sensible and the signifier.[2] The phallus, in its capacity as signifier of lack as well as of the law, is figured in the imaginary by the penis and is, therefore, perceived-conceived by a girl as something extraneous, and as radically heterogeneous. In other words, inasmuch as the girl's phallic pleasure finds both its real and imaginary "support" in the clitoris, that more inconspicuous organ, she is, at once, dissociated from the phallus, understood as a privileged signifier in that conjunction of Logos/Desire that I have named the phallic *Kairos*. I do not mean to say that this conjunction is less marked in girls than in boys. On the contrary, girls often display a greater facility in the (symbolic) register of thought. Nevertheless, the fact remains that the girl's symbolic (in the sense of intellectual) facility is at variance with her sensuous experience; no matter how much pleasure the girl may experience, she is nevertheless deceived by the fact of perceiving her organ as less visible, less impressive, and less appreciated. Consequently, the dissociation between the signifier and the sensuous is accompanied by the belief that the symbolic–phallic order is illusory.

The deception felt by the girl in perceiving herself as disadvantaged (she does not have a conspicuous penis, she is not the

[2]These remarks may be put into relation with recent discoveries suggesting that the right hemisphere plays a greater role in the exercise of language in women than in men. In being more lateralized, men's brains would therefore treat language in a more logical manner, as though dealing with a logical system, whereas, given that the right hemisphere is more implicated in perception-sensation, language use in women would be more associated with sensuousness. It is necessary, however, to interpret such data with the greatest circumspection, given not only the interconnection of neurones, but the fact that biological discoveries are always open to revision.

phallus) reactivates the hallucination of past experiences related to the satisfaction and/or frustration characterizing the girl–mother dyad, that moment of "Minoan–Mycenean" fusion (Freud, 1931, p. 226). As such, the experiences reactivated in this manner consist of sensuous experiences that either preceded the acquisition of language or took place outside of language. This being the case, the discrepancy between what is perceived in the present, under the sway of the phallic *Kairos,* and the hallucination of past perceptions, entails that the phallic monism assigned to the other (the man) that "I am not" thereby marks the being of the female subject with a negation: "I am not what is," "I am, nonetheless, if only by sheer force of *not.*" The extraneous or illusory character of the phallus is perhaps another way of designating this double negation of "nonetheless" and "not."

Thus stated, it is precisely the belief that the phallus and consequently language and the symbolic order are illusory, all in being indispensable, that closes the gap between perception and hallucination. In using the term *belief,* I refer here to the fact that the illusory nature of the phallus is, both consciously and unconsciously, adhered to by women as something that is evident, without any need for proof. This qualification of "illusory" (derived from the Latin *ludere,* "to play," and hence *illudere,* "to make fun of" or "to mock") refers to the fact that everything the phallus gives the female subject access to (the law, power, and a certain pleasure—but also, the possibility of their lack) is ultimately, for her, but a game. It is not entirely nothing, but it is not the be-all and end-all, either, even were this to be veiled, as the phallic mysteries claim it to be. Simply, there is something else, an undefinable, ineffable something else. And as to the phallus—well, by cathecting the phallus, I become a subject of language and of the law: which is what I am. So I play the game: I want my part of the action too. But, it is just a game, just a role that "I" play; a case of play-acting, of make-believe, which, indeed, for the female-subject, is all the so-called truth of the signifier or of the subject-of-speech boils down to. In stating this, I do not mean that women necessarily have a playful (ludic) attitude to life, although this is the case for some. However, when they are not under an illusion, women are disillusioned; which is to say that the seeming "realism" of women is based on these illusions women are able to keep going, to do all that needs to be done, because they don't believe in it, they believe it is an illusion.

There are advantages to such a belief in the illusory nature of the phallus. Girls can, for example, cultivate a secret sensuousness that, if furtive at times, nevertheless spares them from the exacting task that boys must confront in making their erotic pleasure coincide with their symbolic performance. Such a dissociation between sensuousness and the signifier can favor girls' intellectual development, for the two spheres of logical competency and erotism are, in being extraneous from one another, kept distinct. The scholastic superiority of young girls is well known.

On the other hand, the experiencing of the phallus as extraneous has its reverse side, where, far from rendering things easier, it can give rise to an acute phallic ambition bordering on the sadomasochistic martyrdom highlighted by the clinical examples outlined earlier on. Comprising one aspect of what is named in too cursory a fashion "feminine masochism," this sadomasochistic phallic competitiveness can be interpreted as a form of "delusion" inasmuch as it entails the denial (or disavowal) of the difference of the phallus and, thereby, of its illusory status. Such a disavowal, implying an identification with the phallus, amounts to an identification with the phallic position of the man and to a scotomization (or nonrecognition) of the primary preoedipal bond with the mother, often qualified as "primary homosexuality." In refusing to accept the extraneous position of the phallus and/or her psychical bisexuality, the phallic girl (who wants to "have it" too) shows the fervor of a zealot: becoming the saint, martyr, and militant of a signifier, she "organizes" her erotogenic zones in such a way as to deny the illusoriness of the phallus, as though all the better to convince herself that her belief rests upon firm foundations. The result of such a quest for equality with male phallicism is exemplified in the figures of the female paranoiac (the boss, the businesswoman, etc.) and the virile lesbian: partisans of power in all of its more or less dictatorial forms.

The belief in the illusory or extraneous character of the phallus seems to me to be an index of female psychical bisexuality. The reason for this follows from the fact that the dissociation between sensuousness and the signifier which underpins the illusoriness of the phallus is, as we have seen, based on the girl's persistent attachment to the preoedipal fusion with the mother. This attachment is equally an attachment to the code by which such a fusion was given expression: it consists as much of a sensory interaction as of prelinguistic phenomena, such as rhythms and alliteration, which, preceding the acquisition of signs and syntax, form what I have named the "semiotic modality" (1974a,b). The abandonment of this modality, in favor of linguistic signs, occurs in both girls and boys during the depressive position, although, here again, there are probably differences between the sexes that have up to now been insufficiently explored. Later on, the phallic structuring of the subject will complement and reinforce language acquisition while at the same time causing, in girls, what can now be characterized as the reactivation of the depressive position and, thereby, an accentuation of the girl's belief in the *illusory* character of the phallus and language.

It follows that the illusory position women attribute to the phallus can favor the onset of depressive regressions when, in succumbing to the shadowy attraction of the preoedipal object, the girl forsakes the extraneous symbolic order and gives herself up to an ineffable, sullen, and suicidal sensuousness. Some women, on the other hand, display a maniacal investment in illusory phallicism, adhering in this respect to a veritable logic of exhibition, such as that exemplified by the alluring seductress, always immaculately made up, dressed up, prettified, and provocative. In this figure of the female "illusionist" who is completely conscious of the masquerade she employs, we can recognize the "girl-phallus" of which Fenichel and, subsequently, Lacan were to speak. All women know this figure and all of us play on it.

As a final—and precautionary—remark concerning the illusory character of the phallus, I would specify that the particular phenomenon I am describing should be firmly understood as a manifestation of female psychical bisexuality and not be confused with the clinical figures of the false self or the as-if personality, whose etiology always entails a severe splitting of the psychical activity. I have not spoken of "splitting" but of "play," "extraneousness," and "illusoriness." Women's adherence to the illusory character of the phallus does not impede them from functioning in the social order, where they display a certain detached efficiency. Is this not what Hegel referred to in speaking of women as "the everlasting irony in the life of the community"?

The Girl's Twofold Oedipus Complex

The illusory character of the phallus is, however, but one component of the complex configuration of female bisexuality. As is well known, Freud (1931) was to alter his initial conception of the Oedipus complex in the realization that it could not adequately describe the complexity of the girl's development. "We have an impression here that what we have said about the Oedipus complex applies with complete strictness to the male child only. . ." (pp. 228–229). While certain theorists have been encouraged by this remark to reject phallic monism, and therefore the phallic structuring of the female subject, it is obvious that I am not of their opinion. I do propose, however, that the girl's development be seen to entail a twofold Oedipus complex, by which I mean that what I have called *Oedipus-1* (that structuring of the subject inaugurated by the phallic phase and indispensable for both sexes) must be understood as being complemented, in the girl's case, by an *Oedipus-2,* in the sense of a "reworking" or repetition of the oedipal organization that, for this very reason, is open-ended or "interminable."

The mechanism of this *Oedipus-2* can best be grasped by first recalling a certain number of factors. As I have suggested, it is not only the threat of castration but also the experience of the extraneousness of the phallus that prompts the little girl to abandon her clitoral masturbation, renouncing it and turning away from both her real phallicism (from the belief, "I *have* the phallus") and her imaginary phallicism (the belief, "I *am* masculine potency-impotence"). While cultivating her position as a subject of the phallic signifier (with the particular stamp of otherness and illusoriness that she gives it), the little girl, in this phase of *Oedipus-2,* does something more: she changes object. She starts by hating the mother who had previously been the object of her phallic desire who is now viewed with hostility as responsible for her castration as well as for the illusion, with all its implications of deception. Despite her hatred, however, the girl still identifies with mother and, even more, she remains identified with the preoedipal mother with whom she had shared the paradise of the "Minoan–Mycenaean civilization" (Freud, 1931, p. 226). It is from this position of an identification that exists in spite of, and beyond, the hatred for mother that the girl changes object and desires, henceforth not the mother, but what the mother desires, namely, father's love. More precisely, the girl desires that the father make her the gift of his penis-phallus in the form of a baby that the girl will have just as if she were herself the mother. The girl's phallic aspiration therefore takes a new form and continues during this phase of *Oedipus-2,* and one can understand that Freud (1925) postulated that, in opposition to what happens in the case of the boy, where the Oedipus complex is demolished under the influence of the castration complex, the girl's Oedipus complex—what I call *Oedipus-2*—not only is not demolished, but in fact only really commences with the castration complex. In Freud's own words, "the Oedipus complex . . . *in girls is made possible and led up to by the castration complex*" (p. 256).

Taking up this feminine position toward the father is not without its ambiguities. On the one hand, given that it results from an identification with the castrated–castrating mother, at first abhorred and then accepted, it is accompanied by a "marked lowering of the active sexual impulses [and repression] of her previous masculinity [with the concomitant effect that] a considerable portion of her sexual trends in general is permanently injured too" (Freud, 1931, p. 239). Does this mean that the "illusoriness" is supplanted by passivity? And yet, parallel to this rise of passive trends (or, in some cases, depression), the desire of having the penis (penis envy) persists as a variant of phallicism; which proves that active sexual trends are far from having been abolished. This penis envy can take the form of either masculine protest, manifested in the woman's behavior and professional pursuits; or, alternatively and more "naturally," of a desire for a child and motherhood. It is at this point perhaps that the world as an illusory reality for women comes to an end and there opens up the world of real presence.

Representing the real presence of the phallus, the child becomes the object of a cathexis on the part of the mother in a way that no sign or symbol (even if these were phallic) can be. This was evidently understood by the Christian religion, when it made a child its god and, in this way, definitively won women over to its cause. This took place in spite of their profound tendency to disillusionment, which, indeed, amounts to a strong incredulity when they are faced with ideals and disincarnated superegos—what Freud severely criticized as women's poorly developed sense of morality.

The child may therefore, in the case of women, be seen to incarnate the final phallic revolt marking that open-ended, and therefore interminable, phase of *Oedipus-2* ("I want a penis" = real presence) and, in this way, to find in the child another expression of their bisexuality for, quite simply, the child is a woman's penis so that she does not have to renounce her masculinity. At the same time, however, it is via the child that the woman acquires the quality of being "other" than the man; that is, a woman who has given her child, who has emptied herself of it, separated herself from it. This does not mean that motherhood is lived or perceived as a disequilibrium of the identity or, even less, as an open structure; on the contrary, it is most often lived and perceived as a state of completeness, for which the term of *androgyny* is actually more fitting than "bisexuality." Moreover, with the incarnation of the symbolic order in the child-phallus, the woman is presented with the conjunction of her symbolic essence, qua phallic thinking subject, and of her corporeal essence, encompassing her preoedipal sensuality and the sensual mother–daughter dyad as well as the reduplication of mother and daughter in the maternal function. For this reason, and as the continuation of her bisexuality in the androgyny marking her ever-renewed *Oedipus-2,* the woman-mother can be considered the guardian of both the social order and the continuity of the species.

Women's character as social beings culminates in the figure of maternal omnipotence. Today, this figure would seem to find a new vigor in its relaying of the function attributed to the mother as the guarantor of the social and biological order. Modern genetics and gynecology contribute to what may be understood as the mother's aspiration to repair her real presence; abetted by science and technology, the mothering woman fantasizes that she is capable of doing all that is necessary and often exhausts herself in her efforts to not only bring into existence, but equally to improve by means of her child the real presence of the phallus.

And yet, this image of a hypersocial, ultrabiological, and avowedly restorative femininity, while not entirely false, seems to me to overlook two sources of fragility. The first consists of the permanence, in women, of the structure of illusion-disillusionment as regards each and every signifier, law, or desire. The second concerns the vulnerability that necessarily characterizes the woman-mother inasmuch as, in delegating *her* real presence to that of her *child* (to another), she accordingly relives the terrors of castration or, worse, undergoes a violent crisis of identity each time her child's well-being is threatened. In this way, we find once again that the so-called feminine sadomasochism is perhaps precisely the experience of the structural extraneousness of the phallus; for these two sources of fragility affecting the structuring of the female subject are, indeed, the expression of two forms of this experience based, respectively on *Oedipus-1* concerning the disillusionment, and on *Oedipus-2*, concerning the threat to the woman's real presence as delegated to her "other," the child.

It would seem indeed, that female bisexuality falls prey to such ordeals of sadomasochism when not securely anchored on the belief in omnipotence—by which I mean that the various figures of female bisexuality I have outlined are to be understood as so many variants of the position of the female subject in relation to phallic monism. It is perhaps the structural difficulties of this positioning, more than the historical conditions as such, that finally explain the tribulations that have been women's lot throughout the ages.

Going back to the phallic adherence demonstrated in the cases of Armelle and Dominique at the start of my discourse, the suffering of such patients can now be understood as a denial of bisexuality in favor of the fantasy of androgynous completion. In presenting certain striking aspects of the "tribulations of the feminine condition," my aim was to highlight that what one might call, by way of contrast, the "mystery" of female bisexuality can be realized only by avoiding such impasses (alas, only too frequent). Inasmuch as the experience (and the *jouissance* or pleasure) of bisexuality is properly "transphallic," that is, not less phallic but more-than-phallic, it may be described as "mysterious," in the strict sense of the term.[3] Rather than concluding that pain is the ultimate mystery, what I am suggesting is that a resolution of feminine masochism may occur precisely through the achievement of female bisexuality.

Certainly, as with all instances of success, female psychical bisexuality is a fantasy or, if you prefer, a promised land that we have yet to attain. It presupposes the positioning of the female subject in the phallic signifying order (*Oedipus-1*), with all the accompanying pleasures and symbolic gratifications that this extraneous and illusory order procures. But, in addition, it promises a reconciliation with primary homosexuality, a transformation of castration, of depression, and of sexual devalorization, with a consequent revalorization of the maternal role and, thereby, of the woman's role. And this is not all: A cathexis of the real presence of the phallus-child is also necessary, for an experience both of achievement and castration, which, while less illusory, still remains somewhat "estranged." One can appreciate the enormous amount of psychical effort required by such a process, never entirely accomplished, but explaining the strange, disillusioned, and yet lively and reliable air that characterizes certain women.

Correspondingly, a recathecting of orality and anality takes place in women by way of a regressive counterbalance to phallic deception. Language can then become itself cathected in the oral and anal register as a narcissistic pleasure, in distinction to its cathexis in the register of phallic competitiveness. Such a dynamic can give greater importance to "tender" or "affective" tendencies than to "phallic-erotic" ones. The discovery of the vagina as an "interiority" and "unrepresentable volume," that is, "other" than the phallus, is probably also to be placed in this line of development, with the vagina thereby becoming the enigmatic "dark continent" that challenges phallic power as much as it stimulates the imaginary.

Consisting of a veritable vortex of adherence and nonadherence to the phallus (to the signifier, to desire), female bisexuality (were this, indeed, to exist) would be no less and no more than

[3]The word *mysterious* derives from the Greek *mus* "hidden," "enclosed"; from the Sanskrit *mukham* "mouth," "hole," "enclosure," and has given the Slavonic *muka,* "pain," "mystery."

an experience of meaning and its gestation, of language and its erosion, of being and its concealment. In saying this, I have just indicated what is truly at stake in the experience of literature and art, our contemporary and lucid version of the sacred. And I would suggest this as one way of considering why it is the bisexuality of the Gomorrhean Albertine that Proust, in his search for things past, makes the focal point of his narrator's phantasms. Might female bisexuality not, indeed, be the object par excellence of literature and art?

At the same time, the structural relation that I am assuming to exist between female bisexuality and aesthetic experience may open up another avenue of exploration, which I would like to briefly take by way of conclusion. It is my conviction that female unconscious bisexuality allows us to glimpse the psychical mechanisms underpinning atheism, at least the kind of atheism that does not entail a militant antireligious cathexis. This follows from what I have said about a woman's position as regards unconscious bisexuality and phallic monism: far from constituting a cult of the phallus, far from going beyond or from falling short of such a cult, her bisexuality, in its very estrangement, maintains the illusion as an illusion. Am I positing in this manner the "future of an illusion"? But, of course! Whatever one might say, Freud, that inveterate rationalist, was quite right in stating that everyone wants his or her part of illusion, even while obstinately refusing to recognize it for what it is. Women are, however, structurally better placed than men when it comes to exploring the possibilities opened up by illusion. And I am not sure that atheism can ever mean anything else than leaving the Other its place, exploring all its different facets, all its possibilities, and putting them into perspective.

In conclusion, it is the mainspring of such an atheism that I would like to insist upon one last time. For the psychical effort required to produce a subject of speech that no more adheres to the illusion of being than to the being of illusion is extraordinary. Such is the effort required of that psychically bisexual being which is a woman. And thereupon, I acknowledge that what I am saying may not be but an illusion.

References

Freud, S. (1923), The infantile genital organization: An interpolation into the theory of sexuality. *Standard Edition*, 19:139–145. London: Hogarth Press, 1961.

——— (1925), Some psychical consequences of the anatomical distinction between the sexes. *Standard Edition*, 19:243–258. London: Hogarth Press, 1961.

——— (1927), The Future of an Illusion. *Standard Edition*, 21:1–56. London: Hogarth Press, 1961.

——— (1931), Female sexuality. *Standard Edition*, 21:221–243. London: Hogarth Press, 1961.

Kristeva, J. (1974a), *La Révolution du langage poétique*. Paris: Seuil.

——— (1974b), *Revolution in Poetic Language*, trans. M. Waller. New York: Columbia University Press, 1984.

Lacan, J. (1991), *Le Séminaire, livre VIII, Le Transfert*. Paris: Seuil.

Winnicott, D. W. (1986), *Home Is Where We Start from: Essays by a Psychoanalyst*, ed. C. Winnicott. Harmondsworth, U.K.: Penguin Books.

——— (1971), *Playing and Reality*. Harmondsworth, U.K.: Penguin Books, 1982.

Translated by Louise Burchill

4

From Oedipal Problems to Phallic Universe

Pentti Ikonen, Phil.Mag.

Preamble

What follows is rather in the nature of a tractate. The material used will be familiar to readers, from analytical practice, from the analyst's self-analysis, from case studies, and other analytical literature as well as from daily life. I assume, therefore, that the material, as such, it not subject to dispute; and I will refer to it in attempting to present a certain viewpoint, one particular thread plucked out of a manifold texture. I will display it without arguing for it. It must be up to each reader to determine, by self-analysis and by his or her own practice, the fruitfulness of this point of view.

The main theme of my discourse is a serious consideration of certain fundamental findings with regard to the Oedipus complex and phallicism. By these terms I mean the oedipal sexual wish, the urgent need for defense against it with its attendant problems, and the phallic notion of only one kind of genital—the phallus—existing.

My object of investigation is the potential use of phallicism as a defensive organization against the problems of the oedipal phase

(Jones, 1933). As soon as we recognize the child's sexual desire for his parents to be a reality of the psyche, we can begin to discern the problems inherent in it. Here are some of the aspects involved.

Forbidden and Shameful Pleasure

That the sexual wish is directed at the parents means that evil and improper mentations are associated with them. From the outset, the identity of sexuality is that of the forbidden, the unapproved, and the shameful, since it has been defined by these very attributes, in contrast to other sensual pleasures. Only later does it acquire the name of *sexuality,* to become understood as such.

When, in the oedipal phase, the child's attention focuses more strongly and clearly on sexuality and the genitals (the genitals become more cathected by libido and the genital libido begins to differentiate from other forms of libido), the restrictions and prohibitions associated with them are also emphasized more clearly than before, and the forbidden and shameful character of sexuality and its expressions strengthened. Even at the age of latency, a graffiti such as "Johnny loves Mary" is taken as libellous, and later on throughout life, the concern with shame is what regulates the expressions of sex and eroticism.

Mutuality

Mutuality holds an important position in man's psyche. As soon as the child is born, the mother tries to (and indeed does) understand more and more when and why her baby is well or unwell, and to do all she can to care for her baby's well-being. If the mother succeeds in this, she, too, feels content; if not, she feels bad. In this sense, infant and mother do share a common emotional reality (I refer to Alice Balint's [1949] paper and Michael Balint's [1952] work on primary love).

From the infant's point of view, he and his mother inhabit the same emotional space, with pleasure to be sought and unpleasure avoided accordingly. The emotional reality is self-evidently mutual. Only gradually does the child come to realize that this is not so. In some areas of the experiential world, the emotional reality is in fact mutual, but in many it is not. In those areas where mother and child do share a common emotional reality and mutuality obtains, the child feels that he is understood. The same is true of any relationship between two adults; indeed, between any two human beings. This sort of deep, fundamental sense of being understood is one of the most important positive experiences in human life.

In the adult world, we have many ways—beginning with remarks about the weather, or eating together—in which we try to set up a common emotional reality, and even more ways to pretend that it exists. In this context, we may recall an old adage to the effect that were it not for the value of real money there would be no profit in printing counterfeit bills. Between adults, such a shared emotional reality, the mutuality of it, actualizes spontaneously and most powerfully in sexual life, where coitus, and readiness for it, presupposes a mutuality even on a biological level, and lack of mutuality always implies a problem.

If a human being, whether child or adult, is disappointed in his anticipations of mutuality and feels that the failure must be due to himself, it constitutes an insult to his narcissism, and arouses shame. These are emotional upsets that the child must suffer time and time again during the oedipal phase. The incestuous sexual wish for maximum mutual proximity, physically and mentally, invariably leads to the interruption of mutuality, and sometimes to the temporary breakdown of the entire parent–child relationship as a penalty for improper behavior. The fate of oedipal wishes entails the absolute end of mutuality as regards the most important wish of all, and the child's utter ineligibility for mutuality, with all the feeling of exclusion and humiliation this involves.

Sexual Inadequacy of the Child

Also, regardless of restrictions, children do apprehend their inadequacy as sexual partners to adults (Grunberger, 1979). Above all, this emerges in primal scene fantasies and in the power and terror of the adult figures therein, but also in the impressions children have of the parents' genitals, above all of the father's penis. The small boy feels himself to be ineffectual in the sexual act, unable to make an impression, and the little girl is afraid of being "broken." Moreover, the girl feels herself to be devoid of sexual attributes, while the boy feels that his attributes are very insignificant indeed, a motive for envy for both.

To both boy and girl, inadequacy as a sexual partner means humiliation and an offense to his or her narcissism. Recovery demands much psychic work, and leaves as a residue a sort of primary fantasy: for the boy, that he must be efficient and make an impression to be a man; for the girl, that she must be able to endure and suffer a lot in order to be a woman, and also in order to have a child and care for it. These fantasies, processed in various ways, seem, for the most part, to persist throughout life.

The superiority of the oedipal rival also implies a narcissistic insult, which incites the child to rage against one or both of the parents and arouses a wish to "turn the tables"—though on exactly whom or what is unclear—while, at the same time, feeling guilty about all this, and fearing revenge and punishment, in other words, castration.

Phallic Organization

The oedipal disappointments and narcissistic insults described in the foregoing are among the things that the child must learn to live with. In one way or another, they must be worked through, or else some means of defense must be found. In the following, I propose to present the use of phallic organization, for just such a defensive purpose, as well as some of the consequences that arise.

Phallic organization lends itself well to being used as a defense against the oedipal problems, irrespective of how this organization has arisen—whether it is a stage of the libido development, or an organization originally defensive in character.

The defining factor of the phallic organization is that it recognizes only one kind of genital, the phallus (Freud, 1923). This is concretely represented by the penis, and also by the clitoris, which, however, due to its minuteness, at the same time represents the lack of a phallus. Some people have a phallus, others do not. Thus people are categorized as either phallics or castrates, but this bracketing does not necessarily comply with actual gender. In the phallic world, there exists, then, no receptive organ such as the vagina.

If there exists only this one organ, which prepares for action by growing harder, stiffer, and larger, and whose known, or suspected, action is to penetrate into something without a complementary organ to receive it, then the nature of that action must of necessity be piercing, that is, forcible and disruptive (Freud, 1908). It is not a mutual libidinal act involving both participants equally, in accordance with their well-adapted and complementary genitals.

Phallic–oedipal sexual fantasies are in one way or another violent, often openly so, as is evidenced in the primal scenes especially. Boys' war games with swords, pistols, or other weapons are usually (and most naturally) interpreted, by those who wish to make a case for them, as being phallic–sexual in character, and not merely expressive of aggression. In the adult world, too, violence and sexuality are frequently mixed up in general and political discussions on morality, but equally so in the events that form the subject matter of such discussions.

Primal Scene

It is difficult to say to what extent the actual event that precipitated the primal scene fantasy also provoked the psychical dynamics by which the child conceives of coitus; or, alternatively, to what extent the child gradually developed those dynamics and the corresponding conceptualization during the oedipal stage, as a defense against the problems of that phase. The former alternative would mean an instantaneous response to an inconceivable, almost traumatic event, and subsequently, a continuing defensive use of the response obtained in this manner. The second alternative might be likened to a manifest dream, preceded by a—possibly extended—preparatory dynamic process, which, when a suitable launching stimulus presents itself, or is found after active searching, produces the dream in question. The primal scene would then be the intensified manifestation of a defensive organization developed over time, an organization remaining in constant use in later life. In either alternative, the essential point is that the same dynamic organization which actualizes in the formation of the primal scene also plays a central part later on, in the conceptualization of reality, and especially of human relationships.

For my part, I would tend to the view that the child will respond with phallic defense each time the oedipal wishes for mutuality end in disappointment. In this manner, the unfolding sexuality gradually becomes phallicized, and the use of phallic defense expands and establishes itself (in Finland, in my childhood, you could say of a person whose exertions had ended in frustration that he "got a long nose"; in other words, he had to resort to phallic defense).

The child, then, gradually creates his phallic defensive organization under the strain and threat of oedipal disappointments. At the same time, that organization will be colored by his earlier libidinal development. When the longing for mutuality is strong, it may retain many earlier forms, depending on the manner in which it has been possible to achieve mutuality during different stages. Such early forms of mutuality may live on relatively independently alongside phallicism—as infantilisms of a kind—or be mixed in with it, while modifying and disguising it. Consider, as examples, sexual foreplay, or the little perversions of daily life, or, indeed, the human sexual profile in general. Moreover, the child (as later on the adult) will also protect himself against phallicism and "talk" of phallic matters in the "language" of earlier stages of development, even as he employs phallicism to fend off oedipal humiliation: "If I were a great big lion, I'd eat you all."

Violence as Defense

In using phallic organization as defense against oedipal disappointments, the child denies the mutuality which is part of genital sexuality and of which he has no clear conception. It is replaced with ideas of violence and power. Thus the genital mutuality for which the child is ineligible is banalized into violence and the exercise of power. In such terms, the child is no longer excluded to the same extent, since even a small child can give evidence of his power and violence while enjoying the narcissistic and sadomasochistic pleasure they offer. The narcissistic humiliation can be alleviated by phallic displays of power and potency, and, in many cases, a person will spend most of the rest of his life in acquiring such relief.

The idea of forcible penetration that is part and parcel of the phallic organization explains, and simultaneously reinforces, to the child the evil of sexuality: the sexual act hurts one party, the passive one, the phallic object, it pierces, spoils, castrates the person. Sometimes the act injures both parties, so that the phallic one loses at least his or her power, if not the phallus. Intermingled and mixed in with these fantasies are fantasies of the punishments to follow. Some of these are conceived of as natural consequences of sexuality, others as the revenge of rivals, yet others as administered by moral authorities such as parents, educators, and physicians.

Of course, there are a great many ways in which sexuality may cause injury, and equally many reasons why, but the phallic notion carries the conviction that the central sexual event per se is, and ought to be, a destructive act, and that the summit of sexual pleasure is a sadomasochistic breaking and getting broken.

It follows from the phallic equivalence between destructiveness and sexuality that any sort of breaking (spoiling or conquering) will pass for a phallic display of sexual power or potency. This should be kept in mind in all investigations of misdemeanor and violence.

Image of Power

Phallicism colors our image of power. The most impressive manifestations of power are such things as large-scale destruction, invasions, victories, and vanquishings. The power of the sea, for example, is best appreciated in something like a huge tsunami, not in the fact that the ocean supports gigantic ships or that it nourishes a vast range of flora and fauna. A researcher conquers new realms of knowledge, a thinker overthrows the ideas of another. In neither example is mental power evidenced as an ability to reciprocate. The power of nations can hardly be imagined as anything besides their capacity to govern, conquer, or oppress other nations. The mutuality that takes another into consideration is seen as a sign of weakness or guile. After power has been construed as phallic, the conclusion is then drawn that phallicism is indispensable or else there would be no power, no initiative, no violent action in the world.

Hidden Violence

Phallic violence does not necessarily parade in a manifest fashion or even as anything resembling it. It may equally well be realized covertly, as the oppression, the fettering, or hemming in of a partner, or as the maneuvering of someone into a position of dependence. To such ends, even charm and captivation may be taken into service. If one wants to charm somebody, one does not sit down to listen; rather, one attempts to spellbind him or her. What matters is one's own purpose, not the purpose of the other, and so mutuality is of no concern. And as a charmer or enchantress, after achieving the purpose, moves on to find new evidence of his or her irresistibleness (i.e., phallic power), he or she is revealed as a "heartbreaker."

Tool Fixation

The emphasis on the import of a single organ and its function to the neglect of the personality as a whole is clearly evident in those phallic fantasies of children in the oedipal phase that concern the penis: what it looks like, how big it is, how it operates, and how it may be injured or disabled; that is, the fear of castration. These fantasies persist throughout life in forms proper to a person's current age group; in youth and in adult life they are perhaps most evident in "filthy" jokes.

The phallic fantasies of childhood are stimulated by many different factors, chief of which is the strong sensual pleasure associated with the genitals and with fondling them. Masturbation reinforces the feeling that it is possible to receive intense pleasure on one's own, independently of others, solely through a certain organ. Another stimulus is the behavior of the penis itself, its changes in size and appearance. That these changes are independent of conscious will, sometimes clearly related to thoughts and emotions, sometimes irrespective of these as well, seems to emphasize the independence of the penis in relation to the self—of which it, nonetheless, remains a most significant part at all times.

In many phallic fantasies, the phallus is an organ capable of being detached, attached, and exchanged, and the efficacy of the sexual act is dependent on the quality of the phallus, not on its employer. From here, it is but a short way to various fetishistic fantasies as well as to the phallic symbolic values of technical instruments such as weapons, worktools, and vehicles. Certainly, fetishes and phallic symbols do provide protection against castration anxiety, but it would also be worth investigating to what extent the regarding of tools and their relative efficiency as values in themselves, so prevalent in our culture, incorporates a phallic attempt to cancel out and to overcompensate for the humiliation of the oedipal absolute insufficiency. The cathexis of the phallus lends itself well as a defense against the humiliation: "What really matters is the organ itself, not me."

The belief in the paramount importance of the equipment, the tool, implicit in the phallic organization, remains in the sexual area, as well as in many others, throughout the individual's life.

The phallic fixation to equipment, as well as the phallic tool symbolism in general, and in particular the part of it concerned with weaponry—these reflect the shift of the phallic organization from sexual mutuality toward violence, which cares not at all about either mutuality or disqualification from it. In reality, nothing could be less like a weapon than the penis. It is a sensitive and easily damaged organ that must be protected in all situations involving danger and combat. From a sexually realistic point of view, the weaponlike status of the phallus is a defensive and wholly fantastical fabrication. Yet this fantasy thrives mightily in our culture.

As we know, the boy's observation of the lack of masculine genitals in females arouses the fear that he, too, might lose them. This fear is compounded by the idea that the castrates seek revenge for their own inferiority and the superiority of others. Yet the other great significance of the phallus as a support for self-esteem lies in the very fact that not everybody is endowed with one. Human beings—and, to an extent, other living creatures as well—may be categorized into "phallics" and "castrates," and "phallics" are better, more valuable, and privileged. To the oedipal–phallic little boy, to possess an important organ which his mother lacks, but his father and himself both have, is a great help as he attempts to free himself from his mother's orbit. And for a small girl, the desire to free herself from her mother provides a motive for wanting to be like the boys (Chasseguet-Smirgel, 1964).

Again, the insecurity and fear caused by separation from the mother inspire the child to exaggerated phallic fantasies of superiority, and to projecting onto the phallus (and its representation, the penis) things that are really attributes of the mother, from whom the child is trying to separate. Some examples of this are: that the penis of a little boy might secrete a fluid as good as, or better than, that which flows from his mother's breast, or that the urine which issues from it is in fact such a fluid, or that the breasts and the penis are equivalent organs. In adulthood, notions of the healing, invigorating, and beautifying properties of the seminal fluid are natural extrapolations of such fantasies.

The net sum of these imaginations is an instrument nothing short of fantastical: an invincible weapon and tool as well as an inexhaustible cornucopia of goods. Such an instrument is the magic wand of fairy tales, a sort of consummate phallic fantasy, along with a host of similar magical implements: helmets, swords, lamps, and the like. Power and potency reside solely in the instrument. Its possessor or owner may be weak and impotent, but through the magical tool he or she commands, the possessor is able to achieve almost anything. With its aid, he or she is an autopotent operator, independent of any kind of mutuality. And, insofar as technology is able to accommodate it, this is the spirit that informs the production of tools and devices in our technical culture.

Even in the early years of analytic investigation a baby or a child was found, in many cases, to represent to the woman the phallus that she lacks. Later, it was discovered that the child may also be a representation of the woman's inner space (Kestenberg,

1982). The same holds true for the relationship of a little girl to her doll. Because the genital inner space is no part of the phallic world, these stresses on the significance of a child indicate at what point, during analysis, we enter into, or quit, the realm of phallic fantasies.

Passive Phallicism

Also implicit in the phallic defensive organization is the idea of becoming the object of the phallic act, with the attendant emotions and dynamic configurations (Freud, 1924). To a small girl, and equally to a small boy, being a phallic object has the import of being broken, that is, of castration. And, as far as they are concerned, this idea is not far removed from reality. While there is good cause for the terror it exerts, it is attractive nonetheless. The excitement it communicates represents the terrifying summit of dangerous and cruelly sensual pleasure. For some, such a phallic–masochistic picture of the sexual life provides a reason for turning wholly away from sex. Others find here a reason for accepting suffering, and the endurance of it, as part of the sexual life of a phallic object, and yet others a motive for ecstatic fantasies and actings out of agony and danger.

Despite its painfulness, even a passive phallicism will afford protection against the humiliation of oedipal–genital inadequacy—"I *am* a prospective partner, and I *am* attractive." In addition, it makes possible the inversion of the narcissistic pain of humiliation into phallic–narcissistic satisfaction, first in childhood and subsequently throughout life, e.g., in liaisons of love, of friendship, and other kinds of human relationships where oedipal insults loom.

As is well known, the erotic life of mankind is largely tragic. "Plaisir d'amour ne dure qu'un moment. Chagrin d'amour dure toute la vie," says the poet. There are, no doubt, innumerable valid reasons for such a state of affairs, but the phallic sadomasochistic defense should not be discounted as a potential factor.

Generally speaking, passive phallicism extends a natural bridge for the sexualization of various kinds of sufferance. These may be fears, anxieties, feelings of guilt, shame, and envy for whatever reasons, but also varieties of denial and self-victimization, necessary or unnecessary.

Active and passive phallicism will often intertwine. In heroism, for instance, the admiration of power and violence includes the admiration of voluntary exposure to them, of the implicit fearlessness—and, accordingly, a propensity for such surrender. Death and victory will simultaneously and ecstatically illuminate the mind of the sadomasochistic phallic hero. Contemporary horror movies with their elaborate monsters and gargoyles allow a safe identification with the representative of either phallic position, subject or object.

The same narcissistic threat, that of castration, the very reason why the boy resigns his oedipal wishes, can become an enduring passive–phallic fulfillment for him, and in this manner, a narcissistic recompense. The same applies to the girl's penis envy.

The pain associated with the absence of a beloved person, or of one otherwise important—even that of the analyst during a pause in analysis—may be experienced as caused by that person, and transformed into unconscious passive–phallic satisfaction. In such cases, the continuance of pain, the accusations, the quarrels, the actings out, are nothing so much as a wallowing in passive–phallic sadomasochistic pleasure, and a prolonging of it. The same applies to the grief of loss. An endless, agonizing continuation or, rather, sustaining of "heartaches" can bear witness to such a process.

The potentiality of sadomasochistic sexualization of punishment is so well known that we need, in this context, only refer to it in passing, while stressing its possibly phallic character.

Exhibitionism

Children sometimes openly verbalize their oedipal libidinal wishes by confessing their great love, or by stating their intention to marry their father or mother, or both, when they grow up, but more commonly they communicate them by facial expressions, gestures, or various advances. Curiosity, too, may express an oedipal wish, as may jealousy, albeit indirectly.

By his expression, or, if the term is preferable, by his *exhibition,* man signals his attitude and relationship to whatever is at hand, be it other human beings, their thoughts and feelings, or the weather, food, or current politics. From the expressional standpoint, it is essential that the message be understood, and so it contains an expectation of an answer which will indicate a successful transmission. In addition, it involves a probe or query as to how the person for whom the message is intended has reacted to its content.

The child's expressions of his oedipal–sexual wishes are generally fated to remain uncomprehended. If they are indeed understood, they are rejected and disapproved of, as being improper or reprehensible. Nor is a scoffing attitude to the child's oedipal wishes uncommon. Usually, what is ridiculed is the fact that the child does not understand the inadequacy of his desires. Thus, the child's expressions and expectations of a common emotional reality and of the mutuality of oedipal wishes are frustrated time and time again. These disillusionments imply his absolute incompetence for the relationship he longs for, and, therefore, narcissistic offense and humiliation. Against these he can defend by modifying the nature of both his wish and its expression. The wish to arouse a sexual response by the expression, to invite the other into a sexual mutuality, turns into a wish to shock, to astound, or to fascinate and make a suggestive impression on the other, or others. Such situations are familiar to us from both the child's and the adult's worlds. Shock and astonishment can be achieved with mighty phallic and phallic acts, and with castration and its results, and with the various extensions and symbols of all these. Fascination and suggestiveness can be achieved with any power felt to be irresistible, or by allusions to such a power.

Examples are plentiful to say the least, beginning with the displays, hints, and "you-better-believe-it" declarations of "what I've got" or "what I can do" of childhood, and running the gamut up to the great military parades and maneuvers, the athletics games, the fashion shows, and the lavish banquets of the adult world. Obviously, the dynamics of these events and occasions—especially of those that belong to the adult world—are in many ways complex and multidetermined, but in general, the phallic themes are nonetheless clearly in evidence. The defensive character of phallicism is not as easily discerned. It is revealed in the emphasis on autopotency and in the rejection of mutuality for a position of superiority. Both of these are necessary, since mutuality always implies the threatening actualization of oedipal absolute incompetence, with the attendant humiliation and shame. This threat also contributes to the fear of failure and shame associated with phallic exhibition. Conversely, we might say that the very hallmark of phallic exhibition, *differentia specifica,* is the dominance of its defensive function.

Almost without exception, a part of phallic exhibition is the admiration of one's own phallic or fetishistic endowments or prowess. This, and also its defensive character, appears at its most basic level in the boy's or man's admiration of his penis while in the act of masturbating. One male analysand estimated that this accounts for about 80 percent of the act's content, if not more. Defensiveness is evident in the evaluation of the penis that goes with this admiration: whether it looks impressive and potent enough, and whether it is in fact all that it appears to be.

Due to the female physique, the phallic exhibition of a girl cannot, however, be connected to masturbation in a similar manner, nor, in that context, to the genitals and their function.

In both sexes, phallic exhibition is associated with parts of the body that can be imagined as phallic or fetishistic, and with attempts to present these to whatever shape current fashion requires by such means as clothing, various physical exercises, and the use of jewelry and other adornments.

Phallicism Encouraged

It amounts almost to a truism to note that in our Western culture, at least, the boy's disengagement from the libidinal organization that binds him to his mother is supported by encouragement of phallicism (Stoller, 1992). Phallicism is posited as the opposite of childlikeness and reliance on the mother. It is put forward as representing masculinity, power, bravery, and activity, as opposed to femininity, weakness, timidity, and passivity. But since the castrate is also the opposite of the phallic, femininity, weakness, timidity, and passivity become attributes of the castrate (Davis, 1993).

The rebukes to a boy who does not trust his own strength enough, who is not sufficiently detached from his mother, contain both references to childishness and allusions to effeminacy. Typically, such reproaches take the form of epithets that stress the connotations of womanliness, of likeness to the castrated, with all the implied disparagement. English expressions like *sissy* or *mollycoddle* certainly have their equivalents in every culture. The counterbalance is an idealization of phallicism, interpreted as masculinity and often extending to the destructive, inconsiderate, antisocial forms of phallicism. This is illustrated in the joke about the farmer bragging about his precocious son to his neighbor: "My boy already fights like a man, curses like a man, and drinks like a man." Well, and can he read yet?" asks the neighbor. "Why, he's not even that age," replies the father, disdainfully.

This encouraging of phallicism, with its mortifications and idealizations, works much as intended. The boy renounces his mother and the libidinal organization that has bound him to her, and tries to avoid relapsing into them. Phallicism recommends itself—indeed, is recommended—as the solution to getting rid of the libidinal organization of early childhood, as well as from oedipal sexual desires. It is thus advanced as a factor central to the realities of adult life, to sexuality, and to the formation of ideals, and true enough, this is what phallicism becomes.

In his treatise on Oedipus, Devereux (1953) states that, in the boy's unconscious, the father often appears as "a homosexual ogre." I would prefer to be somewhat more specific: this describes the phallic father. And, within the context of the phallic organization, there really is no alternative. In a phallic libidinal relationship, the fate of the weaker is to be castrated. To save himself from castration, the boy wants to identify with the father, to become a homosexual ogre himself. In this manner, too, idealized elements of cruelty and destructiveness find their way into the ideal of the phallic hero.

From the boy's own point of view, and from that of the prevailing culture, all traits to be regarded as feminine, as well as everything that has its origin in mother-identification, constitute a threat to the boy's masculinity; therefore, they must be eradicated. Another possibility is to use them as symbols of a failed castration attempt to stress the preserved phallicism, in a function analogous to, say, a finger cut off at the last joint in a puberty rite, or some such mutilation. In such instances, feminine traits in conduct and dress may become sources of phallic pride.

For a girl or a woman, the idealization of phallicism creates problems. She can scarcely avoid the feeling of belonging to an inferior class, that of the "castrates." She may respond either with resignation or by setting out to prove that the class of the "castrates" is actually not inferior to that of the "phallics," or that she herself in fact does belong to the phallic class. The idealization of phallicism also prompts the girl to develop a sexuality that does not recognize a receptive genital inner space, but rather, and at most, one to grow the phallus-baby. It directs her to seek a phallus for herself in one form or another, or to turn being castrated or abused into a more or less ecstatic masochistic pleasure. Another possibility is to "turn the tables on the 'phallics' " and become a femme fatale or an avenger, to change from an object of phallic injury into an agent of the same, and finding in this a satisfaction both narcissistic and sexual.

Inasmuch as phallicism might be able to protect the girl from regression into earlier libidinal organizations of the child–mother relationship, this is likely to occur mainly through a phallic rejection of mutuality, which would extend even to those earlier organizations. In addition, interpreting the physique of the adult woman as phallic, as also her way of dress and certain behavioral characteristics (i.e., recognizing their fetishistic value) may lead the girl to aspire to these in a phallic sense, and thus to reject all elements of the child in her habitus.

Aggression

Although the phallic concept of sexuality does protect the child's narcissism from the full impact of oedipal humiliation, it also makes the parent, seen as a rival, appear even more terrifying, and stimulates and justifies aggression toward him or her. Phallicism creates an image of a human being driven by violent malice. And as long as one can muster the courage, one has a duty, as well as the right, to defend both oneself and others against such a malicious, or "mean," person.

Phallic meanness is irrational. It is motivated solely by the desire to hurt another, to injure, or even kill him. The motive is not the need for food or money, nor revenge, jealousy, or competition over something, although imagined malice will often masquerade as some such motive: the bad wolf is hungry, the wicked witch is jealous of the maiden's beauty. But hunger or competitive jealousy would not be terrifying in themselves. There are many harmless solutions to them. It is the "meanness," the connoted phallic malice that renders them dangerous. To the phallic, malice, violence, and destructive acts are not means to an end, which would allow of alternatives, but an end in themselves. Malice so imagined may contain other aggressions seen as dangerous, but these are not relevant to the present theme.

Almost as commonly as malice is feared, it is acted out in reality, in attempts to identify with the aggressor—the phallic subject, in this case. There is hardly a child who never becomes the object of such phallic acting out, and to the child it confirms his assumption of "meanness" and the necessity of fighting it or defending against it. In such a fight, it is implicit from the beginning, or the fight turns into a fight over who is to be the phallic subject and who the phallic object; who the dominating one and who the dominated; who the active one and who the victim of the action. We might call this a battle for phallic hegemony, and it rages on as an equally irrational, and often dangerously naive, battle in the adult world.

Phallic Hegemony

The battle for phallic hegemony is energized by the terror and anxiety inherent in the phallic object's position. Being the victim of oppression, violence, and injury, that is, of castration, leaves him or her sullied and spoiled, that is, castrated, by the sexual act; this, moreover, exposes the individual as one who allows him- or herself to be castrated, one who has no pride. An essential portion of the person's value has been removed in coitus; it can be restored, although never entirely, only by a phallic subject accepting him or her as partner, and for women, by the phallus-baby.

If the individual wants to participate in sexual life rather than be excluded from it, as in the oedipal situation, in the phallic world of fantasy, the phallic object has no choice but to accept the violence and castration to which he or she is subjected. There is no alternative here.

Since the phallic relationship proper does not recognize mutuality, but only the relation of castrator versus castrated, with its various derivations, each defeat in the battle for phallic position means, to the phallic subject, castration, in other words, incompetence to be a phallic subject. At this point, phallicism as a defense against oedipal inadequacy can easily collapse, and phallic incompetence becomes condensated with oedipal absolute insufficiency and humiliation.

A Phallic Universe

On what grounds do we consider the examples described above to comply with phallic organization? In all of them, the same dynamic pattern is apparent, whether in sexual form or stripped of its sexual content. With the failure of mutuality, or even as a substitute for a mutuality never pursued, the relationship shifts toward violence, autopotency, and disregard for the other or others. Victory, repression, destructiveness, and demonstrations of all these in displays of power, become ends in themselves. The preoccupation with tools gains in emphasis, at the expense of the subject who employs them. There arises a division into superior, active subjects and inferior, passive objects, and a continual battle for phallic hegemony is initiated. The entire edifice has been erected as a defense against the humiliation that results from utter incompetence for mutuality in an area experienced as being perhaps the most important in a person's life.

This is the pattern by which we structure, without being aware of it, not only human relationships, but equally the rest of our reality; the pattern which, while imagined to be realistic, is idealized and which conforms to the defensive phallic-libidinal organization. This is why I speak of the phallic universe, paraphrasing Janine Chasseguet-Smirgel's (1985) concept of the perverse universe. I agree with her that some defensive libidinal organization, or a dynamic model of it, may dominate our whole conception of reality. The question is whether we are aware of it, and also of against what we are defending.

The basic notion of phallicism, "penetration without a receptive organ," makes coitus a destructive event. It is the confounder par excellence of sexuality and violence, and it excludes the biological premise of sexuality, which is mutuality. In the phallic universe, the notion of mutuality and its implicit idea of taking one's partner into account signify both a compromise and the limitation of one's satisfaction, that is, a kind of counterfeit mutuality. In the genital reality, on the contrary, mutuality signifies the most intense satisfaction. It is at once the very prerequisite of fulfillment and the realization of it.

It is not difficult to discern phallic traits in our culture, nor their effects, useful or harmful. The compulsive perpetuation of destructiveness through acts of conquest, oppression, and violence—whether directed against fellow human beings or against nature—becomes understandable, inasmuch as it relates to phallicism, through the defensive significance of the phallic organization. Each step on the path of mutuality is fraught with the danger of failure, resonating against the background of the oedipal utter incompetence for mutuality and the humiliation and mortification that accompany it. Against these threats phallicism affords a defense by ignoring mutuality.

Battles for phallic hegemony are, manifestly, battles to ensure an increasingly secure phallic position, one increasingly removed from the position of a phallic object, or castrate. At their dynamic core, however, is the rejection of the concept of mutuality, on account of its dangerousness. By its very existence, this battle proves the impossibility of libidinal mutuality. The idealized monuments to phallic glory we find in our culture are simultaneously the vestiges of unresolved oedipal humiliation and shame.

The Vast Significance of Oedipus

It may appear something of an exaggeration to regard the collapse of oedipal-sexual wishes for mutuality as quite so decisive a factor in the life of the individual and of our culture. After all, the life of the child is full of experiences of his inadequacy, of mutuality destroyed, or exclusion from desirable relationships, and of the superiority of competitors. These might well prove sufficient to motivate the desire for autopotency, the use of violence, the relegation of fellow human beings to the disadvantaged position of underdogs, and the canceling of personal weakness by fixation to tools. There are two important respects, however, in which the oedipal libidinal wish for mutuality, with its inherent disillusionment, differs from all other wishes centering on mutuality and adequacy for acceptance. First, it is incontestably one of the most, if not the most, important and intense of the libidinal desires. And second, whereas other wishes for mutuality and the disappointments they result in can be discussed and are consciously and continually worked through in daily life, the oedipal desire is something that neither child nor parents can consciously apprehend.

These two differences help us to appreciate the vast significance of the oedipal problems and of the defensive use of the phallic organization, as compared to other problems that are oedipally neutral. While the root and the energizer of the construction of a phallic universe is conflict, the key to emancipation from it lies in becoming aware of its defensive function and of the object of defense, namely, the oedipal problems.

References

Balint, A. (1949), Love for the mother and mother love. In: *Primary Love and Psychoanalytic Technique,* ed. M. Balint. London: Hogarth Press, 1952, pp. 109–127.

Balint, M., Ed. (1952), *Primary Love and Psychoanalytic Technique.* London: Hogarth Press.

Chasseguet-Smirgel, J. (1964), Female sexuality. In: *New Psychoanalytic Views.* London: Karnac Books.

——— (1985), *Creativity and Perversion.* London: Free Association Books.

Davis, R. H. (1993), *Freud's Concept of Passivity.* Madison, CT: International Universities Press.

Devereux, G. (1953), Why Oedipus killed Laius: A note on the complementary Oedipus complex in Greek drama. *Internat. J. Psycho-Anal.,* 34:132–141.

Freud, S. (1908), On the sexual theories of children. *Standard Edition,* 9:205–226. London: Hogarth Press, 1959.

——— (1923), The infantile genital organization: An interpolation into the theory of sexuality. *Standard Edition,* 19:139–145. London: Hogarth Press, 1961.

——— (1924), The dissolution of the Oedipus complex. *Standard Edition,* 19:171–179. London: Hogarth Press, 1961.

Grunberger, B. (1979), *Narcissism.* New York: International Universities Press.

Jones, E. (1933), The phallic phase. In: *Papers on Psychoanalysis,* ed. E. Jones. London: Balliere, Tindall, & Cox, pp. 452–484, 1950.

Kestenberg, J. (1982), The inner-genital phase—Prephallic and preoedipal. In: *Early Female Development,* ed. D. Mendell. Lancaster, U.K.: MTP Press, pp. 81–127.

Stoller, R. J. (1992), Hooray for love. In: *Affect, Psychoanalytic Perspectives,* ed. T. Shapiro & R. N. Emde. Madison, CT: International Universities Press, pp. 413–437.

5

Moral Masochism and the Affect of Resentment

FRIEDRICH-WILHELM EICKHOFF, M.D.

Motto: *When would they actually achieve their final, most exquisite and most sublime triumph of revenge? Without a doubt, it would be if they were to succeed in putting their own misery, and indeed all misery, on to the conscience of the happy (Nietzsche [1887] On Resentment)*

Freud's Conception of Moral Masochism

According to Freud (1924a), masochism occupies a preferential position in the structuring of human sexuality. He refers to his early finding, dating from the time of the *Three Essays on the Theory of Sexuality* (1905), concerning the existence of libidinal sympathetic excitation of, as it were, anaclitic origin. He writes:

> [S]uch a libidinal sympathetic excitation when there is tension due to pain and unpleasure would be an infantile physiological mechanism which ceases to operate later on. It would attain a varying degree of development in different sexual constitutions; in any case it would provide the physiological foundation on which the psychical structure of erotogenic masochism would afterwards be erected [p. 163].

Its changing psychical manifestations according to the phases of development of the libido—the fear of being eaten up, of being beaten, of being copulated with and giving birth—are well known, as a consequence of a "regression from morality to the Oedipus complex" (p. 169), which occurs to the benefit neither of morality nor of the individual, but in effect as the expression of a loss of conscience to masochism, Freud in this paper ultimately introduced the concept of "moral masochism": "Conscience and morality have arisen through the overcoming, the desexualization, of the Oedipus complex; but through moral masochism morality becomes sexualized once more, the Oedipus complex is revived" (p. 169). Without adducing his considerations about "those wrecked by success" and "criminals from a sense of guilt" from "Some Character-Types Met with in Psycho-Analytic Work," although they manifestly belong in this context, Freud (1916) explained moral masochism as follows:

> Again, masochism creates a temptation to perform "sinful" actions, which then must be expiated by the reproaches of the sadistic conscience (as is exemplified in so many Russian character-types) or by chastisement from the great parental power of Destiny. In order to provoke punishment from this last representative of the parents, the masochist must do what is inexpedient, must act against his own interests, must ruin the prospects which open out to him in the real world and must, perhaps, destroy his own real existence [1924, pp. 169–170].

Moral masochism became for Freud "a classical piece of evidence for the existence of fusion of instincts" (p. 170). It stems from the part of primordial self-destruction, of the death drive that escaped being turned outwards; but, on the other hand, it has the significance of an erotic component, so that even the subject's destruction of himself cannot take place without libidinal satisfaction. In *The Ego and the Id,* Freud (1923) had already ascribed the patient's resistance to recovery in the treatment to a "moral" factor and associated the "negative therapeutic reaction" with the patient's need to protect himself from feelings of guilt connected with an actual or imminent successful outcome of the treatment. "But as far as the patient is concerned this sense of guilt is dumb; it does not tell him he is guilty; he does not feel guilty, he feels ill" (pp. 49–50). This is also the context of the well-known footnote on the "borrowed unconscious sense of guilt," in which the sense of guilt was adopted as the sole and barely recognizable remaining trace of an abandoned love relation; if this can be unmasked, Freud tells us, "the therapeutic success is often brilliant" (p. 50).

In "The Economic Problem of Masochism," the negative therapeutic reaction was according to Freud (1924a) an aspect of moral masochism, an "extreme and unmistakably pathological form" (p. 166). He considered the idea of an unconscious sense of guilt in the patient to be hardly credible and in any case psychologically incorrect; in his view, the unconscious need for punishment covers the situation just as accurately. In the "New Introductory Lectures on Psycho-Analysis," Freud (1933) describes it (the unconscious need for punishment) as an extension of our conscience into the unconscious; it will have the same provenance as conscience and thus match the fragment of aggression which has become part of the super-ego. In this connection, Freud referred also to the relations between problems of the unconscious sense of guilt and morality, education, criminality and delinquency: "And here, at an unexpected point, we have emerged from the psychical underworld into the open market-place" (p. 110).

In "Analysis Terminable and Interminable," Freud (1937) put the final seal on his conception of the negative therapeutic reaction, which plainly originated from his experience with the Wolf Man:

> No stronger impression arises from the resistances during the work of analysis than of there being a force which is defending itself by every possible means against recovery and which is absolutely resolved to hold on to illness and suffering. . . . If we take into consideration the total picture made up of the phenomena of masochism

> immanent in so many people, the negative therapeutic reaction and the sense of guilt found in so many neurotics, we shall no longer be able to adhere to the belief that mental events are exclusively governed by the desire for pleasure. These phenomena are unmistakable indications of the presence of a power in mental life which we call the instinct of aggression or of destruction according to its aims, and which we trace back to the original death instinct of living matter [pp. 242–243].

For Sandler, Dare, and Holder (1973), it is not moral masochism but the negative therapeutic reaction that is the basic psychoanalytic concept. According to these authors' definition, recovery plainly signifies the fulfillment of a forbidden internal wish and is therefore experienced as a danger, which constitutes the motivation for a negative therapeutic reaction (p. 86). They stress the need to distinguish such manifestations from phenomena attributable to inadequate technique: not every possible failure and resistance can in their view be laid at the door of the negative therapeutic reaction.

The Kleinian Perspective on the Negative Therapeutic Reaction

A new perspective was opened up by Joan Riviere (1936), when she investigated the type of resistance embodied in the negative therapeutic reaction on the basis of Melanie Klein's (1935) theoretical assumption about the depressive position as a stage in which the ego is filled with the aspiration to rescue its introjected good objects from destruction by its own oral–sadistic attacks. In her eloquent portrayal of the depressive position,

> [A]ll one's loved ones *within* are dead and destroyed, all goodness is dispersed, lost, in fragments, wasted and scattered to the winds; nothing is left *within* but utter desolation. Love brings sorrow, and sorrow brings guilt; the intolerable tension mounts, there is no escape, one is utterly alone, there is no one to share or help. Love must die because love is dead. Besides, there would be no one to feed one, and no one whom one could feed, and no food in the world. And more, there would still be magic power in the undying persecutors who can never be exterminated—the ghosts. Death would instantaneously ensue—and one would choose to die by one's own hand before such a position could be realized [p. 313].

Riviere dealt with the negative therapeutic reaction mainly in terms of the threat presented by the analytic work to the sense of identity, arguing that the resistance constituted by this reaction could be understood only from the manic position, that of the disavowal of psychic reality on the basis of illusory omnipotence. She saw the will to remain ill as corresponding to the intention to maintain the status quo; any change, because it might bring something unknown, is feared more than actual suffering, so that the patient fears that the prospect of health would not be better but worse—not so much for himself as for his introjected objects, including the analyst. For Riviere, the internal object relations form an integral part of these patients' narcissism. The unconscious love of, and anxiety about, others is not identical with Freud's unconscious sense of guilt, even if the patient's feeling that he does not deserve any love before justice has been done to his love objects is connected with it. Since the analyst represents an internal object, the positive transference must be uncovered in its archaic form. Riviere noted that it is the hypocritical character of the more superficial and more openly displayed layers of transference behavior which makes the treatment of such cases so difficult. Regarding the "borrowed unconscious sense of guilt" as the "product of an identification with some other person, who was once the object of an erotic cathexis," so that the adoption of the sense of guilt is "often the sole remaining trace of the abandoned love-relation"—as Freud put it in the footnote mentioned above—Riviere pointed out that guilt may be manically projected onto an internal object rather than borrowed with the aim of protecting its ideal function, and she warned against the perfidious deceptions of idealization, which cast the analyst in the role of a prophet.

This problem of negative therapeutic reaction was taken up again by Melanie Klein (1957) in terms of envy:

> [E]nvy, and the defenses against it, play an important part in the negative therapeutic reaction, in addition to the factors discovered by Freud and further developed by Joan Riviere. . . . Destructive criticism is particularly evident in paranoid patients who indulge in the sadistic pleasure of disparaging the analyst's work even though it has given them some relief. . . . In others it may play an equally important

> role but remains unexpressed and even unconscious. In my experience, the slow progress we make in such cases is also connected with envy. We find that their doubts and uncertainties about the value of the analysis persist. What happens is that the patient has split off the envious and hostile part of his self and constantly presents to the analyst other aspects that he feels more acceptable. Yet the split-off parts essentially influence the course of the analysis. . . . Other patients try to avoid criticism by becoming confused. . . . For envy, and the attitudes it gives rise to, interfere with the gradual building up of a good object in the transference situation. If at the earliest stage the good food and the primal good object could not be accepted and assimilated, this is repeated in the transference and the course of the analysis is impaired. . . . From the contention that envy spoils the primal good object, and gives added impetus to sadistic attacks on the breast, further conclusions arise [pp. 184–186].

Klein attributed a more prominent role to envy than to jealousy in the shaping of the Oedipus complex, and in particular the frightening fantasy of the combined parents, who are experienced as overwhelmingly powerful. She emphasized the reliving of early affects in the psychoanalytic situation, the process of remembering in feelings, as a result of which the patient can retrospectively overcome earlier renunciations more successfully. She noted that the better integrated ego becomes capable of assuming guilt and a sense of responsibility, which it could not tolerate in childhood, if splitting processes, used mainly as a defense against perception and guilt, lose their power through the analysis.

Even if Klein implicitly stressed the creative aspects of the depressive position, the optimism with which she had begun her work some forty years earlier was now gone; this change of attitude is not unlike that discernible in the pessimism of Freud's comments on the interminability of the analytic search. However, she no longer adduced any theoretical considerations about the drives, and so, logically, the term *masochism* is also lacking, even if the reference to the negative therapeutic reaction forms a bridge to the theme of masochism.

Yet Klein's platonic view of psychic life, namely, that the meaning of the world is created internally and is only then structured externally, leads to a conception of psychic reality different from the scientific approach of Freud, who never lost sight of biology.

The same phenomena, that is, the primary affective data of the psychoanalytic situation, can plainly be understood from different points of view, which in favorable cases complement each other. On this point, Donald Meltzer (1991) has commented that, in Freudian terms, the qualities of external objects ascribed to superego pathology and their manifestations of this quality are introjected, whereas, for Melanie Klein, after her elaboration of the concept of projective identification, these qualities of the superego are a consequence of the setting up of projected parts of the self inside the internal objects. In his view, the fact that they might possibly coincide with the external parents—that, as it were, the shoe fits—may only be taken as an indication that the setting up of such a projection is greatly reinforced if the shoe fits the parents, whereas its internal origin lies in projective identification, so that therapy directed against the severity of the superego or against its wickedness and hypocrisy is substantially a matter of enabling the patient to take back these projections.

In discussing the problem of the negative therapeutic reaction, Adam Limentani (1989) paid particular attention to the countertransference and to the psychoanalyst's affective reactions to the patient's need to remain ill. He pointed out that whereas the majority of analysts—in particular, those from North America—rely more on Freud's concept of unconscious guilt and masochism, most Kleinians tend to resort to the interpretation of envy when they encounter destructive attacks by the patient on their work. I should like to supplement this distinction by pointing out that trauma is evaluated differently in regard to masochism and to the negative therapeutic reaction. North American authors attribute great significance to early traumatization, as is evident from the example of Socarides' (1957) excellent paper "The Function of Moral Masochism," I am quoting below:

> The moral masochist, a product of early childhood deprivation, is caught in a never-ending oscillation between his imperative craving for love and his aggression. The masochistic position is his adaptive response in an effort to express and gratify vital needs, assuage guilt, quiet fear and aggression. To relinquish it, he must experience a new benevolent reality, and, with aggression gradually bound and attenuated by love, he may begin to undo what childhood circumstances have forced upon him [p. 596].

By contrast, the theme of trauma does not play a significant part in the contributions of Kleinian authors.

John Steiner (1993) has assigned so-called pathological organizations of the personality to an intermediate zone between the two Kleinian positions, which he called the borderline position. This is used as a defense not only against the distintegration and confusion of the paranoid–schizoid position, but also against psychic pain and the anxiety of the depressive position, taking the form of the reactivation of fantasies of omnipotence, which afford a certain stability through pseudo-integration, even if on a foundation of omnipotent and perverse mechanisms. The analyst is barely perceptibly drawn into these states of withdrawal and stagnation when he experiences feelings of powerlessness, annoyance, or loneliness, which are to be understood partly as the result of projective identifications. The negative therapeutic reaction is an example of such a withdrawal, which allows the patient to restore his threatened equilibrium pathologically.

According to Steiner, a common feature of pathological organizations is that they prevent mourning processes whereby the parts of the self lost through projective identification can be reintegrated. In the borderline position, reality is at one and the same time seemingly accepted and secretly rejected. Freud (1940) explained this situation by the example of the fetishist's dichotomous attitude toward reality and, in "Splitting of the Ego in the Process of Defence" (p. 277), called it a "way of dealing with reality[,] which almost deserves to be described as artful." A chapter in Steiner's work entitled "Revenge, Resentment, Remorse and Reparation" discusses the feeling of having been deceived, the resentment that leads to protest and rebellion, and the role of aggression in pathological organizations in the form of the tendency to protect the object from overt attacks and to withdraw into complaints that serve for the avoidance of guilt feelings and provide a masochistic satisfaction.[1]

[1]In an essay "Revenge and Resentment in the 'Oedipus Situation' " published after completing my paper, John Steiner (1996) makes a more in-depth investigation of the impasse of resentment by means of a reference to the Oedipus complex facilitating a persecutory and a depressive solution. He mistakes, however, the dissolution of the Oedipus complex in the sense of Freud's article "The Dissolution of the Oedipus Complex" (1924b) with moral masochism conceived in the same year in "The Economic Problem

Bela Grunberger's Conception of Masochism

Grunberger's supervision of a case of masochism, the focus of attention of an entire clinical unit when I was a candidate, made a powerful impression on me, and for this reason a special place is devoted here to his penetrating psychodynamic theory of masochism (1953). A reprint of this paper (and that of Riviere's) can be found in Hanly's outstanding reader *Essential Papers on Masochism* (1995). Grunberger argues that the interlocking of masochism with other clinical disturbances overshadows the attempt to make it a nosological entity in its own right. In a horizontal plane, masochism transcends hysterical patterns, whether or not obsessionally tinged, and underlies every pathology. The same, in his view, applies to a vertical perspective, in which masochism appears as a component of the human condition itself. These ideas can, he says, be extended to a third dimension: during the course of treatment, masochism often persists for longer than other symptoms—that is to say, it transcends them in time. Anyone who is confronted with what Odier called the "notorious and terrible problem of masochism" runs the risk, according to Grunberger, of being attracted by the enigma of the paradoxical linking of suffering and pleasure and of making the search for suffering the nodal point of his investigation. In his considerations, which will then be more speculative than clinical, he is, Grunberger goes on, supported by the complicity of the patient, who readily supplies him with material that, for example, bears witness to the narcissistic gain from illness.

I myself would add that, according to Eidelberg (1933), the masochist enjoys the power he exerts over the object for the purpose of motivating it to inflict punishment, and regains the omnipotence lost by self-induced suffering. For Grunberger, however, the assumption of the narcissistic gain from illness is a rationalization: even if this principle illuminates some aspects of masochism, he does not consider that the resulting explanation

---

of Masochism" (1924a), the essence of which he describes without actually using the term (p. 435). The change between dissolution of the Oedipus complex and regression to the Oedipus complex in moral masochism can well be compared to the alternation between the depressive and schizoid–paranoid positions.

is satisfactory. He continues by saying that the investigator will therefore renounce suffering as the point of departure of his investigation and concentrate instead on pleasure. He points to Freud's (1915) comment in "Instincts and their Vicissitudes": "of course, it is not the pain itself which is enjoyed, but the accompanying sexual excitation" (p. 129).

Apart from the masochist's pursuit of suffering, Grunberger considers his most characteristic trait to be complete inhibition in regard to pleasure of any kind; this is stated to be the most significant feature affecting all phases of libidinal satisfaction, both genital and pregenital. The masochist, he says, makes an initial approach to the securing of pleasure, which like anyone else he seeks to obtain; indeed, he wishes for it even more than most people do. However, at the instant of its achievement, he draws back by a step that is decisive even if only indirectly so. In Grunberger's view, he does this on account of the anxiety that infallibly arises in relation to the object, regardless of the aspect in which that object might appear, and returns to his original attitude, which does not contain a simple renunciation but instead the opposite of pleasure, namely unpleasure. Without going into more detail here, it may be concluded, says Grunberger, that what is thereby achieved is the disappearance of anxiety. The masochist, according to Grunberger, is fleeing from satisfaction in order to protect himself from anxiety. At the slightest attempt to cross the boundary separating him from a genuine satisfaction, anxiety peremptorily makes itself felt. The masochist unconsciously arranges his life in such a way that this dangerous threshold is never reached.

This turning away from pleasure with the aim of avoiding anxiety is presented by Grunberger as the specific masochistic mechanism underlying all clinical manifestations. He says that the anxiety has often been identified as castration anxiety. He notes that others have agreed that the masochist as it were boastfully and ostentatiously misuses castration anxiety to mask the real anxiety. The specific thing for him, however, is the use of castration anxiety for defensive purposes. In Grunberger's opinion, the commonly adduced theory of orality leads to a similar impasse, as when Bergler (1949) considered oral regression to constitute the basic neurosis of psychic masochism. For Grunberger, extreme caution is necessary before confirming the significance of oral frustration in the history of masochistic patients. The picture presented by the unfolding analysis, he goes on, is often that of a castrating mother and a weak, disappointing father. This situation is abundantly described and illustrated until one day it has to be realized that this image is being exaggerated in order to minimize the patient's guilt feelings by the formula, "It was not I who castrated my father but my mother who castrated me."

According to Grunberger's rhetorical argument, self-induced castration anxiety and oral frustration seem to exhaust the phenomenology of masochism. All the specific aspects of masochistic behavior apparently fit into the framework of these two factors. The masochist, he says, arranges his life as if he were castrated and incapable of satisfaction in any field. He is inhibited, poor, suffering, ill, weakened, attacked, and humiliated.

Now Freud (1919b) maintains that a child's fantasies of being beaten by the father are often repressed and can only be brought to light by analytic investigation, whereas beatings by the mother are dramatized, and that observation of the masochistic beating fantasy often arouses the impression that the subject has done something reprehensible, which, although its nature remains vague, means that he deserves punishment. In agreement with these ideas, Grunberger arrives at the interpretation that the object inflicting the blows in the masochist's fantasy is a condensation of telescoped mother and father elements, which the father side is more strongly defended against than that of the mother. For Grunberger, as a result, the unexpected appearance of the father image is fateful for the masochistic scene. After all, the masochistic behavior has the aim of maintaining the defense against the wish for an anal–sadistic appropriation of the father's penis after pregenital castration of the father, and of disguising it. Grunberger never tires of emphasizing the difference between the oedipal parricide and this introjection of the father' penis that is obligatory for both sexes but is charged with a greater sense of guilt in women than in men—an introjection equivalent to pregenital castration of a part object. Birksted-Breen (1996), in her important paper "Phallus, Penis and Mental Space," suggests that it is the introjection of what she calls the penis-as-link, which has a structuring function and promotes mental space and thinking. The masochistic defense is expressed, according to Grunberger, in two ways: (1) I do not wish to castrate my father; nor can I do so, since I myself have been castrated, and moreover by my mother; (2) if I find myself in a conflict situation, then it is with my mother, and this conflict is an oral one. The architect in the masochistic discharge of guilt feelings is pain, which takes the place of pleasure. Suffering instead of pleasure seems, Grunberger says, to be the only permissible value. The overvaluation betrays the return of the repressed, the recathexis of pleasure. Pain becomes a substitute for pleasure; deeper analysis shows that it is the representative of the father's penis, just as the whip is for the perverse masochist. Suffering, he goes on, is utilized, applied in carefully measured doses, modified or stabilized; its intensity corresponds to the degree of anxiety to be neutralized by this technique.

Grunberger mentions those patients who make the most of their castration in the analysis although they derive enormous gains from it. They buy themselves off from castration anxiety by castration equivalents. This, he says, makes it possible to understand an improper aspect of masochism, namely projection: we are confronted less with a turning round of aggression against the person himself than with the projection of this aggression onto the object. This situation, Grunberger continues, lay behind Freud's (1919b) idea that he would not be surprised if it were one day possible to prove that the beating fantasy was the basis of the delusional litigiousness of paranoia. Grunberger writes that the wish for anal introjection of the father's penis is projected onto the bad mother: it is she who seizes the penis. And I myself would add that this corresponds to a Kleinian interpretation in terms of a pregenital sexual relation. Grunberger argues that to be able to obtain the penis, the masochist must introject the bad mother; that is, make a preparatory identification with her. However, he points out that the inability to make this identification is characteristic of the moral masochist. The masochistic mechanism operates like a "screen experience" with the aim of concealing this identification and deceiving the superego. To maintain the projection, the masochist must persist in his suffering and assume the burden of a constant effort to prove to the superego that the castration stems from the mother. Grunberger concludes that the moral masochist differs from the masochistic pervert, who achieves genital pleasure, in that the former's superego cannot be entirely deceived.

Grunberger's formulations readily admit of a supplementation along Kleinian lines. An anal attack on an object, whereby parts of the ego are forced into the object with the aim of taking possession of its contents or of controlling it is a characteristic of projective identification, which has been seen since Melanie Klein's 1946 definition as the prototype of the aggressive object relation and as active in the paranoid–schizoid position from the very beginning. Again, the directing of aggression against a figure condensed out of the two parents is reminiscent of the primal fantasy of the combined parents. Freud's concept of regression from morality to the Oedipus complex is replaced in the Kleinian view by regression from depressive to paranoid processing of guilt. It is as if the concern with masochism had been succeeded by the concentration on psychotic anxieties. Finally, in the post-Kleinian vision of Bion (Grinberg, Sor, and Tabak de Bianchedi, 1975), the alternation between the depressive and paranoid–schizoid positions, deemed to be of equal weight (PS → D, the oscillation between disintegration and integration), has become an important mechanism, upon which Bion commented, with reference to Poincaré's "selected fact," in order to characterize emotional experience. Bion's approach here signified a sense of discovery and was intended to abolish the evaluation of the positions in moral terms.

The Cultural Dimension of Masochism

Leon Wurmser (1993) made a particularly thorough study of resentment in the chapter of his book on masochism devoted to Nietzsche. He shows how Nietzsche's vehement countermasochistic denunciation of resentment and his radical repudiation of justice and guilt constitute a disavowal of the conflictual nature of the human constitution. On the other hand, R. de Monchy (1950) argues that masochism should be seen as a normal mental phenomenon corresponding to the possibility of a healthy narcissism in man's affective attitude to himself:

> There is considerable evidence to the effect that some moral–masochistic impulses are essential if we are to feel content with ourselves and are to make a satisfactory social adjustment. We want to be useful or to be needed by some other person. Whole-hearted devotion to a task is for many people a prerequisite condition of happiness. They want to live for something outside themselves; they want to be able to worship [p. 96].

Such a view agrees in some respects with that of Reik (1941), who regarded sublimated masochism as identical with civilization. Mention may also be made in this connection of Eissler's (1953) detailed study of the moral masochism inherent in Eckermann's relationship with Goethe as an example of a highly successful sublimation. The loss of the conscience to masochism through the erotization of otherwise intolerable guilt has not only an individual but also a collective dimension; this induced Leo A. Spiegel, in his Abraham A. Brill lecture on moral masochism (Spiegel, 1978), explicitly to underline the importance of the cultural atmosphere from which a patient derives his motives.

Finally, we may recall Freud's (1930) extension of clinical concepts to nonclinical subject matter, for example, in *Civilization and Its Discontents.* In this work, the sense of guilt does not appear in a form reduced to its useful signal function but in a fateful cumulation, in that the renunciation of drives demanded by the conscience undergoes a genetic reversal, whereby the severity and intolerance of the conscience are exacerbated, resulting in something like lethal moral masochism.

Chasseguet-Smirgel (1981, 1985, 1987, 1988) writes about a regression of morality to the "archaic matrix of the Oedipus complex." Taking up Freud's 1924 idea of punishment as a regressive substitute for libidinal oedipal wishes, she modifies it to yield the hypothesis that the aim of the moral masochist is the perversion, seduction, and demeaning of the superego, thereby eliminating the difference between father and child, who become sexual playmates. However, the disqualification of the superego does not take place only along the lines of Freud's thesis concerning the resexualization of the Oedipus complex by the provocative seduction to sadism, which robs it of its sovereign, independent character. It also takes place by means of the regressive substitution for the superego of an aspect of the ego ideal that promises reunification of the ego with the primary object.

An ideology molded by moral masochism typified an aspect of the social climate during the historical crisis of the then recently unified Federal Republic of Germany at the time of the Gulf War in early 1991. Dan Diner (1991) has given an outstanding description of the process of "restratification of the collective memory":

> At a time when old certainties were crumbling and sudden imponderables were arising, distant events brought the Germans' own, equally lamentable, past sufferings closer to home. Where in Germany had the victims of the air raids of the Second World War been mourned without those concerned laying themselves open to the charge of revanche? What possibility was there of remembrance of flight and expulsion without venturing into the vicinity of dubious associations of expellees? As long as National Socialism and its crimes were warded off as an abstraction, the need to tend one's own wounds too remained unsatisfied. The Germans having as it were taken up a fixed distance from themselves, Saddam Hussein's Iraq was transformed into an imaginary object that allowed them to approach closer to their own victimhood, to which they had previously had no access. The staging of an identification with the victim, which was in reality the aggressor, was facilitated by the fact that Iraq was opposed by powers which had once stood against Germany, namely a world coalition led by the West [p. 72].

The figure of the false good conscience, elaborated as it were psychohistorically by Diner, can perfectly well be interpreted as a manifestation of moral masochism. The polarization of "hawks" and "doves" was particularly strident; the latter attacked the former for their "occidental ideology" (Schönberger and Kösters, 1992) and "mindless philo-Semitism." The war had to be not only justifiable but also just. Some phenomena were virtually incomprehensible without the assumption of an altered consciousness: white flags of peace as a token of surrender and placards bearing the words "I am afraid" held provocatively aloft in the streets bore witness to the confusion. As stated, the staging of suffering as an indictment of an unjust fate was a perfect embodiment of moral masochism.

The ideological proximity of certain patients who can legitimately be characterized as masochistic to the social climate of the time of the Gulf War in the Federal Republic, where the Pandora's box of nationalism was opening, temporarily allowed these patients to idealize tendencies and resistances of their own. Associated with this ideology was a self-righteousness that blinded those concerned with history and the Holocaust and made them forget the present use of German poison gas—a self-righteousness which, as in an exceptional situation, took precedence over individual psychic contents.

With hindsight, the hypnotic fascination of the Gulf War seems like a passing illness, attributable to the effect of a "parasitic double"; as Freud (1919a) wrote on the subject of the war neuroses—an entirely comparable situation—the old peace-ego defended itself against the "rashness of its newly formed, parasitic double" (p. 209).

References

Bergler, E. (1949), *The Basic Neurosis.* New York: Grune & Stratton.

Birksted-Breen, D. (1996), Phallus, penis and mental space. *Internat. J. Psycho-Anal.,* 77:649–657.

Chasseguet-Smirgel, J. (1981), *Das Ichideal. Psychoanalytischer Essay über die "Krankheit der Idealiät."* Frankfurt am Main: Suhrkamp Verlag.

——— (1985), *The Ego Ideal: A Psychoanalytic Essay on the Malady of the Ideal,* tr. P. Barrows. London: Free Association Books, 1985.

——— (1987), Die archaische Matrize des Ödipuskomplexes am Beispiel des Agierens und des Ausbleibens der psychischen Bearbeitung (The archaic matrix of its Oedipus complex as an example of acts and the failure of psychic work). In: *Aber die Ursprunge des Ödipuskomplexes* (On the origins of the Oedipus complex), ed. J. Stork. Stuttgart: Frommann-Holzboog.

——— (1988), *Zwei Bäume im Garten. Zur psychischen Bedeutung der Vater- und Mutterbilder* (Two trees in the garden on the psychic significance of the images of the mother and father). Munich: Verlag Internationale Psychoanalyse.

Diner, D. (1991), *Der Krieg der Erinnerungen und die Ordnung der Welt* (Aggression in memory and world order). Berlin: Rotbuch Verlag.

Eidelberg, L. (1933), Zur Metapsychologie des Masochismus (On the metapsychology of masochism). *Int. Z. Psychoanal.*, 19:615–616.

Eissler, K. R. (1953), A clinical note on moral masochism: Eckermann's relationship to Goethe. In: *Drives, Affects, Behavior,* ed. R. M. Loewenstein. New York: International Universities Press.

Freud, S. (1915), Instincts and their vicissitudes. *Standard Edition,* 14:109–140. London: Hogarth Press, 1957.

——— (1916), Some character-types met with in psycho-analytic work. *Standard Edition,* 14:309–333. London: Hogarth Press, 1957.

——— (1919a), Introduction to *Psycho-Analysis and the War Neuroses. Standard Edition,* 17:205–210. London: Hogarth Press, 1955.

——— (1919b), "A child is being beaten": A contribution to the study of the origin of sexual perversions. *Standard Edition,* 17:175–204. London: Hogarth Press, 1955.

——— (1923), The Ego and the Id. *Standard Edition,* 19:1–59. London: Hogarth Press, 1961.

——— (1924a), The economic problem of masochism. *Standard Edition,* 19:155–170. London: Hogarth Press, 1961.

——— (1924b), The dissolution of the Oedipus complex. *Standard Edition,* 19:171–179. London: Hogarth Press, 1961.

——— (1930), Civilization and Its Discontents. *Standard Edition,* 21:57–145. London: Hogarth Press, 1961.

——— (1933), New Introductory Lectures on Psycho-Analysis. *Standard Edition,* 22:1–182. London: Hogarth Press, 1964.

——— (1937), Analysis terminable and interminable. *Standard Edition,* 23:209–253. London: Hogarth Press, 1964.

——— (1940 [1938]), Splitting of the ego in the process of defence. *Standard Edition,* 23:271–278. London: Hogarth Press, 1964.

Grinberg, L., Sor, D., & Tabak de Bianchedi, E. (1975), *Introduction to the Work of Bion.* Perthshire, Scotland: The Roland Harris Educational Trust.

Grunberger, B. (1953), Esquisse d'une theorie psychodynamique du masochisme (Outline of a psychodynamic theory of masochism). *Rev. Française Psychoanalyse,* 18:193–214.

Hanly, M. A. F., Ed. (1995), *Essential Papers on Masochism.* New York & London: New York University Press.

Klein, M. (1935), A contribution to the psychogenesis of manic-depressive states. *Internat. J. Psycho-Anal.,* 16:145–174.

——— (1957), *Envy and Gratitude.* London: Tavistock.

Limentani, A. (1989), On some positive aspects of the negative therapeutic reaction. In: *Between Freud and Klein. The Psychoanalytic Quest for Knowledge and Truth.* London: Free Association Books.

Meltzer, D. (1991), Jenseits des Gewissens. Das Konzept des Über-Ichs und seine Bedeutung für die psychoanalytische Arbeit (Beyond the conscious: The concept of the ego and its role in psychoanalytic work). *Anal. Psych.*, 22:79–99.

de Monchy, R. (1950), Masochism as a pathological and as a normal phenomenon in the human mind. *Internat. J. Psycho-Anal.*, 31:95–97.

Nietzsche, F. (1887), *Zur Genealogie der Moral,* Vols. 1–3. Munich: Schlechter, 1973.

Odier, C. H. (n.d.), *L'homme esclave de son infériorité* (Man as slave to his sense of inferiority). Paris.

Reik, T. (1941), *Masochism in Modern Man.* New York: Farrar & Rinehart.

Riviere, J. (1936), A contribution to the analysis of the negative therapeutic reaction. *Internat. J. Psycho-Anal.*, 17:304–320.

Sandler, J., Dare, C., & Holder, A. (1973), *The Patient and the Analyst. The Basis of the Psychoanalytic Process.* New York: International Universities Press.

Schönberger, K., & Kösters, C. (1992), *Der "freie" Westen, der "vernönftige" Krieg, seine "linken" Liebhaber und okzidentaler Rassismus.* Marbach, Germany: Author.

Socarides, C. (1957), The function of moral masochism: With special reference to the defence process. *Internat. J. Psycho-Anal.*, 39:587–596.

Spiegel, L. A. (1978), Moral masochism. *Psychoanal. Quart.*, 47:209–236.

Steiner, J. (1993), *Psychic Retreats. Pathological Organisations in Psychotic, Neurotic and Borderline Patients.* London: Routledge.

——— (1996), Revenge and resentment in the "Oedipus situation." *Internat. J. Psycho-Anal.*, 77:433–443.

Wurmser, L. (1993), *Das Rätsel des Masochismus* (The puzzle of masochism), foreword, M. Eicke. Berlin, Heidelberg, New York: Springer-Verlag.

Translated by Philip Slotkin, M.A., M.I.T.I.

6

The Concept of Libido in the Light of Contemporary Psychoanalytic Theorizing

Otto F. Kernberg, M.D.

What follows is an overview of my effort to develop a contemporary psychoanalytic theory of drives, linked both with affect theory and with a developmental model based upon psychoanalytic object relations theory. Such a synthesis between Freud's (1920, 1923, 1933) dual drive theory and object relations theory has by now, of course, a long tradition that includes the contributions of Melanie Klein (1940, 1945, 1946, 1957), Winnicott (1958, 1965, 1971), Jacobson (1964, 1971), and Mahler (Mahler and Furer, 1968; Mahler, Pine and Bergman, 1975). Some leading object relations theoreticians, however, such as Fairbairn (1954), Sullivan (1953, 1962), Guntrip (1961, 1968, 1971), Greenberg (Greenberg and Mitchell, 1983), and Mitchell (1988), have concluded that object relations theory and drive theory are essentially incompatible with each other. Interpersonal psychoanalysis —the contemporary version in the United States of the cultural psychoanalysis of an earlier generation—rejects Freud's drive theory (Greenberg and Mitchell, 1983); and I believe that self psychology (Kohut, 1971, 1977) also may be considered a type of object relations theory that rejects Freud's theory of the drives.

The contemporary reevaluation of Freud's dual drive theory that has occurred mostly in France is relevant to the relationship between object relations theory and drive theory. Perhaps particularly the work of Laplanche (1970, 1987, 1992), and Green (1973, 1986, 1993) has emphasized the central importance of unconscious destructive and self-destructive drive manifestations in the form of attacks on object relations, and the central role of unconscious erotization in the mother–infant relationship in libidinal development, all of which, in my view, tends to link drive theory and object relations theory in intimate ways.

Another important development within psychoanalytic theory has been the growing emphasis on affects as primary motivators, and the centrality of the communicative functions of affects in early development, particularly the infant–mother relationship (Krause, 1988; Krause and Lutolf, 1988). This emphasis has linked affect theory and object relations theory quite closely, despite the persistent controversy between those who see affect, particularly peak affect states, as essential representatives of the drives, and those who stress the psychophysiological nature of the affective response, and attempt to replace drive theory with an affect theory.

I would like to stress the centrality of linking drive theory and object relations theory, for there are undesirable consequences of keeping these two major trends of psychoanalytic thinking apart: an object relations theory devoid of a theory of drives tends to devolve, as I see it, into a theory of interpersonal functioning that may stress the unconscious aspects of intersubjectivity, but is usually attracted by sociological models of development, in which the unconscious world of the present transference developments is seen as a replica of aspects of actual past interactions. This leads to neglect of the formation of unconscious mental structures. This development, in my experience, tends to accentuate superficial aspects of unconscious functioning (the role of adaptation and reality) and to minimize awareness of the uncanny aspects of primitive hatred and the primitive nature of early erotic and sadomasochistic unconscious fantasy. Without a theory of drives, such an object relations theory tends to underemphasize both aggression and eroticism, while stressing pregenital, preoedipal, dyadic relations as the origin of the dynamic Unconscious.

On the other hand, a traditional drive theory that does not explore the implications of object relations theory and affect theory for its conception of drives, eventually tends to relegate drives to mythical structures, such as the equation of the Unconscious with the structure of a natural language (Lacan, 1966), or an assumption of primary, innate development of the drives as inherited phylogenetically determined primary fantasies. Finally, a replacement of drive theory by an affect theory relegates motivation to its sources in biological structures, underemphasizing the importance of unconscious phantasy, and the psychological nature of human desire.

Now I wish to outline in some detail my efforts to synthesize a contemporary theory of drives with a developmental object relations theory model, and to describe the role of affects in the construction of the world of object relations and in constituting the substrate of the drives (Kernberg, 1976, 1990, 1992). To begin, I stress Freud's (1920, 1923, 1933) differentiation between drives and instincts: he conceived of instincts much as they are seen today, as biological motivational systems, innate, discontinuous, and species specific. They are differentiated in terms of patterns of "consummatory behaviors" which are fixed, innate patterns of perception and behavior organized by their interaction with environmental triggering factors. Higher biological centers mediate broad, alerting, exploratory behaviors that then, under the influence of specific environmental conditions, lead to the triggering of the actual consummatory behavior patterns. Biological instincts, in their modern conception, are integrated, sequentially organized behavior patterns derived from the linkage of their component inborn dispositions under the influence of triggering environmental conditions.

Drives, in contrast, are conceptualized as highly individualized, malleable and displaceable unconscious motivational systems, continuous in their motivational function. In Freud's terms, they occupy an intermediate realm between the physical and psychological, and are manifest only by their derivatives, namely, representations and affects. A contemporary psychoanalytic view of drives, as perhaps most significantly put forward by Melanie Klein (1945, 1946, 1957) and Laplanche (1970, 1987), conceives of them as affectively charged unconscious phantasies that involve desired and feared relations between the self and internalized objects. I have described the relationship of a self representation with an object representation in the context of a dominant peak affect state as the basic unit of unconscious fantasy.

Freud classified drives into libido or life drive and the (problematically called) death drive, the basic drive toward self-destruction. Libido and the death drive must be differentiated from sexuality and aggression as biological functions. Laplanche's discussion of Freud's reasons for abandoning his earlier classification of drives into ego drives and sexual drives is convincing, as is his argument regarding the origin of drives. He describes them as intrapsychic motivational structures originating in the context of the total dependency of the infant, not only on the care of the mothering person, but on the unconscious messages from mother experienced as enigmatic stimulations reaching the infant from birth on. These early experiences determine the earliest unconscious fantasy by a process of accumulation of early overwhelming experiences, their retrospective unconscious elaboration, and the gradual differentiation of the dynamic unconscious from a primary ego–id matrix.

I find this general formulation eminently compatible with my proposal that intensely pleasurable experiences of the infant in the relationship with mother generate primary, "all good" units of self and object representations, while peak experiences of pain and fear generate "all bad" ones. Within these primary units, self and object representations are not yet differentiated from each other. Early splitting operations maintain the segregation between experiences negatively and positively charged with intense affect. Only in a later stage, splitting between idealizing and persecutory experiences is complemented by the differentiation between self and object representations within each experience, and this latter differentiation contributes to the delimitation of ego boundaries and reality testing. These highly charged primitive affective experiences recede deeply into the repressed unconscious, while those conscious and preconscious interactions of the infant and mother that take place under conditions of low-level affective activation serve adaptive purposes and are incorporated into the conscious and preconscious ego.

In my view, the gradual integration of the "all good," idealized, pleasurable affective experiences of mother with the unconscious erotic meanings injected via mother's "enigmatic" messages, will constitute libido as a drive. In the same way, the integration of painful, terrifying, rageful affective experiences with the unconscious meanings of mother's hostile, enigmatic responses will constitute the death drive. The expression of the death drive as a primitive layer of persecutory superego precursors along with the projective mechanisms attempting to externalize these internal persecutors will give rise to the deepest layers of potential self-destructiveness, paranoid tendencies, and defensive efforts to eliminate or destroy relationships with significant others. These motives are part of a gradually developing dynamic between the search for erotic linkages with significant others, and the attack upon those linkages with the ultimate goal of total elimination of all need for others together with the experiencing self. The term *death drive* for these antilibidinal, *anti-Eros* forces seems justified (Green, 1993).

As to affects, contemporary affect theory sees them as philogenetically recent systems of regulation in mammals that assure the protection of the infant during its long stage of dependency, functioning as a mode of communication and as major motivational influences throughout life. Affects include a subjective experience of pleasure or nonpleasure that motivates the infant to move toward or away from a determinate stimulus or situation. Each affect includes a typical pattern of neurovegetative and psychomotor responses, with expressive movements that communicate the affective state to the caregiver, and correspond to the innate capacity of both infant and caregiver to read each other's affective response. Inborn affective responses thus foster both the linking of early self experiences with the pleasure-giving object as well as the tendency to destroy those linkages under conditions of intensely experienced danger, pain, or frustration. It is at the moment of peak affect states that self and object representations are linked and fixated in early memory structures and elaborated secondarily in unconscious fantasy. Thus the libidinal and the aggressive drives are formed not simply by the accumulation and integration of affect states per se, but by the ongoing development of fantasied, feared and desired, idealized and persecutory relations with significant objects.

I mentioned that in contrast to the nature of instincts (discontinuous, homogeneous for the species, innate, and inalterable), drives have an essentially psychic nature: they are continuous, individualized, and subject, throughout development, to alteration through displacement and condensation. Practically, this means that the primitive affect states of elation, fear, rage, sadness, shame, surprise, disgust, and sexual excitement are elaborated and modified in the context of their integration with internalized object relations. These in turn are condensed and integrated in the context of the commonality of their affect states. In other words, the relationships with different objects in the context of hatred or of love are integrated as fantastic primitive object representations relating to representations of the self. The affects themselves are condensed, converging into two key series of emotional experience: erotic desire, on the one hand, and murderous hatred, on the other.

Freud described the origin of libido in erogenous zones, the pressure toward the achievement of pleasure, the specific aim, and the object of the drive. The basic units of self and object representations and the affects linking them bring together these characteristics of drives. The erogenous zones represent, as Laplanche has pointed out, the general erogenous quality of the body. The desire for an erotic fusion with mother takes the specific fantasy contours of those erogenous zones most involved, at a certain point of time, in the intimate relation with her. The infant's fantasied relation to mother's body under the impact of early erotic stimulation will profoundly influence the nature of erotic fantasy, as it incorporates, later on, these retrospectively interpreted early experiences. The intensity of the affect of erotic desire represents the intensity of the drive at any particular point; the particular erogenous gratification involves the libidinal aim, and the origin of the drive lies not in the specific erogenous zone but in the entire relationship of the primitive psychic apparatus of the child with the first needed and then desired object. The erotic desire "leans" on the biological apparatus of sexual excitement (Laplanche, 1992), and the integration of the experience of the primitive affect of elation with the perception of the erotic bodily response to the relationship to the breast creates the prototype of erotic desire that, later on, will "lean" on the focused sexual response of the genital organs. In this connection, it is ironic, although not surprising for a psychoanalyst, that the highly complex affect of sexual excitement remains almost completely ignored in most studies on development of affects.

As erotic desire "leans" on the biological apparatus of sexual excitement, so hatred "leans" on the primary affect of rage as it is aroused in the context of the earliest object relations. Rage is one of the fundamental affects, an inborn biological response that acquires its function as the originator of hatred only in the context of the internalization of persecutory, "all bad," internalized object relations. The affect of hatred, a complex, central aspect of the death drive, involves in its most primitive forms the desire not only to destroy the object, but to destroy even the awareness of the relationship with the hated object, and, in a profound sense, to destroy the self as the organ of perception of hatred. Sadistic pleasure already reflects the condensation of such primitive hatred with erotic desire, as masochistic pleasure reflects the erotization of the most primitive desire for self elimination together with all elimination of self awareness.

The basic (self representation/object representation) units of internalized object relations thus include the constituent affective components of the drives. One might say that the affect of sexual excitement is the central affect of libido in the same way as the affect of primitive hatred constitutes the central affect of the death drive. The id is conceptualized in this model as the sum total of repressed, desired, and feared primitive object relations. The gradual integration of successive layers of persecutory and idealized, prohibitive and demanding, internalized object relations become part of the primitive superego, while internalized object relations activated in the service of defense consolidate as an integrated self structure within the ego, surrounded by integrated representations of significant others. In short, the id or dynamic Unconscious, the superego, and the ego are constituted by different constellations of internalized object relations, so that the development of the drives and the development of the psychic apparatus—the tripartite structure—occur hand in hand.

We can now see how contemporary affect theory constitutes a bridge between biological structures and intrapsychic structures, and why affect theory cannot replace drive theory. Primitive affects are inborn psychophysiological structures; regardless of which classification of affects one accepts. They reflect multiple moments of arousal in the relations to any particular object that are less important than the consistent, deeply repressed, stable unconscious relations to the parental objects that transcend any particular affective reaction to it. Affects, shorn of the object relations in the context of which they enter the psychic apparatus, cannot reflect, by themselves, the nature of unconscious fantasy, of motivating desire. Unconscious desire leans on primitive, affectively invested object relations, and this "leaning" quality is best illustrated, I believe, by the relationship between affects and drives that I have proposed.

Perhaps the erotic response illustrates most clearly how unconscious desire "leans" on the biological function of sexuality, but transcends it by far in its importance in human sexual life. We know that, in addition to the normal development of the anatomical aspects of the sexual organs, a normal level of testosterone is a precondition for normal activation of genital excitement, and that the intensity of sexual excitement is reduced with long-term insufficiency of testosterone in both genders. However, it is also evident that sexual excitement is influenced much more by unconscious and preconscious fantasy than by fluctuations in the hormonal level.

In fact, the study of severe personality disorders has found that, in patients with extremely severe pathology of internalized object relations, especially those who have experienced severe physical and psychological trauma, the erotic response may be extinguished in spite of an absolutely normal physiological apparatus. Clinically, the freer the capacity for polymorphous perverse infantile sexual experiences, the better the prognosis for the treatment of severe personality disorders. Patients who seem to have a primary inhibition of the erotic potential are the most intractable cases (Kernberg, 1984, 1992). Braunschweig and Fain (1975) have illustrated how the unconscious relationship between infant and mother activates the capacity for the erotic response, and have contributed fundamentally, in my view, to clarifying the nature of core gender identity as well as object choice. Stoller (1975, 1979) has demonstrated how unconscious aggressive conflicts contribute, in their confluence with the erotic response to determine the nature of sexual excitement.

Unconscious fantasy has its origins in earliest infancy. Contrary to Freud's view of the infant as originally isolated and disconnected from his human environment, contemporary psychoanalytic infant observation has confirmed the connectedness of the human infant, the high degree of differentiation of his perceptive capacity—including cross-modal sensorial transfer—from the very beginning. These observations (Stern, 1985) make the concept of an original autistic phase and a succeeding symbiotic phase of development as proposed by Mahler highly questionable. There is much evidence of the infant's ability to make differentiations between self and object during alert states of low-level affect activation. It is interactions in peak affect states of euphoria and rage that dissolve differentiation into "symbiotic" fantasies of merger.

In other words, I think that symbiotic and nonsymbiotic (differentiated) modes of relationship alternate from the beginning of life on, and that unconscious fantasy starts out when a shift into the symbiotic mode is prompted by moments of maximum distress or pleasure, with their corresponding peak affects. I see such symbiotic states of experience as the preconscious origins of what gradually will become the dynamic Unconscious, the starting point in which the memory traces of intense affects are laid down in the context of fused self and object representations. I am including here the infant's gradually ever more complex perception of the interactions between him and mother, in which unconscious messages from mother are stored, to be retrospectively activated by later traumatic experiences and reinterpreted in the light of the ongoing development of unconscious fantasy (Laplanche, 1987, 1992). Cognitive experiences and memory traces from states of low affect activation that powerfully influence the developing ego's adaptive functions will gradually enter into conflict with unconscious fantasy, and will indirectly influence compromise formations that enable unconscious fantasy to infiltrate the developing ego. In my view, splitting mechanisms dominate and precede the development of repression as the major defensive operation of the ego in the sealing off of the dynamic unconscious.

Mother's unconscious fantasy, expressed in the enactment of unconscious object relations in her interactions with her baby, may be "read" and unconsciously interpreted by the infant. Because of the infant's innate capacity to read affective communication, severe distortions in mother's affective life may distort the organization of the affective life of the infant, and severe pathology of mother's internalized object relations may thus participate crucially in the setting up of the unconscious life of the infant.

Language as communication of subjective experience and in the creation of early intersubjectivity comes to be superimposed upon affective communication. The condensation of different internalized object relations under a similar affective sign, and the displacement of affective reactions from one object to another are replicated in the linguistic categories of metaphor and metonymy. From this viewpoint, one might reverse the Lacanian assumption that the unconscious is structured like a natural language by pointing to the fact that there are aspects of language structured like unconscious affects. The eruption of affect into language structure and the linguistic styles that defend against the affects of unconscious internalized object relations constitute a rich clinical area; here the analyst can explore the expression of unconscious fantasy and desire in the manifest content of the patient's free associations, his linguistic style, and his nonverbal behavior. In this process, the rôle responsiveness of the psychoanalyst listening to his patient's communications is codetermined by the capacity to "read" the unconscious affective messages that powerfully influence the countertransference.

The model I have presented so far enables us to formulate more precisely, I believe, the mutual influences of psychic structure and biological developments, of unconscious fantasy and the neurophysiology of affects. The relative intensity of sexual and aggressive drives may be considered as mediated by temperament, that is, by inborn dispositions to intensity, rhythm, and thresholds of affective responses. The influence of traumatic experiences on drive development is mediated by the intensity of traumatically induced affects in a first phase, and later, by their unconscious modification by retrospective interpretation of these traumatic experiences (Laplanche, 1992).

While temperament operating through the disposition to intensity of affect, on the one hand, and trauma, on the other, are significant contributors to the vicissitudes of drives, the overriding influence on drive development resides, I believe, in the intense, unconscious elements of the relationship between mother and infant. Within this relationship, the paternal figure as "excluded third person" (Kernberg, 1997) makes its appearance not only as part of the reality of the infant's life, but also as part of the unconscious reality of mother's image of the infant's father and her own—and the influence of these images on her unconscious erotic relationship to her infant. And again, in this unconscious communication, mother's affective messages may be crucial in the organization of the infant's affective responses.

When the analyst interprets the nature of the transference–countertransference relationship from an "external" perspective he symbolically replicates the role of the oedipal father, who disrupted the preoedipal, symbiotic relationship between infant and mother, and thus originated the archaic oedipal triangulation. (I have earlier [1997] referred to the French psychoanalytic perspective [De Mijolla and De Mijolla Mellor, 1996] that conceptualizes the analyst functioning as the "third person.") Patients with neurotic personality organization possess an internalized "third person," expressed in their capacity to split the self into an acting and an observing part; this indicates the firm establishment of a triangular structure, the advanced oedipal stage of development. The analyst's self-reflective exploration of his countertransference reflects the same triangulation.

Patients with a borderline personality organization, however, strive to maintain a symbiotic link with the analyst, and tend to experience the analyst's enactment of the interpretive role as a violent disruption of that symbiosis. Their strenuous resistance against the analyst's interpretive activity is partly in the service of avoiding the traumatizing effects of discovering the relationship of the parental couple and their own envy of it, the differences between sexes and generations, the shock of the primal scene, and the most primitive level of frustration and anxiety in the form of fear of annihilation related to the establishment of triangulation.

The clinical and metapsychological concept of normal and pathological narcissism that I have discussed elsewhere (Kernberg, 1984, 1992) is a major implication of the theory I have outlined here. At a metapsychological level, narcissism refers to the libidinal investment of the self, and to the vicissitudes of normal and pathological investment of the self with both libidinal and aggressive drive derivatives. At the clinical level, *narcissism* refers simply to the normal or abnormal regulation of self-esteem, and, more specifically, to the particularly frequent and severe pathology of self-esteem regulation that we describe as the narcissistic personality disorder.

As I have proposed in earlier work, normal narcissism implies the investment with libido of a normally integrated self that includes both the good, ideal and the bad, devalued self representations as these are integrated into total object relations in the development of object constancy. The normal integration of mutually split-off internalized object relations requires that self representations invested with libido predominate over those invested with aggression, and their integration implies a recruitment, one might say, of aggression at the service of libido. Normal self-esteem regulation is guaranteed by the integration of the tripartite psychic structure that, in turn, is based upon such integrative processes within ego and superego.

In contrast, in pathological narcissism, the pathological grandiose self as described originally by Herbert Rosenfeld (1964) reflects a condensation of the libidinal sector of self representations, while the bad, devalued, and persecutory aspects of internalized object relations are repressed, dissociated, and projected. Here, narcissistic grandiosity largely replaces object love, with its genuine investment in others, its desire for their approval, and its capacity for gratitude. Nevertheless, in most cases of pathological narcissism there is still a search for relations with others that have a libidinal, if selfish, character.

In more severely pathological cases, the pathological grandiose self is infiltrated with aggression, and this is reflected clinically in a search for autonomy and power at the expense of investment in relations with others: powerful destructive tendencies incorporated in the patient's psychic equilibrium gravely endanger relations with others as well as the patient's own survival. This constellation corresponds, I believe, to what Green (1993) has described as negative narcissism or the narcissism of death, and has led me to describe the syndrome of malignant narcissism and its relationship to the antisocial personality structure (1992). The point here is that normal and abnormal types of personality structure are intimately linked to the vicissitudes of internalized object relations, and to the quantitative equilibrium between libidinal and destructive drives.

I have described in earlier work (1992) how the primary affect of rage, by repetitive activation, may become transformed into hatred; and how hatred may, in turn, affect cognitive and perceptive functions leading to the internalization of primitive or persecutory objects. Repetitive experiences of violence and mistreatment may become part of psychic structure by the dual nature of identification, that is, the fact that identification is always both with an object and with the self in affective interaction with that object.

In fact, perhaps the most important practical implication of object relations theory is the conception of identification as a series of internalization processes ranging from earliest introjection to identification per se, to the development of complex identity formation. Each step includes the internalizing of both self and object representations and their affective interactions under the conditions of different developmental levels.

In the transference of healthier patients, with a well consolidated ego identity, the diverse self-representations are relatively stable in their coherent mutual linkage. This fosters the relatively consistent projection onto the analyst of the object representation aspect of the enacted object relationship. In contrast, patients with severe identity diffusion lack such linkage of self representations into an integrated self. They tend to alternate rapidly between projection of self and object representations in the transference, so that the analytic situation seems chaotic. Systematic interpretation of how the same internalized object relation is enacted again and again with rapid rôle reversals makes it possible to clarify the nature of the unconscious object relation, and the double splitting of (a) self representation from object representation and (b) idealized from persecutory object relations. This process promotes integration of the split representations which characterize the object relations of severe psychopathology (Kernberg, 1987, 1995).

I have tried to show how the proposed theory linking drives, affects, and object relations has direct relevance for psychoanalytic practice in addition to providing an instrument for the classification of personality disorders on a psychoanalytic basis (Kernberg, 1996). The central task of psychoanalytic treatment is the systematic elaboration of the transference, that is, of unconscious pathogenic internalized object relations from the past that are activated in the here-and-now. The psychoanalyst listens simultaneously to what the patient says, to how he says it, and to his own affective response to the patient; these ''messages'' constitute the raw material that will enable the analyst to clarify the nature of the dominant object relation in the transference. But transference analysis, as Laplanche (1992) suggested, always includes an additional element: the unconscious communication from the analyst. This is not to be confused with countertransference in the ordinary sense: it is the reproduction of the situation in which the infant experienced the enigmatic messages of the mother. This archaic relationship, repeated in the here and now and acknowledged as such, leads to the analysis of the deepest levels of unconscious fantasy. The transference is never fully resolved (Laplanche, 1992), but ends up reinvested elsewhere when the patient has acquired sufficient freedom from his pathogenic conflicts.

References

Braunschweig, D., and Fain, M. (1975), *La nuit, le jour* (the night, the day). Paris: Presses Universitaires de France.

De Mijolla, A., & De Mijolla Mellor, S. (1996), *Psychoanalyse.* Paris: Presses Universitaires de France.

Fairbairn, W. R. D. (1954), *An Object-Relations Theory of the Personality.* New York: Basic Books.

Freud, S. (1920), Beyond the Pleasure Principle. *Standard Edition,* 18:1–64. London: Hogarth Press, 1955.

——— (1923), The Ego and the Id. *Standard Edition,* 19:1–59. London: Hogarth Press, 1961.

——— (1933), New Introductory Lectures on Psychoanalysis. *Standard Edition,* 22:3–184. London: Hogarth Press, 1961.

Green, A. (1973), *Le discours vivant* (Living discourse). Paris: Presses Universitaires de France.

——— (1986), *On Private Madness.* London: Hogarth Press.

——— (1993), *Le Travail du negatif* (The work of the negative). Paris: Editions de Minuit.

Greenberg, J. R., & Mitchell, S. A. (1983), *Object Relations in Psychoanalytic Theory.* Cambridge, MA: Harvard University Press.

Guntrip, H. (1961), *Personality Structure and Human Interaction.* London: Hogarth Press.

——— (1968), *Schizoid Phenomena, Object Relations and the Self.* New York: International Universities Press.

——— (1971), *Psychoanalytic Theory, Therapy, and the Self.* New York: Basic Books.

Jacobson, E. (1964), *The Self and the Object World.* New York: International Universities Press.

——— (1971), *Depression.* New York: International Universities Press.

Kernberg, O. F. (1976), *Object Relations Theory and Clinical Psychoanalysis.* New York: Jason Aronson.

——— (1984), *Severe Personality Disorders: Psychotherapeutic Strategies.* New Haven, CT: Yale University Press.

——— (1987), An ego-psychology object relations theory approach to the transference. *Psychoanal. Quart.,* 56:197–221.

——— (1990), New perspectives in psychoanalytic affect theory. In: *Emotion: Theory, Research and Experience,* ed. R. Plutchik & H. Kellerman. New York: Academic Press, pp. 115–130.

——— (1992), *Aggression in Personality Disorders and Perversion.* New Haven, CT: Yale University Press.

——— (1995), *Love Relations: Normality and Pathology.* New Haven, CT: Yale University Press.

——— (1996), A psychoanalytic theory of personality disorders. In: *Major Theories of Personality Disorders,* ed. J. F. Clarkin & M. F. Lenzenweger. New York: Guilford Press, pp. 106–140.

——— (1997), The psychoanalytic classics revisited: The contributions of Ronald Fairbairn. (Unpublished).

Klein, M. (1940), Mourning and its relation to manic–depressive states. In: *Contributions to Psychoanalysis, 1921–1945.* London: Hogarth Press, 1948, pp. 311–338.

——— (1945), The Oedipus complex in the light of early anxieties. In: *Contributions to Psychoanalysis, 1921–1945*. London: Hogarth Press, 1948, pp. 339–390.

——— (1946), Notes on some schizoid mechanisms. In: *Development in Psychoanalysis,* ed. J. Riviere. London: Hogarth Press, 1952, pp. 292–320.

——— (1957), *Envy and Gratitude.* New York: Basic Books.

Kohut, H. (1971), *The Analysis of the Self.* New York: International Universities Press.

——— (1977), *The Restoration of the Self.* New York: International Universities Press.

Krause, R. (1988), Eine Taxonomie der Affekte und ihre Anwendung auf das Verständnis der frühen Störungen (A taxonomy of affects and their application to an understanding of the origins of psychological distress). *Psychotherapie und Medizinische Psychologie,* 38:77–86.

——— Lutolf, P. (1988), Facial indicators of transference processes in psychoanalytical treatment. In: *Psychoanalytic Process Research Strategies,* ed. H. Dahl & H. Kachele. Heidelberg: Springer, pp. 257–272.

Lacan, J. (1966), *Écrits.* Paris: Éditions du Seuil.

Laplanche, J. (1970), *Vie et mort en psychanalyse* (Life and death in psychoanalysis). Paris: Flammarion.

——— (1987), *Nouveaux fondements pour la psychanalyse* (New foundations for psychoanalysis). Paris: Presses Universitaires de France.

——— (1992), *Seduction, Translation, Drives,* ed. J. Fletcher & M. Stanton. London: Institute of Contemporary Arts.

Mahler, M. S., & Furer, M. (1968), *On Human Symbiosis and the Vicissitudes of Individuation.* New York: International Universities Press.

——— Pine, F., & Bergman, A. (1975), *The Psychological Birth of the Human Infant: Symbiosis and Individuation.* New York: Basic Books.

Mitchell, S. A. (1988), *Relational Concepts in Psychoanalysis.* Cambridge, MA: Harvard University Press.

Rosenfeld, H. (1964), On the psychopathology of narcissism: A clinical approach. *Internat. J. Psycho-Anal.,* 45:332–337.

Stern, D. (1985), *The Interpersonal World of the Infant.* New York: Basic Books.

Stoller, R. J. (1975), *Perversion: The Erotic Form of Hatred.* Washington, DC: American Psychiatric Press.

——— (1979), *Sexual Excitement.* New York: Pantheon.

Sullivan, H. S. (1953), *The Interpersonal Theory of Psychiatry.* New York: W. W. Norton.

——— (1962), *Schizophrenia as a Human Process.* New York: W. W. Norton.

Winnicott, D. W. (1958), *Collected Papers: Through Paediatrics to Psycho-analysis.* New York: Basic Books.

——— (1965), *The Maturational Processes and the Facilitating Environment.* New York: International Universities Press.

——— (1971), *Playing and Reality.* New York: Basic Books.

7

The Oedipus Complex and Male Homosexuality

Richard C. Friedman, M.D.
Jennifer I. Downey, M.D.

The topics of the Oedipus complex and male homosexuality have been part of the core of psychoanalysis since its inception by Freud. In light of recent developments in a number of fields, many extra-analytic, a fresh look at both areas seems timely.

Let us begin by commenting on the so-called "positive" Oedipus complex from a developmental perspective. In the 1970s we learned as analytic candidates that persistently unresolved oedipal conflicts led to global psychopathology. Homosexuality was conceptualized as *evidence* of such unresolved conflicts. Resolution of oedipal conflicts led to identification with the parent of the same sex. This was associated with the formation of an adequate superego structure and with the programming, so to speak, of heterosexual orientation. The persistence of a homoerotic image in conscious mental life as a stimulus for erotic fantasy, whether masturbation or otherwise, was presumed to be motivated by unconscious anxiety stemming from unresolved oedipal and preoedipal conflicts. The psychodynamics and narrative constructions that the literature had stressed are familiar to psychoanalytically informed readers (Socarides, 1968).

Basically, the general paradigm was that intense castration anxiety and separation anxiety or both, and anxiety resulting from the perceived threat of self-disintegration of all three kinds of anxiety, led to pathological identification with the parent of the opposite sex. The representation of the parental imago varied from patient to patient. Equation of the penis with the breast by men was stressed as an underlying motivation for fellatio (Bergler, 1956). Transient enhancement of gender-valued self-regard and sense of security was presumed to result from physical incorporations of the penis, either via anal intercourse or fellatio.

The *severity* of the patient's homosexual "disorder" was thought to be more or less related to the degree with which the homosexual-heterosexual ratio in the consciously experienced erotic fantasy life was predominately or exclusively homosexual.

Thus, it was expected that the successful analysis of a homosexual individual would lead to resolution of oedipal and preoedipal conflicts and change of sexual orientation to heterosexual (Wiedeman, 1962, 1974; Bayer, 1981).

Reasons for Revising the Paradigm

There are many reasons by now for concluding that the preceding paradigm is largely invalid. Let us stress *two* that were emphasized by Friedman (1988) in his book on male homosexuality.

1. Many *patients,* probably most, who had been discussed in the psychoanalytic literature in terms of their homosexual orientation actually suffered from major mental disorders, such as depression and diverse personality disorders. Often, these patients were integrated at a low borderline level of organization. Thus, the population described tended to be skewed toward the disturbed side of the health–illness spectrum. Psychodynamic formulations of such homosexual patients were often applied to all homosexual people.

2. Commonly, patients who were predominately or exclusively homosexual entered psychoanalysis with pronounced conflicts that produced suffering and impaired capacity to love and work.

Analysis led to conflict resolution and symptom improvement but often without alteration of sexual orientation.

How are we to understand this? Let us say here that we are aware that the topic of change in sexual orientation seems controversial to many analysts at this time. The perspective we wish to adopt is not political but, rather, empirical. The literature in this area has been extensively reviewed (Acosta, 1975; Haldeman, 1991).

Several years ago Friedman (1988) suggested that description of a *patient's* history of sexual fantasies, activity, perception of identity as homosexual or not, and social role be made independently of description of psychopathology. More specifically, Friedman suggested that level of ego integration, type of character defenses and sexual fantasies and activity be conceptualized as orthogonal (that is, independent) axes of behavior.

Being aware of a substantial body of data (even then) indicating that people predominately or exclusively homosexual often function at high levels of ego integration (and we are speaking here not just about social adjustment, but about meaningful integration of ego functions), many never seeking assistance from mental health clinicians, Friedman (1988) limited most theoretical speculation (at that time) to the clinical domain. It should be noted that such pioneer sexologists as Havelock Ellis (1938) and Magnus Hirschfeld (1914) had discussed higher functioning people who were then called "homosexual" and today would be called "gay or lesbian." Both the early sexologists and their modern psychoanalyst counterparts, however (e.g., Richard Isay, 1989), have directed attention primarily to higher functioning men but not women. The psychoanalytic literature on lesbianism is much more sparse than the literature on male homosexuality, and is almost exclusively focused on highly disturbed patients. We take this to be due to reporting bias and not different distributions of higher and lower functioning lesbian people than in the gay or general population (Magee and Miller, 1996; Downey and Friedman, 1998).

Having reached the (then) unexpected conclusion that male homosexuality is not associated with global psychopathology, and that sexual orientation often does not change during analysis,

Friedman (1988) was led to infer that the homosexual erotic image in adults who are predominately or exclusively homosexual is usually not constructed in response to unconscious unresolved conflict. This inference, quite radical at the time, led to a critical reassessment of Freud's ideas about psychological development.

All roads in this area lead to Rome—or, specifically, Delphi, that is, to the Oedipus complex. In order to consider the Oedipus complex in relation to *homosexuality,* it is necessary to think critically about more general aspects of oedipal theory first. It is to this topic that we now turn. "Oedipal theory" may refer to many aspects of experience and behavior, of course. With our focus on sexual orientation, it is the explicitly *sexual* aspects of Freud's theory that we shall hereby stress. We use the term *sexual* in a delimited way—*not* as general bodily pleasure, but, rather, as a conscious experience of lustful, erotic feeling that is associated with physiological events in the central nervous system (CNS) and throughout the body (Masters and Johnson, 1966).

Let us now reassess some of Freud's ideas about sex and aggression during childhood and adulthood. We will begin by summarizing some extrapsychoanalytic material relevant to the line of argument.

The Adult Sexual Experience—Hormonal Considerations

In men and women the feeling of erotic desire or "lust"—a specific affect—is dependent on the presence of "adequate enough" levels of androgen (Money, 1987). In women, androgen levels are much lower than in men and the effects of androgen are modified by the hormones of the menstrual cycle. The simple fact of differential hormonal profiles following puberty leads men and women to experience sexuality quite differently. In pointing this out, we are not suggesting that hormones in themselves are unitary "causes" of erotic motivations. They exert important influences, however, and ones that clinicians must be aware of.

To a large extent, psychoanalytic "drive–instinct" theory, insofar as it emphasizes the insistent, persistent urgency of drives seeking discharge, conforms to *male* sexual experience. Indeed, the psychoanalytically naive but biologically informed reader might interpret the discussions of drive-instinct in much of the early psychoanalytic literature as the expression of the psychobiological activities of testosterone, unopposed by the hormones that fluctuate with the menstrual cycle (Friedman and Downey, 1995).

Condensations from the Oedipal and Preoedipal Past in the Sexual Experience of Adults

Erotic stimuli are processed according to personal narratives, called "sex scripts" by Stoller (1985) and composed of "impulses, desires, defenses, falsifications, truths avoided and memories of past events, erotic and nonerotic—going back to infancy" (p. viii). During adulthood people tend to return over and over again to the content of a quite specific erotic narrative theme. The recurrent erotic theme includes the fundamental features of sexual object and situation, as well as the sex of the erotic object. In our culture the concepts of the triangular and of the forbidden are both important influences on the structure of sexual narratives.

In adult sexuality the past is always conflated with the present. The condensation of past objects and situations, and imagined (forbidden) objects and situations and part objects, with present actors in erotic narratives, provide dramatic and endlessly fascinating dimensions to personal scenarios of lust, passion, and desire. It is probably never possible for someone to recall his or her childhood sexual life without its being colored by the condensation, or fusion, between childhood and adult affects, images, and self and object representations (Stoller, 1975, 1979; Kernberg, 1995).

During sexual arousal we are probably more in touch with "oedipal" and "preoedipal" self and other representations and infantile organization of affects and defensive operations than at any other time. The sexual experience is full of "thrills and regressions" (to borrow Balint's [1959] expression) and promises types of syntheses that are not otherwise available to us.

Just as there is no way of reexperiencing the *physiology* of childhood after one has become an adult, however, so it is not possible to actually reexperience the psychology of childhood and particularly childhood sexual experience. Thus, inferences about development made from the psychoanalysis of adults must always be qualified by the ever-present likelihood of retrospective distortion.

Sexual Experience Involves Integrated Patterned Activity

During adulthood, erotic activity and imagined or fantasized erotic activity seem to function as basic mental components, depicted as it were on an erotic canvas. As is true with other areas of motivated patterned activity, however, sexual activity that appears to be a single, unitary behavior actually consists of components of smaller behavioral units that under usual, natural circumstances connect seamlessly with each other.

To put this somewhat differently, the story line of "scripts," whether sexual or otherwise, consists of connected "frames," each of which in turn is made up of "subframes"; smaller mental units. One can liken this to chemical compounds composed of elements.

We humans seem to imagine or *fantasize* about activities that our mammalian relatives actually carry out. (Of course, we can also enact such activities, but fortunately not too frequently on the analytic couch.) The point is, however, that study of selected *activities* of nonhuman animals may shed some light on dissecting out the determinants of discrete *elements* that interconnect to form complex patterns of sexual activity.

In male nonhuman primates, for example, sexual intercourse may be scientifically described as consisting of contact (placing two hands on the hips of the partner), mounting, erecting, intromission, penile thrusting, and ejaculation/orgasm. Thus the complex pattern of activity that constitutes the final sexual act actually involves intricate integrations carried out by mind and brain. One major way of investigating how the brain integrates sexual behavior, involves stimulation and ablation studies carried out in our closest mammalian relatives, nonhuman primates.

Stimulation–Ablation Studies

In one group of experiments, lesions were made in the medial preopic-anterior-hypothalamus (MP-AH). This area of the brain was selected for study because it was known to be involved in the regulation of sexual behavior in a number of species (Slimp, Hart, and Goy, 1978).

Lesions in this area led to impaired *copulatory behavior.* This in itself was an important observation, but this research was especially innovative because the investigators made meticulous observations of another type of sexual behavior—masturbation. They used video cameras and other methods to study this behavior and found startling results. Discrete lesions in the MP-AH that clearly diminished copulatory behavior did *not* diminish masturbatory behavior, including masturbation to ejaculation. The meaning of this crucial observation to the researchers was that the MP-AH is specifically involved with sexual behavior directed toward a partner and is not a neural locus for all forms of sexual behavior (Slimp, Hart, and Goy, 1978).

Different anatomical sites for masturbation to orgasm and for copulation illustrate that complex integrations at the level of brain and mind are necessary in order for sexual activity to occur properly. Although great diversity in sexual developments exists most frequently, masturbation occurs earlier in the individual's development than does copulation. The temporal discontinuity between solitary erotic experience and sociosexual activity is paralleled by an anatomic dysjunction between the two domains.

Childhood Sexuality Viewed from the Vantage Point of Adulthood—Retrospective Distortion

The question arises, when do the crucial brain–behavioral integrations characteristic of adult sexuality first occur in the life cycle? Although the answers to this are not definitively known, what we do know of the behavior of young animals, including human children, and the neurohormonal "hardware" that influences this behavior, suggests that only rudimentary, initial parts of integrative procedures are carried out during the earlier phases of childhood, including the "oedipal" phase. Key steps are made in these complex processes immediately prior to puberty and continue during early adolescence when the crucial integrations are usually completed.[1]

All of modern science is indebted to Freud for his courageous discussions of childhood sexuality. As we have come to learn more about sexuality, however, certain types of *discontinuities* between childhood and adult sexual experience suggest themselves. Although the beginnings of erotic sexuality occur during childhood—in children and in nonhuman primates—they tend to occur in the form of *components* or *elements* of sexual activity that are not fully integrated with each other. The differences between childhood and adult sexual activity and experience are important. One of these differences is that the full experience of erotic arousal depends to a great degree on the presence of androgen in the bloodstream and this occurs during the physiological processes of puberty (or prepuberty; McClintock and Herdt, 1996).

The Oedipus Complex Reconceptualized

We would like to turn attention now away from the adult sexual experience and toward the developmental aspects of Freud's theory of the Oedipus complex.

Given the profound changes that Freud made in other aspects of psychoanalytic developmental theory during his career, the absence of such change with regard to the mechanisms of the Oedipus complex over a forty plus year period is astonishing (Gay, 1988). (Many psychoanalysts would agree with Freud's steadfast adherence to his original ideas about the psychological significance of the myth of Oedipus.)

Psychoanalytic practitioners have to look no further than their most recent experience with patients to find example after example of unresolved oedipal conflicts expressed in free associations and dreams. Many clinicians might wonder why questions about

[1]By "completed" we do not mean to be complete in terms of the capacity for rich and mature object relations, but complete only in terms of the capacity to experience and express adult sexual activity in the manifest sense.

the ubiquity and relevance of the Oedipus complex are even raised.

Let us turn the light of critical reassessment on the *erotic* and developmental domains to respond to this question. We are about to argue *against* the universal occurrence of a biologically determined incestuous wish.

In a recent review of anthropological and sociobiological data published as a lead article in *The American Journal of Psychiatry*, Mark Erickson (1993) argued that secure bonding during infancy is associated with incest *avoidance* later in life. Only when early bonding is disrupted is incest likely to occur. Although Erickson did not study fantasy, he pointed out that Freud viewed castration anxiety as the major motivation for incest avoidance. He questioned Freud's emphasis on innately determined incestuous desire and suggested that the motivation to commit incest might not in fact be intense or even present among children who have experienced consistently secure early bonding. Incestuous motivations and fantasies might be evidence for disruption of early bonding and therefore psychopathological. He also noted that incest rarely occurs in nonhuman primates.

Erickson's review added an important dimension to arguments of earlier critics who had questioned oedipal developmental theory. Oedipal theory, at least as conceptualized by Freud, was substantially weakened by increased knowledge about the development of *gender identity* (Stoller, 1968; Money and Ehrhardt, 1972), *superego formation* (Kohlberg, 1976, 1981), *personality structure* (Millon, 1981), *the etiology of the neuroses and psychoses* (DSM-IV, 1994), and by the emergence of the field of sociobiology (Wilson, 1975).

Recently, R. Wright (1994), a sociobiologist, commented:

> Why would boys want to have sex with their mothers and kill their fathers? Genes that specifically encourage this aren't exactly destined to spread through a hunter–gatherer population overnight?
>
> When boys reach adolescence, they may, especially in a polygamous society—find themselves competing with their fathers for the same women. But among these women is *not* the boy's mother; incest often produces deficient offspring, and it's not in the son's genetic interest to have his mother assume the risks and burdens of pregnancy to

> create a reproductively worthless sibling. (Hence the dearth of boys who try to seduce their mothers) [pp. 315–316].

The same author emphasized that childhood scenarios of competition between father and son for mother usually do not have sex as the goal.

Cumulative recent research and clinical experience, therefore, has raised fundamental questions about the Oedipus complex. What specifically is the role of the Oedipus complex in development? Is the Oedipus complex biologically determined or even strongly biologically influenced or not?

Because of new knowledge about sexual orientation the need to reconceptualize oedipal theory is of particular importance (D'Augelli and Patterson, 1995; Cabaj and Stein, 1996).

Is the Oedipus Complex a Unitary Entity?

Most psychoanalysts conceptualize the Oedipus complex as Freud did, as an irreducible psychological unit. Erotic desire for the mother, parricidal wish, and resulting castration fear are hypothesized to occur in a single construct or, if you will, a "complex." This is biologically determined and universal.

In a recent critical review, we proposed that what to Freud seemed unitary can be conceptualized as a form of experience that consists of several key components. These components are integrated cognitively in various ways during development. Most relevant to the concept of the Oedipus complex are the erotic, the aggressive, and the anxiety components (Friedman and Downey, 1995). Of these components, the erotic element that Freud thought to be so crucial actually seems to us to be not necessarily central and not necessary as a trigger for the aggressive and anxious components experienced during childhood. Let us explain further.

As mentioned earlier, sexual behavior occurs in immature animals but not in its full form. For example, in nonhuman primates, immature animals typically carry out some but not all of the sequences necessary for adult-type copulation. The nonhuman animal data have some interesting parallels in the sexual activity of children. Thus, a recent investigation of the frequency of various sexual behaviors in normal 4- to 6-year-olds revealed that touching genitalia or displaying sex parts of each other occurred reasonably often. Behaviors characteristic of adult sexuality were rare, however, and when present generally signified sexual abuse (Yates, 1993).

The important research of Galenson and colleagues (1993) demonstrated that children frequently engage in intentional genital self-stimulation prior to the "oedipal phase" of development. Galenson's research also suggested that at least some of these children probably experience early forms of erotic fantasy. Although the importance of this research cannot be overemphasized, it should not be taken to mean that erotic fantasy and activity during childhood—whether oedipal or preoedipal, is *normative.* Orgasm may occur during very early childhood. How frequently it actually does during natural circumstances is another question. Even Galenson's careful observational research has not established that orgasm *usually* occurs during most early childhood sexual activity.

Freud extended the meaning of what is sexually considered to be "erotic" to include many related but not specifically sexual dimensions of behavior and experience, including gender identity role and attachment behaviors. If we adopt a more circumscribed use of the term *erotic* limiting it only to those experiences which are associated with feelings of sexual desire and arousal (that is, erotic affect as opposed to diffusely pleasureful feelings), there is good reason to believe that only some children, by no means all, experience meaningful erotic arousal during or prior to the oedipal phase of development. We hypothesize that even when such arousal is experienced, sexual desire for a *parent* (as a primary stimulus) is highly variable. What little evidence exists seems to us to suggest great diversity in the emergence of childhood sexuality. The age at which the various components of erotic motivations become more salient probably varies substantially between children, and important differences between boys and girls are present. Thus, boys are exposed to testosterone *prenatally;* girls are (for all intents and purposes) not. The significance of this finding for sex differences in the threshold of childhood sexual arousal has thus far received scant attention.

In any case, for boys *and* girls as well, we hypothesized that the erotic component of the Oedipus complex is not a normatively occurring, innately determined event during the oedipal phase of childhood as Freud proposed.

Organizational and Activational Effects of Sex Steroids

There is an important additional reason for thinking that erotic desire is probably a separate component of mental life, not fully integrated with aggressive motivations during the oedipal phase, and not primarily responsible for serving as a trigger of what are usually considered "oedipal" competitive–aggressive fantasies and fears of retaliation—during childhood. This line of reasoning concerns the neurobiological regulators of human sexuality, compared with the neurobiological regulators of competitive-aggressivity.

We suggest that the aggressive–competitive dimensions of the "Oedipus complex" do not in fact require a trigger of forbidden erotic desire in order to be activated. Rather, they occur along a developmental line of their own, intersecting with a sexual developmental line at different times in different people. The aggressive –competitive line is biologically determined and phylogenetically continuous across many mammalian species, including the primates. The control of sexual behavior, however, is different across mammalian species. This is particularly true of sexual behavior in primates including humans—compared to nonprimates such as rats and guinea pigs, for example (Friedman and Downey, 1993).

Let us now focus more on aggressive–competitive behavior in males. The aggressive–competitive line of development unfolds in boys at times when there is virtually no testosterone in the bloodstream—during preoedipal and oedipal phases of development, for example. It may be thought of as an expression of an effect of hormones on the "hard wiring" of the brain. Rodents and rhinos, zebras and horses, guinea pigs and rats, nonhuman primates and human beings all express marked sex differences in play virtually from the time that they become freely mobile. Male animals engage in rough-and-tumble activity to a far greater degree than female. The developmental line, from early rough-and-tumble activity to aggressive interactions pre- and postpubertally, separates male and female animals through development (Friedman and Downey, 1993).

The aggressive fantasies and activities that occur in male humans, including parricidal fantasies usually thought of as oedipal, seem to us to be part of this developmental line, which is independent, although sometimes overlapping, with the developmental line that determines sexual activity and fantasy.

From a neuroendocrine perspective it is important to emphasize that the behavioral effects of rough play—and, in many boys, frank aggressivity—are a consequence of prenatal organizational effects of androgen. What this means is that in men prenatal testosterone secreted from the fetal testes leads the brain to be organized in such a way that, after birth and during childhood, behavior associated with masculinity is expressed. This behavior does not depend on the surge of sex steroid hormones of puberty.

In contrast, sexual behavior in its fully integrated form seems to require the activational effects of testosterone during or after puberty, in addition to the earlier occurring organizational effects. Thus, the brain must first be organized in a particular way. Much later, during and after puberty, the individual becomes fully motivated to engage in sexual interactions with the intensity and complexity of adulthood.

Sexual Fantasy in Adulthood and Childhood

Sexual narratives, that is, fantasies, always contain condensations of past experience. Not only do these condensations involve various object and part-object relationships, but also affects from many stages of development. Cognitive bridges form during different phases of development and function to connect these disparate elements.

Cognitive bridges may function in several major ways. First, they may provide connections within a behavioral system such as that of sexual activity. An example of it would be the connection between sexual arousal and sexual intercourse. In the adult one motivates the other and the two are condensed in fantasy. We suggest, however, that diversity exists among children with regard to the age when this bridge is constructed.

A different type of bridge involves the connection between two independently developing behavioral systems that become welded to each other in late childhood or even later. An example of such a cognitive bridge would be a rageful feeling at the representation of the father triggered by erotic desire for the mother. In a more general sense this would present as aggressive fantasies directed at males triggered by sexual desires for females.

Understanding the development of childhood sexuality and aggression and the relationship between the two may be thought of as "unpacking" components of information which in adulthood regulate and determine the synthesis of a sexual fantasy narrative. To borrow an analogy from jewelry, we might think of the sexual and aggressive components found in children's mental lives as individual polished stones, while the synthetic framework adulthood provides is like the setting which organizes and locates the stones in a particular frame and pattern (the sexual narrative).

Clinical Considerations

Let us now return to the clinical situation. In so doing, we will try to integrate the two levels of our discourse: the scientific-developmental and the psychoanalytic-clinical.

Let us consider gay men who have been analyzed with greatly improved capacities to love, work, experience pleasure, but whose erotic life remains, in its object, unaltered. How are we psychoanalysts to conceptualize this empirical phenomenon?

The model that we outlined earlier on emphasizes diversity with regard to developmental erotic phenomena. Modification of the "original" paradigm of universal primary erotic desire for the mother, to accommodate this diversity, does not necessitate abandonment of oedipal-like conflict as a core unconscious mechanism in the psychological functioning of adults.

With regard to the erotic component of the Oedipus complex, we have emphasized that there is probably great variability in the intensity of sexual feelings between children, and in the way in which sexual fantasies are integrated and elaborated. We have questioned the universality of incestuous desire for the parent of the opposite sex.

What about incestuous desire for the parent of the same sex? Richard Isay (1989) has suggested that some boys are primarily erotically attracted to their fathers. Whether this actually happens or not remains to be established. We suspect that this sometimes happens. Isay has pointed out that his hypothesis is compatible with recent research on genetic and hormonal determinants of homosexuality (Friedman and Downey, 1994). To some degree this may be true; however, this research does not directly bear on erotic attractions to a parent. Isay's hypothesis is, in a sense, more conservative than ours. It retains the idea of primary incestuous motivation and substitutes the father for the mother.

We propose, rather, that many boys whose primary sex object is male are not primarily erotically attracted to their fathers, but to others, including male siblings, friends, other peers, and fantasized figures, including "imaginary playmates." We also suspect that just as with heterosexual men, the childhood fantasies of boys on a homosexual path consist of "components" that await integration and elaboration, at least during the oedipal age range.

What about the unconscious aspects of retaliation? Clinical experience suggests that the representation of the retaliatory parent is often of the father, and that the imagery associated with retaliation involves bodily damage, that is, castration. Often, as might be expected, the paternal and maternal representations are fused; and as has been extensively discussed by others, the manifest image of the threatening father might also symbolically represent the preoedipal mother.

The basic modifications in theory that we have proposed focuses primarily on the nature of unacceptable wishes, and on the determinants of the consciously perceived erotic object. Regarding imagery associated with retaliation, however, we have also suggested that the symbolic form with which such fear is experienced often involves somatic representations, including the genitalia (usually the penis). The years during which oedipal-like conflicts are experienced are crucial for integration and representation of the body image. Consistent with our belief that incestuous wishes are *not* universal or biologically determined, we do not accept the theory that the symbolic representation of bodily damage, even including genital damage, is necessarily and inevitably triggered by such wishes. We hypothesize that many types of fears are symbolically represented somatically by young children, and that diverse wishes are experienced as unacceptable and therefore likely to provoke severe punishment.

Although we question many aspects of oedipal theory, we do not challenge the general consensus concerning the developmental significance of movement from dyadic to triangular types of conflictual relationships during the oedipal phase. Altering the paradigm, however, such that the triangular conflict does not require a trigger that is explicitly sexual, modifies it substantially from what Freud had in mind, and we believe brings it into better alignment with modern knowledge.

Psychobiology and Developmental Psychoanalytic Theory Reconsidered

The ideas about development that we have put forward thus far were stimulated by data in two domains: clinical psychoanalysis, and psychobiology. If boys are not universally programed to be erotically attracted to their mothers, it is theoretically consistent that many men who are predominately or exclusively homosexual should experience psychoanalysis without erotic object change. The clinical data that we have outlined are compatible with findings in two psychobiological areas: behavioral genetics, and psychoneuroendocrinology. Let us begin with genetics.

The term *heritability* refers to the proportion of phenotypic variance that is due to genetic variance. Recent research indicates that homosexuality is *moderately* heritable. Let us attempt to place this finding in some perspective. Of all areas of science that elicit suspicion in humanists, genetics has arguably been assigned the most villainous role. This is because of a tendency in political theorizing to search for single causes of daunting social problems and find these in "biology." "Genetics" thus assumes the unwanted role of weapon in an ongoing battle about the distribution of good services, rights, and privileges in society. We don't believe this should be the case.

The idea of "heritability" contains within it, if you will, the notion of behavioral variance. This suggests a somewhat different model of the mind than the one sometimes used by clinicians. Consider sex differences, for example; many behaviors vary among men and also among women. Graphs of these behaviors lead to curves whose means are somewhat different. These differences, however, do not allow one to predict the performance of individuals. A particular woman, for example, may have more spatial and mathematical ability than 99 percent of men. Nonetheless, differences exist between men and women generally. Analytic clinicians, often intuitively, refer to models of an ideal norm. No such ideal is inherently suggested in the example we just gave.

The fact that a trait is heritable does not necessarily suggest that it is impervious to environmental influence. The heritability of tallness, for example, may be detectable only if all members of a population experience adequate nutrition during their growth phases.

In light of recent advances in behavioral genetics (Bouchard and Propping, 1993), it should come as no surprise that in men and women homosexuality appears to be moderately heritable. Recent studies of familiality (Pillard, Poumadere, and Caretta, 1982; Pillard and Weinrich, 1986), and of MZ and DZ twins and triplets reared together (Bailey and Pillard, 1991; Whitam, Diamond, and Martin, 1993), and a few instances of MZ twins separated and reared independently (Eckert, Bouchard, Bohlen, and Heston, 1986), provide a solid database supporting such a conclusion. In addition, genetic "linkage" studies have been reported, but the story here is still incomplete since negative findings have also been published by independent investigators unable to replicate the original research (Rice, Anderson, Risch, and Ebers, 1995). The MZ–DZ studies, however, were carried out by independent investigators. But before attempting to speculate about the possible meanings of all this, reporting some personal experience of one of the authors (Friedman, 1988) might be of help. Research involving a gay young man revealed that he had an identical twin who was heterosexual. The twin was prevailed upon to enter a study of "sexuality." The heterosexual twin was unaware of the sexual orientation of his brother, believing him to be a heterosexual bachelor. Each man's sexual fantasies had been homo- or heterosexual since childhood; each was sexually active. We mention them here in order to emphasize an aspect of their life narratives. When interviewed alone and in the company of the other, each described the same personality characteristics of their father and reported that he had treated each of them identically. The gay man described his father as quiet, detached, unrelated, aloof. Father and son rarely spent private time together because, after work, the father would retreat to his workshop in the basement. Although invited, the gay man was disinterested in using the tools his father obviously loved, preferring to stay upstairs, either playing the piano or conversing with his mother. The heterosexual man described his father as quiet, strong, deep, dignified, and involved with him (although not necessarily at a verbal level). He usually joined his father in leisure activities in the shop in the basement of their home. The twins therefore agreed that their father was a "quiet man." The "value" that each assigned to the "quietness" was radically different, however, and the attribution of motivation that each made was also different. To the child who grew up to become homosexual, his father was detached and uninvolved. To the child who grew up to become heterosexual, his father was dignified and strong.

Who knows what a dispassionate scientific observer might say? All that we can conclude is that the inner world of the children, the representational world, was different, and that in an experiential way it was as if they had "different" fathers.

In the scientific literature on the family background of gay compared to heterosexual men, childhood relationships with fathers are frequently (although by no means invariably) reported to have been problematical in various ways (Friedman, 1988). How are we to interpret this discrepancy with regard to questions pertaining to "etiology" of homo- or heretosexuality? Many interpretations are possible, but we may conclude with some certainty that one cannot simply accept the personal narratives of adults at face value.

With regard to psychodynamic issues, the new genetic data clearly dramatize the importance of the distinction between psychodynamics and etiology. Mental structures that are expressed in unresolved oedipal conflicts, for example, may be the product of primary genetic determinants that are immediate and direct or delayed and indirect, or may not be under genetic control at all. In the instance of the twins we just mentioned, for example, the origins (that is, etiology) of the different valuing of their object representations during childhood was not clear. Such phenomena require prospective interdisciplinary investigation.

Psychoneuroendocrinology and Homosexuality

The complexity of our evolving paradigms is bound to increase if we turn to the area of psychoneuroendocrinology.

Sex differences in the structure and function of the central nervous system (CNS) that derive from the effects of gonadal steroids secreted during a critical period of prenatal life occur throughout the vertebrate kingdom. Among the manifestations of these CNS effects are certain differences in both sexual and nonsexual behavior. In the human, testosterone secretion in the male fetus increases between the twelfth and twentieth week of pregnancy. A substantial body of evidence has been amassed from studies of humans as well as nonhuman mammals supporting a prenatal androgen hypothesis of male homosexuality. A highly compressed summary of this hypothesis is that some variant of prenatal androgen control occurs, such that too little, at a critical time, leads to homosexuality in men; whereas too much leads to homosexuality in women. The hypothesis assumes that the prenatal hormonal effects influence the brain, but not the genitalia. We will not summarize the various lines of research relevant to the prenatal androgen hypothesis here. There have been a number of recent reviews of this subject (Geschwind and Galaburda, 1985; Gooren, Fliers, and Courtney, 1990; Gorski, 1991; Byrne and Parsons, 1993; Meyer-Bahlberg, 1993; Friedman and Downey, 1993).

We do want to stress, however, the importance of the need for a highly complex multivariate developmental model of sexual orientation. A complex model is necessary since prenatal sex steroid hormones also influence childhood sex stereotypic play. This effect is robust.

Both gay men and lesbians tend to have histories of childhood play that do not conform to stereotypic sex patterns. This has been termed "sex role nonconformity" by researchers and is *not* inherently pathological. This "nonconformity" refers to norms naturalistically established by families and peers, not by clinicians and investigators (Bell, Weinberg, and Hammersmith, 1981; Whitam and Zent, 1984; Bailey and Zucker, 1995). The research on prenatal hormones and childhood play is so compelling, and its implications are so far reaching, that we want to say a word more about this line of work.

Our cognitive capacities lead us to form gender-role behavior in childhood, out of the same predispositions that influence sex stereotypic play in young mammals generally. The determinants and consequences of childhood gender role behaviors, and the mental representations that are associated with them have become one of the more intriguing puzzles of modern psychology.

A summary of relevant issues about gender dimorphism in play follows:

1. Sex typed childhood play is heavily influenced by prenatal hormones (i.e., testosterone).
2. Prenatal hormonal influences extend to areas that include activity level, predilection to throw the body through space, emotional responses to objects and striking one's own body, even the predilection to experience pleasure from prototypically sex-typed adornments such as jewelry, and from playing "house" and participating in other rehearsals for maternal behaviors. Same-sexed competitive motives and fears are probably part of the developmental line stemming from these influences.
3. This whole developmental array of behaviors involves interactions and representations that are not primarily "caused" by influences that Freud emphasized as central—such as perception of the genital difference or primary sexual desire for the parent of the opposite sex. They seem not to fit well with models involving drive-energy, libido, etc.
4. The influences that shape childhood identifications, disidentifications, and fantasy elaborations, influences that, in turn, are of essential importance for the creation of personal narratives, in light of the importance of prenatal neuroendocrine determinants of behavior, need to be reconceptualized.
5. Any model that attempts to clarify the origins of sexual orientation must take into account childhood play and childhood gender role behavior.

6. In some people, however, prenatal hormones might influence sexual orientation directly without influencing childhood play.
7. Genes might exert their effects via prenatal hormones in some people and via direct action on the brain in others.

In connection with the above, it could be mentioned that one area where psychoanalysis has already made substantial contributions is that of Childhood Gender Identity Disorder (GID). Although of enormous interest in itself, the fact is that *most* homosexual men do not have histories of such a disorder. However, some patients who have the disorder do grow up to become homosexual adults (Green, 1985, 1987). The psychodynamic issues in this field constitute a specialized domain, and we refer those with particular interests in this area to the writings of Susan Coates (1992) and child psychoanalysts.

Conclusion

We would like to conclude by commenting on psychoanalysis and psychobiology. Freud often borrowed embryological ideas and used them metaphorically. We often adopt his frame of reference about psychobiology without necessarily being fully aware of it. MacLean's (1965) famous "triune brain" paradigm seems a good example. MacLean said:

> Man finds himself in the predicament that Nature has endowed him essentially with three brains which despite great differences in structure must function together and communicate with one another. The eldest of these brains is basically reptilian, the second has been inherited from lower mammals and the third is a late mammalian development.
>
> Speaking allegorically of these three brains within a brain, we might imagine that when the psychiatrist bids the patient to lie on the couch he is asking him to stretch out alongside a horse and a crocodile. The crocodile may be willing and ready to shed a tear and the horse to neigh and whinny, but when they are encouraged to express their troubles in words, it soon becomes evident that their inability is beyond the help of language training. Little wonder that the patient who has personal responsibility for these animals and who must serve

> as their mouth piece is sometimes accused of being full of resistance and unwilling to talk [p. 197].

An occasional "whinny" emerging from our consulting rooms (sometimes in a duet) seems proof to many of us that MacLean's model is correct.

And well it might be but it is not all inclusive! The frame within which biology is presented here, and by Freud as well, did not emphasize childhood play, for example. Yet of all human behaviors, one of the most important that is thought to be biologically influenced and similar to early life activities of other mammals, is play. As adults, we may be similar to crocodiles and horses, but as children we are like puppy dogs, colts, and kittens.

The new extra-analytic scientific advances that we have discussed here have implications that extend far beyond the way we think about the Oedipus complex and homosexuality. We seem to have reached a point where renewed collaboration between psychoanalysts and psychobiologists is needed. This seems certain to move our field well beyond the two-instinct theory, which seems to us a marker for the psychobiological frontier during Freud's lifetime.

As students of fantasy, we psychoanalysts have a particularly vital role to play in this interdisciplinary collaboration. Working alongside our extra-analytic colleagues, particularly those in brain imaging, cognitive neuroscience, and neurobiology, we will perhaps be able to construct a valid developmental model that is both scientific and psychoanalytic. Until then, we are called upon to tolerate substantial ambiguity and mystery. In other words, although circumstances are different, the challenges we face seem quite similar in certain ways to those of the first generation of psychoanalytic pioneers.

References

Acosta, F. X. (1975), Etiology and treatment of homosexuality: A review. *Arch. Sex Behav.,* 4:9–29.

American Psychiatric Association (1994), *Diagnostic and Statistical Manual of Mental Disorders,* 4th ed. (DSM-IV). Washington, DC: American Psychiatric Press.

Bailey, J. M., & Pillard, R. C. (1991), A genetic study of male sexual orientation. *Arch. Gen. Psychiatry*, 48:1089–1096.

——— Zucker, K. J. (1995), Childhood sex-typed behavior and sexual orientation: A conceptual analysis and quantitative review. *Dev. Psychol.*, 31:43–55.

Balint, M. (1959), On genital love. In: *Primary Love and Psychoanalytic Technique*. London: Tavistock, pp. 109–120.

Bayer, R. V. (1981), *Homosexuality and American Psychiatry: The Politics of Diagnosis*. New York: Basic Books.

Bell, A. P., Weinberg, M. S., & Hammersmith, S. K. (1981), *Sexual Preference, Its Development in Men and Women*. Bloomington, IN: Indiana University Press.

Bergler, E. (1956), *Homosexuality: Disease or Way of Life?* New York: Hill & Wang.

Bouchard, J. R., & Propping, P. (1993), *Twins as a Tool of Behavioral Genetics*. New York: John Wiley.

Byne, W., & Parsons, B. (1993), Human sexual orientation: The biologic theories reappraised. *Arch. Gen. Psychiatry*, 50:228–239.

Cabaj, R. P., & Stein, T. S., Eds. (1996), *Textbook of Homosexuality and Mental Health*. Washington, DC: American Psychiatric Press.

Coates, S. (1992), Gender identity disorder in boys: An integrative model. In: *Interface of Psychoanalysis and Psychology*, ed. J. W. Barron, M. N. Eagle, & D. L. Wolitzky. Washington, DC: American Psychological Association, pp. 245–265.

D'Augelli, A. R., & Patterson, C. J. (1995), *Lesbian, Gay and Bisexual Identities Over the Lifespan*. Oxford: Oxford University Press.

Downey, J. I., & Friedman, R. C. (1998), Female homosexuality: Classical psychoanalytic theory reconsidered. *J. Amer. Psychoanal. Assn.*, 46:471–506.

Eckert, E. D., Bouchard, T. J., Bohlen, J., & Heston, L. (1986), Homosexuality in monozygotic twins reared apart. *Brit. J. Psychiatry*, 148:421–435.

Ellis, H. (1938), *Psychology of Sex*. New York: Emerson.

Erickson, M. T. (1993), Rethinking Oedipus: An evolutionary perspective of incest avoidance. *Amer. J. Psychiatry*, 150:411–416.

Friedman, R. C. (1988), *Male Homosexuality: A Contemporary Psychoanalytic Perspective*. New Haven, CT: Yale University Press.

——— Downey, J. I. (1993), Neurobiology and sexual orientation: Current relationships. *J. Neuropsychiatr. Clin. Neurosci.*, 5:131–153.

——— ——— (1994), Homosexuality. *New Eng. J. Med.*, 331:923–930.

——— ——— (1995), Biology and the Oedipus complex. *Psychoanal. Quart.*, 64:234–264.

Galenson, E. (1993), Sexuality in infancy and preschool-aged children. In: *Sexual and Gender Identity Disorders: Child and Adolescent Psychiatric Clinics of North America,* ed. A. Yates. Philadelphia: Saunders, pp. 385–391.

Gay, P. (1988), *Freud: A Life for Our Time.* New York/London: W. W. Norton.

Geschwind, N., & Galaburda, A. J. (1985), Cerebral lateralization: Biological mechanisms, associations and pathology. I. A hypothesis and a program for research. *Arch. Neurol.,* 42:428–459.

Gooren, L., Fliers, E., & Courtney, K. (1990), Biological determinants of sexual orientation. *Ann. Rev. Sex Res.,* 1:175–196.

Gorski, R. A. (1991), Sexual differentiation of the endocrine brain and its control. In: *Brain Endocrinology,* 2nd ed., ed. M. Motta. New York: Raven Press, pp. 71–104.

Green, R. (1985), Gender identity in childhood and later sexual orientation: Follow-up of 78 males. *Amer. J. Psychiatry,* 142:339–341.

——— (1987), *The "Sissy Boy Syndrome" and the Development of Homosexuality.* New Haven, CT: Yale University Press.

Haldeman, D. C. (1991), Conversion therapy for gay men and lesbians: A scientific examination. In *Homosexuality: Research Implications for Public Policy,* ed. J. C. Gonsiorek & J. D. Weinrich. Newbury Park, CA: Sage, pp. 149–161.

Hirschfeld, M. (1914), Die Homosexualitaet des Mannes und des Weibes (Homosexuality in men and women). In: *Handbuch der gesamtem Sexualwissenschaft in Einzeldarstellungen (Complete Manual of Sexual Knowledge),* Vol. 3. Berlin: Lorius Marcus.

Isay, R. (1989), *Being Homosexual.* New York: Farrar, Straus & Giroux.

Kernberg, O. F. (1995), *Love Relations, Normality and Pathology.* New Haven, CT: Yale University Press.

Kohlberg, L. (1976), Moral stages and moralization: The cognitive–developmental. In: *Moral Development and Behavior; Theory, Research and Social Issues,* ed. T. Lickona. New York: Holt, Rinehart & Winston, pp. 31–53.

——— (1981), *The Philosophy of Moral Development: Moral States and the Idea of Justice. Essays on Moral Development.* New York: Harper & Row.

MacLean, P. D. (1965), New findings relevant to the evolution of psychosexual functions of the brain. In: *Sex Research: New Developments,* ed. J. Money. New York: Holt, Rinehart & Winston, pp. 197–218.

Magee, M., & Miller, J. C. (1996), Psychoanalytic view of female homosexuality. In: *Textbook of Homosexuality and Mental Health,* ed. R.

P. Cabaj & T. S. Stein. Washington, DC: American Psychiatric Press, pp. 191–207.

Masters, W. H., & Johnson, J. E. (1996), *Human Sexual Response.* Boston, MA: Little, Brown.

McClintock, M., & Herdt, G. (1996), Rethinking puberty: The development of sexual attraction. *Curr. Direct. Psycholog. Sci.,* 5:167–183.

Meyer-Bahlberg, H. F. L. (1993), Psychobiologic research on homosexuality. *Child Adolesc. Psychiatr. Clin. N. Amer.,* 2:489–500.

Millon, T. (1981), *Disorders of Personality.* New York: John Wiley.

Money, J. (1987), Human sexology and psychoneuroendocrinology. In: *Psychobiology of Reproductive Behavior: An Evolutionary Perspective,* ed. D. Crews. Englewood Cliffs, NJ: Prentice-Hall, pp. 323–344.

——— Ehrhardt, A. A. (1972), *Man and Woman: Boy and Girl.* Baltimore, MD: Johns Hopkins University Press.

Pillard, R. C., Poumadere, J., & Caretta, R. A. (1982), A family study of sexual orientation. *Arch. Sex. Behav.,* 11:511–520.

——— Weinrich, J. D. (1986), Evidence of familial nature of male homosexuality. *Arch. Gen. Psychiat.,* 43:808–812.

Rice, G., Anderson, C., Risch, N., & Ebers, G. (1995), Male homosexuality: Absence of linkage to micro satellite markers on the X-chromosome in a Canadian study. Presented at Annual Meeting of International Academy of Sex Research, Provincetown, MA.

Slimp, J. C., Hart, B., & Goy, R. W. (1978), Heterosexual, autosexual and social behavior of adult male Rhesus monkeys with medial preoptic-anterior hypothalamic lesions. *Brain Res.,* 142:105–122.

Socarides, C. (1968), *The Overt Homosexual.* New York: Grune & Stratton.

Stoller, R. J. (1968), *Sex and Gender. On the Development of Masculinity and Femininity.* New York: Science House.

——— (1975), *Perversions.* New York: Pantheon Books.

——— (1979), *Sexual Excitement.* Washington, DC: American Psychiatric Press.

——— (1985), *Observing the Erotic Imagination.* New Haven, CT: Yale University Press.

Whitam, F. L., Diamond, M., & Martin, J. (1993), Homosexual orientation in twins: A report on 61 pairs and three triplet sets. *Arch. Sex. Behav.,* 22:187–206.

——— Zent, M. (1984), A cross-cultural assessment of early cross-gender behavior and familial factors in male homosexuality. *Arch. Sex. Behav.,* 13:427–439.

Wiedeman, G. H. (1962), Survey of psychoanalytic literature on overt male homosexuality. *J. Amer. Psychoanal. Assn.,* 10:386–409.

——— (1974), Homosexuality: A survey. *J. Amer. Psychoanal. Assn.,* 22:651–696.

Wilson, E. O. (1975), *Sociobiology: The New Synthesis.* Cambridge, MA: Harvard University Press.

Wright, R. (1994), *The Moral Animal.* New York: Vintage Books, pp. 315–316.

Yates, A., Ed. (1993), *Sexual and Gender Identity Disorders: Child and Adolescent Psychiatric Clinics of North America.* Philadelphia: Saunders.

8

On Homosexual Dread and Homosexual Desire

CHARLES W. SOCARIDES, M.D.

In this paper, I suggest a provisional psychoanalytic explanation for the clinical/affective state of *homosexual dread,* especially as it relates to nonpsychotic individuals. Such dread is a response to conscious homosexual thoughts and fantasies, which in homosexual individuals ordinarily lead to homosexual enactments with a sense of gratification, but not in those who experience homosexual dread. In contrasting homosexual dread with homosexual desire, I emphasize several theoretical constructs regarding both homosexuality as a developmental disorder, and describe homosexual dread as a symptom formation arising from structural conflict—a compromise formation to conflicts over homosexuality. I attempt to explain, in effect, why two individuals with the same fantasy system respond with completely different affective states to unconscious homosexual wishes shedding further light on the problem of the ego-acceptance of perverse impulses, a major factor in the formation of all sexual perversions. Clinical examination of homosexual dread patients leads to additional clarification of the true homosexual condition.

Homosexual Dread

During a lengthy psychoanalytic career of treating homosexual men, I have often been confronted with a singular and remarkable phenomenon, namely, homosexual fantasies and desires in *nonhomosexual* men, with a neurotic personality organization, fantasies and desires that arouse anxiety centered on the conviction that they are "homosexual." I have found that these neurotic patients, in whom this chief complaint dominates the clinical picture, are generally misunderstood by even experienced clinicians and, as a result, their treatment is both frustrating and ineffective; stalemated, it ultimately becomes simply supportive in nature. The importance of anxieties associated with this situation had been touched upon by Freud throughout his career, and special attention was given to it in one of his last essays as having relevance to man's healthy sexual functioning and happiness. In "Analysis Terminable and Interminable," Freud (1937) said:

> In males, the striving to be masculine is completely ego-syntonic from the first; the passive attitude, since it presupposes an acceptance of castration, is *energetically repressed,* and often its presence is only indicated by excessive over-compensations [pp. 250–251; emphasis added].

He also noted earlier:

> A man's heterosexuality will not put up with any homosexuality, and *vice versa.* If the former is the stronger it succeeds in keeping the latter latent and forcing it away from satisfaction in reality. On the other hand, there is no greater danger for a man's heterosexual function than its being disturbed by his latent homosexuality [p. 244].

Homosexual dread is insistent and obsessive in quality, intruding upon the individual's consciousness without apparent reason. It enters with force and conviction, is not subject to reasoned argument, and, similar to a hypochondriacal preoccupation, catapults frenzied and despairing patients into repeated consultations in order to prove or disprove what is perceived by them to be a malady of possible fatal proportions. Dreading the diagnosis of "homosexual," they enter therapy with the hope that this condition can somehow disappear. In this connection, it should be noted that there are exacerbations and remissions of this symptom either as a result of therapy or sometimes spontaneously without treatment. Careful psychoanalytic examination, including a developmental history, reveal that these individuals have been able to function heterosexually, and have usually done so throughout their lives although they may have suffered from periods of relative sexual impotence. Their history does not conform to the typical history of homosexuality of the obligatory type. Almost all of them have never engaged in homosexual acts during their entire lives; or if they have done so it has been on isolated occasions, often at puberty or shortly thereafter, with little pleasure and even deep abhorrence and self-disgust.[1] Rare homosexual acts in adulthood are acts of "riddance," overcoming the dreaded fear by undergoing the dreaded event. As with most children, they give a history of some childhood same-sex experimentation on rare occasions. Their concern and anxiety are of such proportions that many of them consider suicide as the only possible solution to what they perceive as a grave crisis.[2]

In these patients, the homosexual fantasies occur suddenly and episodically, usually becoming manifest in middle or late adolescence, while distracted, taking a walk, or reading a book. Patients complain that they come "as if out of the blue" and produce severe anxiety. They are often compelled by their dread to look within themselves for "true homosexual feelings" by peering at

[1]In contrast, Eidelberg (1954) remarked on the clinical picture produced by the ego's total acceptance of perverse impulses. In comparison to character neurotics, perverts "are aware of being peculiar, queer, or better than normal . . . although not normal. . . . Many consider themselves better than normal and claim that their life is more 'gay,' their climax more intense, their intellect superior, and their moral standards higher than that of the common man" (pp. 249–250).

[2]It is my growing belief that such cases, when not brought to the attention of the analyst, may well make up a large majority of suicides of college populations reported in the press as individuals who are suffering from gender-identity problems *(New York Times,* February 22, 1987). According to the "Report of the Secretary's Task Force on Youth Suicide" (Feinleib, 1989), "In a study of gay and bisexual male adolescents, 30% attempted suicide at least once. Gay male adolescents were two to three times more likely than their peers to attempt suicide. . . . Of all adolescent suicides or attempted suicides, concern about homosexual orientation is a major cause."

other men's genitals, continually examining themselves in an obsessive manner, as to whether they are attracted to men, and reacting to the gaze of others with a dread feeling that they might indeed be considered "homosexual" or that there is something "terribly wrong" with them. Often they test themselves with fantasies of having sexual relations with other men to see if indeed they are truly homosexual, responding to any genital response in themselves with fresh attacks of dread and near panic. They begin to fear that others may be looking at them as if they are indeed "queer" and their statements on this point nearly assume the proportions of paranoid ideation.

Homosexual fantasies and urges immediately erode their self-confidence, their ability to work, and their affection with girl friends and other friends. At first they assert that they never had any attraction toward men, nor any homosexual desire before the onset of these ideas. Some consider themselves "zero on a Kinsey scale," and believe that they grew up "just like any other kid," began masturbating and fantasizing about women at puberty, their attraction to women being "full and complete with a great urgency." As adolescence progressed, they somehow had difficulties in approaching young women, feeling isolated from their peers, and occasionally jealous of other men who had success with women. On some occasions, they got angry at members of their own sex who "took away women from them."

Obligatory homosexuals,[3] in contrast, also initially perceive homosexual desire as something unusual or different from other boys' interests in the opposite sex, but this desire ultimately becomes a powerful wish to be near to, close by. They yearn for genital manipulation or other bodily contact with same-sex partners. Homosexual desires in these patients often do not become fixed until or after puberty when they begin to assume their final homosexual form (Freud, 1905). Many homosexual individuals date their awareness of "being homosexual" to a very specific "organizing experience" (Socarides, 1988), usually before puberty, in which they had contact with another boy, often someone

[3]Those in whom the sexual pattern is stereotyped, unconsciously motivated, and who cannot function sexually with opposite-sex partners or, if forced to do so, function with little or no pleasure, and are mistakenly labeled "bisexuals.'

a few years older—an experience which provided emotional comfort, excitement, erection, and ejaculation. "Organizing experiences" are those early sexual activities (often of a traumatic nature) recovered in analysis, which played a crucial role in later design of the perversion. They not only provided genital excitement but, by virtue of the accompanying affective release, supplied an initial sense of self-cohesion, a means of relating to the internal world and external objects. As such experiences help to create the "end-product" (Freud, 1919), they may be considered to play an essential role in the "choice" of the perversion (Socarides, 1991). While such homosexual individuals may experience conflict, it is usually an external one, in which there is a fear of disapproval by peers, by one's family, or by society. While some homosexuals struggle against this knowledge and believe, at first, that they may have been "cursed," they continue to remain consciously aware of their desire and yearning, ultimately engaging in sexual practices which lead to pleasure, relief of tension, and the alleviation of depression and other symptomatology. It should also be noted that homosexual men may also develop associated neurotic symptoms due to the failure of the perverse activity to completely neutralize their earliest childhood anxieties and conflicts.

In both kinds of patients, those with homosexual dread and those with homosexual desire, the presenting sexual fantasies and preoccupations are essentially the same, thereby lending confusion to the diagnosis: sucking a man's penis, kissing a man, being close to a man, thoughts of anal penetration, and sexual excitement in the presence of individuals of the same sex. The striking difference is that in the former such fantasies are responded to with fright and dread amounting to panic proportions, while in the latter with urgent pleasurable anticipation. Both seek psychoanalytic help; the former to remedy what they perceive to be a devastating and troubling incursion into their essentially normal heterosexual life, and the latter to determine if something might possibly be done to remove a sexual perversion which puts them into a position of societal disadvantage, extraterritorial to the male–female design and the biological realities surrounding them. This is not to say that the true homosexual does not have anxieties, but his anxieties are of a different sort. Some homosexuals are prompted to enter therapy because of disturbing symptoms of anxiety and elaborations of this anxiety into episodes of depersonalization, regressive desires to isolate themselves from others; fears of self-dissolution, splitting phenomena, sudden awareness of a breakthrough of a feeling of femininity; episodes of sadistic–masochistic behavior in their sexual encounters; tendencies to severe mood swings or depression, bursts of rage-anxiety. Some begin to perceive that the homosexual act itself serves to save them from a mysterious fragmentation, and that a magical restoration occurs whenever they engage in homosexual relations. In others the homosexual needs have become increasingly insistent, imperative, and intrude into their everyday functioning, thus producing anxiety as well as interfering with every aspect of their lives. In addition, some homosexuals come to be aware that they are not simply responding to an instinctual need but are dominated by a tension which they can neither understand nor control.

Review of the Literature

The condition of homosexual dread[4] deserves more than the cursory psychoanalytic explanation it has received over the years. It has been mistakenly referred to, when severe, as "homosexual panic," with which it may be easily confused. Homosexual panic is not homosexual dread for it occurs in *homosexual* individuals who are experiencing, as Blum (1981) put it, "passive surrender to the love object with its implications of threat of primary identification with a loss of identity because of merger with the love object [the mother]" (p. 274).

I have described this condition in previous writings (Socarides, 1978, 1988), without labeling it as "panic," as being caused by a threat of reengulfment by the mother. It is a psychosomatic fusion, if you will, secondary to regression, for the nuclear conflict

[4]This term, coined by the author (1995), follows an earlier description by Greenson (1964). The word *dread* is used to connote something not simply fearful, horrible, or terrifying; a situation which may well evoke anxiety concerning a doubtful event from which one hopes to escape. It carries with it the additional meaning of a thought-event for which one feels completely unprepared (e.g., death).

of obligatory homosexual patients consists of the desire for and fear of merging with the preoedipal mother in order to reinstate the primitive mother–child unity (Socarides, 1968, p. 492). Similarly, Kernberg (1975) notes that: "homosexual self-love may lead to homosexual panic which may represent fear of fusion with a loss of boundaries" (Kernberg, 1975), without differentiating between homosexual dread and homosexual panic. Others (Frosch, 1967; Meissner, 1978; Blum, 1981) have also noted that a dread of being homosexual appears frequently in borderline patients and represents a stage in the development of paranoid symptomatology.

When mild, dread has been erroneously considered to be an "epiphenomenon"—anxiety due to a failure of heterosexual functioning precipitated by sexual, social, or professional failure, or the threat of such failure with its misinterpretation of "masculine failure"; hence the anxiety has been termed "pseudohomosexual anxiety" (Ovesey, 1976).[5] But, I contend, pseudohomosexuality is not homosexual dread, either. It is a conscious concern and deliberation over masculine functioning with its attendant preoccupations and anxieties, often of a relatively mild nature, quite easily removed by explanation and reassurance. It results simply from, as Ovesey (1976) put it, a masculine failure which has been symbolically misinterpreted as homosexuality.

Such individuals do not suffer from true homosexuality, nor do they display the symptoms of homosexual dread, with its accompanying threatened fragmentation of the ego, and regressive disturbances. In contrast to these mild manifestations of concern over homosexual ideas, homosexual dread may reach such proportions as to suggest the existence of an incipient oncoming psychosis with disturbances in ego boundaries and threatened loss of reality testing. In those of paranoid disposition, there is

[5]"Pseudohomosexuality" is not to be confused with anxiety secondary to the emergence of homosexual content in the dreams of neurotics or phobics during the course of psychoanalytic treatment which has been erroneously considered to constitute the "homosexual component of the neurosis"—an interpretation favored during the early years of psychoanalysis and arising from the false notion of "inherited (constitutional) bisexuality." I agree with Rado (1956), that "the fear voiced by many patients that their genetic constitution includes a 'homosexual component' has no foundation in fact" (p. 210).

an overt panic based on a hidden (unconscious) dread of anal rape. In schizophrenics the threat of anal rape may grow into fixed sexual delusions of persecution and ideas of reference.

Gillespie (1964) has commented that the heterosexual activity of these (dread) patients could be regarded as "pseudoheterosexuality," arising from superego and ego ideal demands on a preoedipally determined homosexual.

> The psychosexual development of such cases is basically that of the perverse overt homosexual; they achieve heterosexual activity with the help of fetishistic mechanisms; that is the female is treated as a fetish representing the phallus with which her whole body is equated, and an ego-split arises during intercourse. Paternal superego demands for masculinity are satisfied in this way [p. 207].

While I do not believe that my homosexual dread patients engage in fetishistic heterosexuality, I am impressed with Gillespie's statement that: "some forms of heterosexual behavior are, in a sense, spurious, and represent defensive activities on the part of an arrested homosexual; whereas, some homosexual activities are equally spurious and are defenses of an essential heterosexual" (p. 207).

I am in complete agreement with his statement that homosexual activities seem to be "natural" to some individuals because of a preoedipal fixation, while in others, homosexual activity is defensive, a regressive defense against an oedipal problem.

Greenson (1964) has observed that for most psychiatric patients in our society appearance of homosexuality in their treatment stirs up a "peculiar kind of dread" (p. 191). His explanation was that for such patients awareness of homosexuality threatens their gender identity. This is true of neurotics, paranoid patients, and even some types of homosexuals, each of whom handle the problem differently. Greenson also noted that the ones who do not seem to have any anxiety about their gender identity are the bisexuals and the typical overt homosexual. "In neurotics," he said, " 'I am a homosexual' is perceived as an oppressive, earth-shaking revelation and leads to a sense of impending panic" (p. 192). It amounts to a feeling of losing a component of the self, a connection one had taken for granted. Something central to the sense of self, the individual's gender identity is implied. Greenson concluded that the sexual object determines the gender of these individuals, while in the case of the overt homosexual:

> [N]either the gender of the usual object nor the enactment of fantasies of being of a different sex influences his gender identity. He knows he is a man even though he may play different roles. It seems, for him, his anatomy is the determining factor. The same is true for bisexuals [while the neurotic adult seems to need some awareness of] sexual attachment to a person of the opposite sex in order to maintain his gender identity [pp. 194–195].

Chasseguet-Smirgel (1986) also has noted and commented on the absence of dread of perverse activities in the true pervert: "This fear is absent from those whose sexual identity *has never been established,* i.e., perverts. It is at its height in those 'non-perverts' in whom the sexual identity is more fragile" (p. 91; emphasis added).

In my opinion, the explanation for the lack of dread in true homosexual patients lies partially in the fact that they have already resolved the question of gender identity by making an unconscious identification with the female (mother) and are finding their forfeited masculine identity through identification and the incorporation of the partner's body and penis in the homosexual enactments (Anna Freud, 1951, 1954; Socarides, 1968, 1978). The object relationship, therefore, is a narcissistic one, from object to self (the homosexual object representing the self). Homosexuals therefore suffer no feeling of loss or dread of loss of self in homosexual enactments, but, on the contrary, are engaging in a creative reification of the self.

On the other hand, the symptom complex of homosexual dread involves emergence into consciousness of a repressed homosexual ideation secondary to the regression of the ego to earlier phases of development. This occurs in patients who once experienced severe negative affective (depressive) states in their earliest years (Socarides, 1985), secondary to severe parental deprivation, trauma, and threats to sexual identity. How are we to explain the sudden emergence of unacceptable formerly repressed homosexual ideation in these patients? The defense mechanism of negation plays a crucial role in the presenting symptomatology of homosexual dread patients.

As Freud (1925b) said in connection with the problem of fetishism, "the content of a repressed image or idea can make its way into consciousness on condition that it is negated . . . with the help of negation only one consequence of the process of repression is undone" (p. 235).

Passage through the oedipal phase, the demands of adult heterosexual functioning, and other vicissitudes lead to a progressive deterioration of compensatory defensive measures—hyperheterosexuality, narcissistic overestimations, reaction formations—and a failure of the repressive mechanism. Conflict, previously handled by repression, is now dealt with by negation, an essential feature of this condition. Sexual thoughts and fantasies of an oral, anal, and narcissistic content belonging to the early childhood years, which functioned to assuage feelings of abandonment and despair, have broken through the repressive barrier and emerged into consciousness.

Latent Homosexuality

Dread patients may be easily confused with those who are latent homosexuals. Latent homosexuality means the presence of the underlying psychic structure of either the preoedipal or oedipal type of homosexual (Socarides, 1978), who does not have overt orgastic activity with a person of the same sex. The shift from latent to overt homosexuality, and the reverse, depends on several factors: (1) the strength of the fixation at the preoedipal level (quantitative factor), the severity of anxiety, and the intensity of regression from the later oedipal conflict; (2) the acceptability of the homosexuality by the ego, the superego (conscience mechanism), and the ego ideal; and (3) the strength of the instinctual drives, libido, and aggression. Such individuals may never, or rarely, engage in overt homosexual activity. The latent homosexual may or may not have any conscious knowledge of his preference for individuals of the same sex for orgastic fulfillment. On the other hand, there may be a high level of elaboration of unconscious homosexual fantasies and homosexual dream material, with or without conscious denial of its significance (Socarides, 1980). The individual who is a latent homosexual may go through his entire life without realizing his homosexual propensities, managing to function marginally on a heterosexual level, sometimes marrying and having children. Another pattern is that of the individual who, fully aware of his homosexual preference, abstains from all homosexual acts. Others, as a result of severe stress, infrequently and transiently do engage in overt homosexual acts, living a major portion of their lives, however, as latent homosexuals. In the latent phase, they may maintain a limited heterosexual functioning, albeit unrewarding, meager, and usually based on homosexual fantasies. They may utilize homosexual fantasies for masturbatory practices or may abstain from sexual activity altogether, although conscious of their homosexual need and desire.

"Ego-dystonic" Homosexuality

The ego's dread of homosexual thoughts and fantasies should not be misunderstood as constituting an "ego dystonic" form of homosexuality, a term unfortunately introduced out of sociopolitical debate within the American Psychiatric Association in 1973. It was introduced to connote those individuals who are consciously distressed over being homosexual. This term is psychoanalytically inaccurate as all patients with obligatory homosexuality, as well as all those with obligatory perversions, are suffering from an ego syntonic condition whether it is consciously acceptable in the social sense or not.

The term *ego syntonic* has long been used in psychoanalysis to denote behavior which is compatible with the integrity of the self.

As I have noted earlier (Socarides, 1978):

> when one speaks of the ego-syntonicity of homosexuality or any other perverse act, . . . we are dealing with two components: conscious acceptance and unconscious acceptance. The degree of conscious acceptance of a perverse act varies with a person's reactions to societal pressure and consciously desired goals and aspirations. The conscious part of ego-syntonicity can be more readily modified than its unconscious component. Analysis of homosexual patients reveals that

> ego-syntonic formations accepted by the patients are already the end result of unconscious defense mechanisms in which the ego plays a decisive part. In contrast, where superego or id play the decisive role, the end result is often an ego-alien symptom. The splitting of the superego promotes ego-syntonicity. The superego is especially tolerant of this form of sexuality as it may represent the unconscious acceptable aspect of sexuality derived from the parental superego. The split in the ego and the split in the object lead to an idealized object, relatively free of anxiety and guilt. The splitting of the ego leads also to an ego relatively free of anxiety, which is available for the purposes of an incestuous relationship at the cost of the renunciation of a normal one [pp. 168–169].

Obsessional Neurosis

While homosexual dread thoughts have the quality and intensity of obsessive ideas, tormenting the individual, they are not part of an obsessional neurosis. Obsessional ideas are first of all derivative. As Fenichel (1945) said,

> Sometimes they have preserved their character as impulses; sometimes they have lost it, and consist only of intense ideas that have to be thought about; their persistence represents the energy of some other associatedly connected impulsive idea that has been warded off [p. 268]. . . .
>
> The defensive forces did not succeed in making the patient unaware of what is going on within them; they did succeed, however, in transforming the original drive into a compulsive form; the nature of this transformation is a problem of the mechanism of symptom formation and compulsion neurosis [p. 269].

Fenichel also provides a relevant example:

> A patient who suffered from the fear that he might be give the impression of being a homosexual had the following obsessive thought whenever he became acquainted with a man whom he had not met before. "With this man I could have homosexual intercourse." He did not feel any sexual excitement or impulse, and was entirely unaware of the fact that the obsessive idea expressed a wish. Other

> obsessions and compulsions do not seem to express a distorted instinctual urge but are . . . an assurance of the defending forces. Compulsion can be described as a command from within [p. 269]. [The ego] is compelled to do or to think, or to omit certain things; otherwise it feels menaced by terrible threats [p. 268].

Homosexual dread patients are not "menaced by terrible threats" if they do not carry out their homosexual fantasies. The carrying out of such fantasies would have even more dire consequences than the dread itself. Furthermore, in an obsessive neurosis, the obsessive thought is always a disguise and substitute for something else. For example, in compulsive neurosis the impulse to murder women is a distorted expression of incestuous desire. The first half represents a gratification of the Oedipus wish, the second half the punishment the patient dreaded. In summary, obsessive ideas bear a certain similarity to the ideation expressed by homosexual dread patients, but the structure of the two conditions is quite dissimilar.

Gender Identity and the Function of Perversion

Perverse fantasies leading to the affective state of homosexual dread are a breakdown product, with consequent anxiety secondary to the lifting of repression and regression to earlier phases of development. They signify that a serious threat to sexual identity, already formed but precariously held, has occurred. In contrast, in all my homosexual patients, there is a failure to form a gender-defined self-identity in accordance with anatomy leading to a conscious–unconscious sense of femininity or deficient sense of masculinity. This may be more apparent in some individuals than in others, but emerges as a central finding in my psychoanalyzed cases of homosexuality despite structures and personality traits which attempt to compensate for this inadequacy. Even a masculine-appearing homosexual, for example, reveals deep feminine unconscious identification during analysis. Although the foundation for gender-defined self-identity is laid by the age of 3 or 4, gender-defined self-identity is not a fixed entity but is subject to minor fluctuations, even into adulthood and later life (Stoller,

1964, 1967, 1968; Galenson and Roiphe, 1973, 1979; Mahler, Pine, and Bergman, 1975; Edgecumbe and Burgner, 1975; Socarides, 1978).

There are two levels which must be attained for the sense of identity, the first being the awareness of being a separate and individual entity, and the second the beginning of a gender-defined self-identity. Galenson and Roiphe (1973), in their psychoanalytic observational studies of infants and young children over a 10-year period, have illuminated the factors in the preoedipal phase that lead to the awareness of sexual identity. It is my observation from the study of homosexual dread patients that they have achieved an appropriate gender-defined self-identity but it is a vacillating structure, a precarious accomplishment, and they have passed through the oedipal phase and are able to make a heterosexual adjustment.

True homosexual perverts, on the other hand, have not been so fortunate. They have been unable to master intrapsychic separation and as a result suffer from a continuation of a primary feminine identification with the mother (Lampl-de Groot, 1946; Jacobson, 1950; Greenacre, 1953; Kestenberg, 1956; Van der Leeuw, 1958; Socarides, 1960) normally resolved through a successful traversing of the separation–individuation phase (Mahler, Pine and Bergman, 1975) by the age of 3. Edgecumbe and Burgner (1975), at the Hampstead Child Therapy Clinic, have noted: "development of self and body representations, and of identifications, make a crucial contribution to the establishment of differentiated sexual identity. . . . The process of acquiring a differentiated sexual identity rests largely on the child's capacity to identify with the parent of the same sex" (pp. 163–165).

They verify that the acquiring of a sense of gender-defined self-identity begins during the child's second year, continues through the anal phase, and reaches it peak during the phallic phase. Although in agreement with Mahler's concept, they differ with respect to timing, Mahler holding that the sense of sexual identity is formed somewhat later, beginning in the earliest period of the phallic phase.

The homosexual pervert enacts his perversion for ego survival. There is a reconstitution of a sense of sexual identity in accordance with anatomy through achieving masculinity through incorporation of the penis and identification with the male sexual partner. This further lessens castration fear. In preoedipal type-I homosexual perverts, the major defense mechanisms are introjection, projection, and identification. The pathological use of splitting is due to a fixation to, or defect in, the developmental process, interfering with the sense of identity and the development of object constancy (Socarides, 1988).

The homosexual patient, laboring with these difficulties in self-object differentiation, and in order to promote an emerging autonomous self, uses perverse sexual desires and fantasies which arise from his extreme and persistent narcissistic needs. His enactments represent an attempt to find a tranquil integrity of being and are therefore highly desired and sought after. The crises of diffusion of the self receives soothing experience. They are a substitute for action in the external world, helping to fill a void in the patient's life. They resolve an intense crisis and, through incorporation and identification with the partner's body and penis, achieve masculine identification and a sense of wholeness.

The homosexual's erotic experience can be understood as providing two functions: (1) a warding-off function forestalling the dangers of castration, fragmentation, separation anxieties, and other threats; (2) a compensatory function consisting of intrapsychic activities which help maintain and decrease threats to the self-representation, and object representations. They are an artificial means of self-esteem regulation and enhancement. In homosexual desire a fear of the engulfing mother is resolved by finding a man to incorporate, idealize, and identify with, lending calm and a soothing experience to the patient.

Through acting out, the overt homosexual stabilizes his sense of self through his perverse enactments, reinforces his pathological object relations, overcomes destructive aggression and feelings of vulnerability, and brings pleasure to an internalized self-object (Kohut, 1971; Kernberg, 1975; Socarides, 1988). The homosexual act represents an overcoming of a severe intrapsychic crisis (in contrast to the case of the homosexual dread patient) by displacing and projecting the inner need and tension onto another person or object, by concocting what Khan (1965) has termed "active ego-directed experimental play action and object-relations" (p. 28), in which the "technique of intimacy" plays a major role. Affective release into the external world diminishes internal threats provoked by destructive aggression. Pathological internalized object relations which lead to despair and hopelessness are mitigated. The perversion, in contrast to those with homosexual dread, is experienced as a creative and reparative act and is thoroughly acceptable to the ego. Similarly, the absence of healthy self-esteem in relation to internal parental figures is lessened through creating a pseudo-object relationship and mutual pleasure. It furthermore establishes a "rudimentary mode of communication with the external object" (Khan, 1979, p. 408). The homosexual, despite his attachment to the preoedipal mother, however, does not experience meaningful communications with either parent, and no internalization of the object takes place. There is no true ego enhancement, and the perversion must be incessantly repeated. Such acting out in true obligatory homosexuals is facilitated by: (1) deficiencies in the ego, due in part to the lack of neutralized energy which has impaired the ability to control immediate responses and instinctual discharge of aggression; (2) lack of internalization of superego function and a splitting of the superego, so that the perversion is sanctioned by the split-off part representing parental attitudes. In a primitive manner acting out helps maintain the cohesiveness of the ego and supplies it with the opportunity to initiate reparative needs toward a real object.

The Role of the Superego

As noted by Freud (1940), superego splitting is essential for the performance of the perversion. True homosexuality, in my opinion, cannot be understood without reference to the superego.

Gillespie (1956) further commented:

> The choice by the ego of a particular piece of infantile sexuality is dictated to an important extent by the ego's judgement of what would please, or at least pass relatively unchallenged by parental imagoes, eventually internalized for superego formations. The attempt to please the superego is especially obvious in masochism but it operates in other perversions also. This formulation must be understood to refer to pregenital archaic superego formations as well as to postoedipal ones concerned with the supposed parental attitude to genital sexuality [p. 399].

The perversion therefore avoids the anxiety and guilt that would otherwise arise. The superego of the preoedipal homosexual is primitive, characterized by splitting, processes that may involve not only the ego and the object, but the superego as well.

While homosexual dread patients suffer from severe guilt feelings, a sense of unworthiness, wishes for self-punishment, and extreme degrees of self-loathing because of their homosexual fantasies, the opposite is true in those with homosexual desire. In true perverts there is an absence of superego injunctions as regards the enactment of the perversion itself, while guilt feelings may be unacceptable as regards the expression of aggression. The conflict of developmentally arrested patients is largely an external one (Socarides, 1978). This is explainable in part by the fact that there has been insufficient structuralization of the psychic apparatus in these developmentally arrested patients. Homosexual perverts with severe neurotic or borderline personality organization show a marked absence of internal conflict, for their behavior is not regulated by a superego identified with the moral power of the parents (moral self-regulation) since these patients can be seen not to have developed beyond the first stage of superego formation (Sandler, 1960).[6] A more mature superego development leads to the profound reaction to perverse impulses in homosexual dread patients.

As Dorpat (1976) has pointed out, "[perverts] evoke and employ object representations to comfort, punish, control, or guide their activities in a manner similar to (but less reliable than) superego formation" (p. 871).

The dilemma of homosexual perverse patients is temporarily resolved by the use of external objects (self-objects), including sexual self-objects, whose function is to substitute for missing structures in the functions they perform. The narcissistic (self-object) transferences (mirroring and merging) encountered in psychoanalytic therapy of perverse individuals are manifestations of this underlying developmental defect. Furthermore, the absence-presence of a defective superego (an automatic self-regulatory mechanism of conscience) creates serious therapeutic

[6]Reinforcing this view is a contribution by the Kris Study Group of the New York Psychoanalytic Institute in a report entitled "Superego Analysis" (Hoffman, 1993) in which it is noted that "the superego as we know it has little effect on the question of the 'right or wrong' of early perverse impulses" (p. 47; Hoffman, preliminary communication).

obstacles, for these patients may remain unaffected as regards alleviation-removal of their perverse practices, at least temporarily, through the transference relationship. In contrast, those with homosexual dread are easily influenced by a transference mirroring relationship with the analyst, even during the early phases of treatment.

The symptom of homosexual dread may occur in individuals at all levels of personality organization, from neurotic, to narcissistic, to borderline, and especially in those with psychosis.[7] I shall concentrate exclusively on a class of patients with essentially neurotic or narcissistic personality organization and tendencies to regression, but in whom repression predominates over splitting, and projection is not a significant defense mechanism, except on rare occasions. I shall cite the case of James in some detail, as he clearly demonstrates a classical picture of homosexual dread and the cataclysmic effect this affect has on the total functioning of the individual.

The Case of James: Homosexual Dread in a Patient with Neurotic Personality Organization

My first contact with James, a successful Midwestern businessman, occurred in 1984, when, as a man of 39, he wrote me, "Approximately one year ago, I realized I had within myself deviant feelings which surfaced as a result of my divorce. My reaction to these feelings was a total breakdown, and since that time I have made progress in regaining some stability. I have been basically told that I would have to live with my condition—that I am a homosexual."

The patient wrote of his complaint with a sense of urgency as well as a sense of fatalism. He furthermore complained of what appeared to be a conversion symptom: his legs tingled continuously, from his ankles through to his groin. "The intensity varies,

[7]Space limitations preclude discussion of such cases. Freud's (1911) celebrated case of Schreber may well be reinterpreted as illustrating homosexual dread in a man with a psychotic personality organization rather than a psychotic reaction in a homosexual man, i.e., one who had previously repressed his true homosexuality. Lothane's (1992) excellent study "In Defense of Schreber: Soul Murder and Psychiatry" is also confirmatory of this view. It is his belief that Schreber's central problem was a psychotic depressive reaction.

as do the areas of these feelings. I perceive this to be a physical expression of my fears and anxiety, and simply do not know how to rid myself of them."

From his earliest years James, a highly intelligent and articulate man, had to endure both physical and psychological traumas in the form of severe illnesses and operations as well as feelings of anxiety and depression secondary to his mother's incapacity to care for him. His father was absent from home for the first three years of the patient's life because of military service. James developed severe ear infections at 7 months of age, pneumonia at 11 months, for which he was hospitalized for three weeks, whooping cough at 5 years, with hospitalization for two months, tonsillectomy at age 6, and appendectomy at age 7. His mother was incapacitated when he was 2 because of a hysterectomy, and she frequently lay in bed depressed, unable to care for the boy's needs, during which time he was routinely given over to a nanny, until the age of 7. He remembers himself as an unhappy, depressed, anxious, crying child, unable to mix with others and never feeling confident with his peers. Shy and introverted, he sucked his thumb until the age of 10, was often sick and occasionally vomited. Bored and unhappy in nursery school and kindergarten, he would on occasion burst into bouts of aggressive behavior with temper tantrums.

Upon his father's return, James was instantly antagonistic to him, frequently exclaiming "You are not my daddy." He began to witness severe arguments with the mother due to the father's alcoholism and his inability to perform his medical practice adequately. Because of a feeling of deep disappointment in his father, he experienced great hatred for him and swore that he would "never go to his funeral." The only person he loved and was attached to was his nanny, whose death when he was 14 left him despondent for nearly six months. Indeed, during his childhood apparently both parents were feared and often hated. He remembers a repetitive dream of childhood: "I'm on a steel superstructure of a building in a bed being pushed along by mother, who suddenly pushed me over the side into an abyss. She had a black hat on and this was a nightmare and I remember falling."

At puberty he discovered that he had considerable athletic ability, ultimately becoming a star football player, a sport in which he continued to excel and engage in up to his college years. Feeling that he was "boring and unattractive" and unacceptable to girls, he engaged in a program to improve his physique by lifting weights from age 14 to 19.

His sexual history reveals that he never had any actual homosexual experiences, although at age 11 he briefly participated in a mutual genital examination with a boy of approximately his own age. A dream from that time, however, has homosexual content: "a guy is in the bed and he says 'why don't you stick your finger up my ass?' And I said 'no.' He sticks his own finger up his ass with a look of pleasure and shame combined." His adolescence, however, was replete with incestuous feelings for his mother as well as for his nanny, and he dreamt about "playing with her genitals." By 14, he had conscious desires for sexual intercourse with his mother and the mother of a neighborhood friend, and he masturbated to these fantasies. In midadolescence, he also saw the mother's vagina for the first time while she was sitting on a couch, and was frightened and excited by its appearance, so it became a focus of a chronic masturbatory fantasy of sexual intercourse. Although his mother, he states, was a "cold person," she often sat with her legs apart allowing him to look into her vagina which produced an erection. While there was an abundance of fantasies of sexual intercourse with not only his mother and nanny but with many women, young and old, he had no girl friend until age 19 and never engaged in sexual intercourse with a woman before age 21—his sole gratification being masturbation. While away from home for the first time in college, he suffered his first attack of homosexual dread while quietly reading a *Newsweek* magazine featuring stories on the "Gay Movement." Overwhelmed with the sudden thought that he was a "homosexual" he broke into severe anxiety. This attack left him frightened, confused, and desperate, unable to play football, quitting the team in despair, and ultimately by the second year failing in his studies. By his junior year, his "mental torment" gradually receded and he was able to finish school.

During his senior year in college, he had his first satisfactory heterosexual experience and upon graduation married a college classmate. Moving back to his home town, he began a prosperous business. He was 22 years old at the time. He immediately began to engage in extramarital sexual relations with several women for two to three years. His favorite practice was that of mutual genital exhibitionism with one of his secretaries, simultaneously viewing her and himself, masturbating himself, and then on occasion masturbating her. During this period of successful business ventures he felt "powerful," "like hot shit," self-important and self-confident, until his business life "got out of hand" and he became a "slave to it." During these first five years he began to lose sexual interest in his wife and felt guilty for "abandoning her" within himself.

Other extramarital affairs continued during the next few years of marriage which served to reassure him that he was a well-functioning heterosexual man and wipe away the memory of past homosexual feelings as well as forestall new ones. Milder feelings of anxiety occurred, however, in response to dreams or fantasies of autofellatio. Such fantasies during late adolescence and young adulthood represent a threatened return of his horrifying conviction "I am a homosexual," and he could not easily escape them. For example, while viewing a movie with his wife, a man came on the screen and he thought, "God, this is a lovely guy." His next thought was, "Maybe you're a queer," to be followed by, "What do queers do, they suck penises and you like to suck your own penis in your dreams." Memories and fantasies breaking into consciousness made him feel as if he were "falling apart," and his legs would become numb up to his thighs. On other occasions he had dreams of wearing a skirt and his once powerful legs, which had been his source of pride in athletic competition, had become "feminine."

The second major attack of homosexual dread at age 38 for which he came to treatment occurred while driving in his new car, lonely and depressed, several weeks after his divorce. Suddenly he experienced severe anxiety and the panic-producing thought, "You're queer, it's over." This was accompanied by a strong feeling that "I'm attracted to men . . . I feel like killing myself." Unable to work, he "tested" himself by frequenting bars, tormented with the idea that he must want somehow to perform fellatio with a man, all the while assuring himself that if any man approached he would viciously fight him off. For several weeks he dreamt of sucking penises including his own. Within a month anxiety gave way to depression; he lost fifty pounds, developed stomach pains, and sobbed in despair. Significantly, a few months before his divorce he had admitted his father to a rehabilitation hospital and helped him discontinue his medical practice until he could recover. Both his divorce and the incapacity of his father left him feeling increasingly helpless and abandoned. Unable to work, he lived in a hotel where his companions were alcohol and a gun brought back from Germany by his father. On occasion he sought the company of an older woman who provided solace and comfort, allowing him to sleep on her chest and be cuddled. At other times, his agony was so great that he contemplated suicide, placing his father's pistol in his mouth, ready to pull the trigger. In total resignation, he tried to accept the advice of several local psychiatrists, namely, that he simply "accept his homosexuality" and "live with it."

He came to see me on a twice-a-week basis for lengthy sessions, traveling a long distance for a two-and-a-half year period during which his fear of being a homosexual gradually receded as the structure and developmental history of homosexuality, in contrast to his neurotic fear of homosexuality, was explored. A strong positive (father) transference provided him with ego support and, reassured, he gradually reestablished himself in business. During this period of central importance he was "falling in love" with a "beautiful woman" who provided him with the fullest sexual and emotional experiences he had ever known as well as reestablished his identity as "heterosexual." While much was made clear during this first period of therapy, including an understanding of his narcissistic pathology, the central dynamics and understanding of this patient's homosexual dread, its origins, meaning and content, was never uncovered. The dread of being a homosexual, however, gradually disappeared and he discontinued therapy, being quite content with himself and once again functioning even more effectively in his work.

Ten years passed before I saw this patient again. A third serious attack had occurred one year after his second marriage. Depressed and regressed, he felt that the precipitating stress for this attack was the sudden resignation of one of his associates, which left him feeling betrayed and inferior. This was compounded by a verbal attack by a woman on his staff with whom he had had sexual relations many years earlier and for whom he felt considerable affection. These events led to a severe depletion of his self-esteem, made him sob uncontrollably with feelings of overwhelming guilt, shame, and the sense that he had been abandoned by both men and women upon whom he depended for his self-confidence. Both occurred, however, in the context of his finding his wife "repulsive" to him sexually. The total symptom picture was essentially the same as the first period of analysis, namely homosexual dread without homosexual enactments, disturbances in sensation in his legs, and an even more severe degree of inconsolability and gloom together with fantasies of sucking his own penis and performing fellatio on other men. Anxiety and depression were extreme and he felt unconsciously guilty for destroying his relationship with his wife. He correctly ascertained that his symptomatology represented both his sense of failure as a man and a wish to become a woman himself, a frequently discussed topic in his first analysis.

Clearly, the first treatment had only symptomatically relieved this man of his illness, and it was the abrupt and traumatic fragmentation of his former relationships with both men and women, including his wife, together with the eruption of severe aggression toward men over their desertion and betrayal of him, which led to guilt, an inability to perform his work, regressive experiences and a need for punishment. He increasingly feared the demands of his wife and was constantly concerned with his inability to function sexually with her. He recalled that during the marriage ceremony itself, the fear that other men were more masculine and more confident led to a short-lived episode of intense pathological jealousy of a former employer who was present at the wedding. This represented a deep sense of his own inadequacy in the masculine role and a projection of "I do not love him, she loves him," together with an abdication of the masculine position which was then perceived in the unconscious as a loss of sexual identity: "If I'm not a man I must be a woman. Therefore I must want men." These ideas led to the conviction "I must be a homosexual."

Discussion

James's symptom of homosexual dread is not explainable by early psychoanalytic formulations derived from Freud's (1905) analysis of the psychodynamics of perversion and the role of castration anxiety. For neither does castration anxiety nor the resultant avoidance and fear of women as sexual objects constitute the dread of which he complained. Neither was anxiety of the vagina dentata or revulsion toward the female genitalia responsible for his prevailing terror. It was the fear of a narcissistic sought-after love object's denial of him, as well as his fear and hatred of the mother, together with his failure to attain such an object in a love relationship which catapulted him into such terror. The loss of supporting structures (intense heterosexual activities and fantasies) led to a sense of loss and attempts at self-restitution through the activation of early "internalized soothing structures."[8]

Such early internalized structures are the autoerotic activities of early childhood—sucking one's own penis, wishing to suck other men's penises, sucking at the breasts of many women, multiple heterosexual relations. Beneath this gratification was an unresolved hostility toward the opposite sex, which appeared in the patient's dreams and in actual life. While James was a model of kindness, caring, and generosity to both parents, he had a deep ambivalence and hatred toward both mother and father because of feelings of abandonment. Homosexual dread was a result of a desperate search by the ego not only for the lost mother, but also for one's projected masculinity.

Such patients as James may be seen to have a distinctly recognizable defense organization in which they engage not only in heterosexual but also in fantasy-homosexual sexual activities, all the while fearing both types of sexual activity. There is a combination of isolation, denial, and disavowal with respect to their drives.

In other words, James had homosexual thoughts from early childhood—polymorphous perverse thoughts—which then resurfaced to replace his more acceptable and pleasurable fantasies of

[8]Hershey (1985) has clearly delineated how traumas in the early mother–child interaction play a role, predisposing such a person to the formation of internalized soothing structure, which the ego suddenly activates and externalizes in later life situations.

heterosexual activity. Homosexual fantasies had earlier on been compartmentalized, their implication denied, only to return at a later stage in his life with the failure of repression and its replacement by a less functional and less effective defense mechanism, that of negation.

In my patient, the first experiences of early childhood were unspecified painful ones caused by severe early parental deprivation with separation anxiety, threats of annihilation, traumatic experiences,[9] severe guilt feelings, depressive affective states, and a complete sense of worthlessness. The dangers experienced were dangers from within, with unspecified feelings of hunger, oral needs, and guilt feelings, which were then transformed and transmuted into dread homosexual wishes. James was suffering from a hunger for lost objects at the same time that he was experiencing homosexual dread feelings with severe loss of self-esteem. Early childhood disappointments and total lack of narcissistic supplies left him unconsciously apathetic, depressed, and drained of energy, leading to attempts to satisfy his hunger by regression to a state of hallucinatory wish-fulfillment (fantasies of autofellatio and the wish to suck other men's penises). His passive oral needs were an attempt to force a necessary supply by objectionable means (i.e., homosexual ones). Many of these needs were at first satisfied in adult life by heterosexual means, but ultimately those of a homosexual nature appeared in consciousness with much shame and guilt. They were an attempt to ward off more severe feelings of deprivation through the incorporation of the paternal phallus in order to internalize and make up for the loss of masculine identity and strength, a desire which in true homosexual individuals leads to pleasure and temporary fulfillment. In dread patients, in contrast, homosexual fantasies are experienced as a threat of the loss of self representation and sexual identity, together with the further loss of narcissistic supplies, and loss of the heterosexual love object. James fled from his wives and experienced guilt over the destruction of a relationship which was meaningful to him. Anxiety over his limbs represented the threat of

[9]Greenacre (1968) has described how traumas such as operations, severe bleeding, and prolonged severe illnesses occurring between the ages of 2 and 4 play an important role in perverse impulse formation as well as lead to great uncertainty about their [individual's] bodies and especially their genital equipment" (p. 309).

the loss of body ego boundaries as well as his turning into a woman. The trauma that he experienced (the feeling of abandonment and deprivation and the sense of impending annihilation) was revived and abreacted during the analytic sessions. The melancholic feeling of annihilation produced a paralyzing depression and endless weeping over the loss of both parents, as well as anxieties over "being a homosexual," and fantasies of becoming a woman himself.

The disturbance in competent male functioning and the fear of his marriage partner led to passive feminine longings for the father, a wish to incorporate the father's phallus, constituting a defensive mechanism employed by the ego.

Throughout his early life, James utilized sensory experiences to reify and give tangible substance in order to ward off the threat of a failing sense of self (e.g., sucking his thumb till a last age, and oral fantasies of various kinds) as well as to overcome feelings of despair and abandonment. These helped maintain the cohesion and stability of a self menaced with abandonment and regressive disintegration. Earlier perverse homosexual fantasies made him feel secure but disavowed, and then returned from his unconscious. They were unacceptable to his conscious ego and resulted in the symptom of homosexual dread. In an earlier period of life, they were utilized as a defense against the emergence of deeper fears of personal annihilation, abandonment, profound grief and depressive reactions with a severe loss of self-esteem. The regressive revival of polymorphous perverse and homosexual fantasies occurred secondarily to turning away from the female in his adult life with a resurgence of hatred of the paternal figures and the threat of abandonment they represented. They occurred especially when he felt threatened, engulfed, cornered, or captured by women.

The case of James is remarkably similar to that reported by Rosenfeld (1949) in his excellent study of paranoia, paranoid anxiety, and narcissism and their relation to male homosexuality. Rosenfeld's patient, similar to my own, never engaged in homosexual activity, had long periods in which he was completely heterosexual, but found it extremely difficult to tolerate demands and frustrations imposed on him by marriage and by having another child, becoming increasingly aware that he was unable to love a woman. Such attempts led to repugnance, hate, depression, and a turning away from women in hopelessness and despair, after which homosexual dread symptoms emerged. In his depression, anxiety, and sense of worthlessness, he felt he had destroyed the breast of the mother and the paternal phallus. His inability to restore his mother and relationship to his father also led to feelings of self-loathing and guilt, and the feeling that he was not a man and could not use his penis in a satisfactory manner with women.

As in Rosenfeld's case, my patient developed a positive transference to me, the analyst, as a virile and encouraging father. This helped him to restore his interest in women, his sexual potency, and removed his fear that he was becoming a woman. In this connection, Rosenfeld reported that his patient's homosexual search was related to an idealization of a fantasied good father—a figure once lost, whom the patient sought but never found. The homosexual fantasies began to disappear when the structure of the relationship with the mother was fully understood, and when anxiety, guilt, and depression over the loss of the mother (once again renewed in the failure of his attraction to a woman), and his loss of self had been repaired. This was accompanied by an understanding of his attempt to incorporate the father's phallus in homosexual wish/dread activities in order to ward off further regression to an undifferentiated phase. In accomplishing these goals, the patient's whole personality was again restored, including his body ego boundaries, and the threatened loss of self was averted. In both cases, Rosenfeld's and my own, the threat of passive, submissive, socially despised, and superego-unacceptable submission to sadistic, masochistic, degrading humiliation at the hands of other men in homosexual acts resulted in dread.

Homosexual dread, therefore, is not a defensive reaction against the enactment of unconscious true repressed homosexuality (the perversion), for the ordinary developmental sequence in the development of homosexuality as a perversion has never taken place. It is a defense against further regression of the ego to an undifferentiated state and loss of ego boundaries with regressive revival of early oral and anal incorporative fantasies, including homosexual ones. In securing the phallus of the father in homosexual fantasies, the patient unconsciously attempts to incorporate the paternal phallus and thereby consolidate a masculine identity in order to make up for early childhood deprivations, depletion sensations, depression, abandonment, and despair. The wish to incorporate the father's penis collides with superego injunctions and makes for a sense of degradation or humiliation, and is damaging to the patient at all levels.

The dread patients I have seen used early infantile autoerotic sexual experiences together with precocious sexual heterosexual fantasies as psychic organizers which contributed to the structuralization of a sense of self and the warding off of feelings of depression, annihilation, and abandonment. They tended to concretize the self in its appropriate gender-identity through earlier techniques of self-affirmation by sexual means. In regression, caused by a failure of sexual functioning in their adult life, they engaged in reinstituting primitive methods of affirmation of the reality of their own existence and their gender identity. Dreaded homosexual activities became the means by which these individuals attempted to consolidate the sense of gender identity, albeit with great anxiety.

Summary

I have presented a provisional psychoanalytic explanation for the clinical–affective state of homosexual dread—the presence in consciousness of homosexual thoughts and fantasies in nonhomosexual men. I described the meaning, content, and possible origin of this clinical state, separating it from homosexual panic, ego dystonic homosexuality, latent homosexuality, pseudohomosexuality, as well as obligatory preoedipal homosexuality, conditions with which it may be confused. I suggested a provisional etiology, symptomatology, and course of this condition by utilizing a clinical case history typical of such patients. The defense mechanism of negation is central to the clinical picture. In contrasting homosexual dread with homosexual desire, I emphasized several theoretical constructs regarding both obligatory homosexuality as a developmental disorder, and I also described homosexual dread as a symptom formation arising from structural conflict. I attempted to explain why two individuals with the same fantasy system (those with homosexual dread and those with homosexual desire) respond with completely different affective states to unconscious homosexual wishes, and in so doing shed further light on the problem of ego acceptance of perverse impulses, a major factor in the formation of all obligatory sexual perversions. I touched upon and elaborated factors important for ego acceptance or ego nonacceptance of perverse impulses such as superego function, need–tension gratification, achievement or nonachievement of true object relations, the functions of erotic experience in perversion, defenses prominent in both conditions, as well as the achievement or nonachievement of appropriate gender-defined self-identity.

References

Blum, H. (1981), Object inconstancy and paranoid conspiracy. *J. Amer. Psychoanal. Assn.,* 29:789–813.

Chasseguet-Smirgel, J. (1986), The archaic matrix of the Oedipus complex. In: *Sexuality and Mind: The Role of the Father and the Mother in the Psyche.* New York/London: New York University Press, pp. 74–91.

Dorpat, T. L. (1976), Structural conflict and object relations conflict. *J. Amer. Psychoanal. Assn.,* 24:855–875.

Edgecumbe, R., & Burgner, M. (1975), The phallic–narcissistic phase: The differentiation between preoedipal and oedipal aspects of development. *The Psychoanalytic Study of the Child,* 30:61–180. New Haven, CT: Yale University Press.

Eidelberg, L. (1954), *A Comparative Pathology of the Neuroses.* New York: International Universities Press.

Feinleib, M. R. (1989), Report of the Secretary's Task Force on Youth Suicide. In: *Prevention and Interventions in Youth Suicide,* Vol. 3, ed. M. R. Feinleib. Washington, DC: U.S. Department of Health and Human Services, Public Health Service, pp. 89–1623.

Fenichel, O. (1945), *The Psychoanalytic Theory of Neurosis.* New York: W. W. Norton.

Freud, A. (1951). Homosexuality. *Bull. Amer. Psychoanal. Assn.,* 7:117–118.

——— (1954), Problems of technique in adult analysis. In: *The Writings,* Vol. 14. New York: International Universities Press, 1968.

Freud, S. (1905), Three Essays on the Theory of Sexuality. *Standard Edition,* 7:123–243. London: Hogarth Press, 1953.

——— (1911), Psycho-analytic notes on an autobiographical account of a case of paranoia (dementia paranoides). *Standard Edition,* 12:1–79. London: Hogarth Press, 1958.

——— (1915), The unconscious. *Standard Edition,* 14:159–215. London: Hogarth Press, 1957.

——— (1919), "A child is being beaten," A contribution to the study of the origin of sexual perversions. *Standard Edition,* 17:175–204. London: Hogarth Press, 1955.

——— (1925a), Negation. *Standard Edition,* 19:233–239. London: Hogarth Press, 1961.

——— (1925b), Some psychical consequences of the anatomical distinction between the sexes. *Standard Edition,* 19:241–258. London: Hogarth Press, 1961.

——— (1937), Analysis terminable and interminable. *Standard Edition,* 23:209–253. London: Hogarth Press, 1964.

——— (1940), An Outline of Psycho-Analysis. *Standard Edition,* 23:139–207. London: Hogarth Press, 1964.

Frosh, J. (1967), Delusional fixity, sense of conviction and psychotic conflict. *Internat. J. Psycho-Anal.,* 48:475–495.

Galenson, E., & Roiphe, H. (1973), Object loss and early sexual development. *Psychoanal. Quart.,* 22:73–90.

——— (1979), The development of sexual identity: Discoveries and implications. In: *On Sexuality: Psychoanalytic Observations,* ed. T. B. Karasu & C. W. Socarides. New York: International Universities Press, pp. 1–17.

Gillespie, W. H. (1964), Symposium on homosexuality, parts 2–3. *Internat. J. Psycho-Anal.,* 45:203–209.

——— (1956), The general theory of sexual perversion. *Internat. J. Psycho-Anal.,* 37:396–403.

Greenacre, P. (1953), Certain relationships between fetishism and the faulty development of the body image. In: *Emotional Growth: Psychoanalytic Studies of the Gifted and a Great Variety of Other Individuals,* Vol. 1. New York: International Universities Press, 1971, pp. 9–31.

——— (1968), Perversions: General considerations regarding their genetic and dynamic background. In: *Emotional Growth: Psychoanalytic Studies of the Gifted and a Great Variety of Other Individuals,* Vol. 1. New York: International Universities Press, 1971, pp. 300–314.

Greenson, R. R. (1964), On homosexuality and gender identity. In: *Explorations in Psychoanalysis.* New York: International Universities Press, 1978, pp. 191–197.

Hershey, D. (1985), On a type of heterosexuality, and the fluidity of object relations. *J. Amer. Psychoanal. Assn.*, 37:147–171.

Hoffman, L. (1993), Superego analysis: Preliminary communication. Paper presented to the Ernst Kris Study Group, New York Psychoanalytic Institute.

Jacobson, E. (1950), Development of the wish for a child in boys. *The Psychoanalytic Study of the Child,* 5:139–152. New York: International Universities Press.

Kernberg, O. (1975), *Borderline Conditions and Pathological Narcissism.* New York: Jason Aronson.

Kestenberg, J. S. (1956), On the development of maternal feelings in early childhood. *The Psychoanalytic Study of the Child,* 11:257–291. New York: International Universities Press.

Khan, M. M. R. (1965), Intimacy, complicity and mutuality in perversions. In: *Alienation in Perversions.* New York: International Universities Press, 1979, pp. 18–30.

——— (1979), *Alienation in Perversions.* New York: International Universities Press.

Kohut, H. (1971), *The Analysis of the Self: A Systematic Approach to the Psychoanalytic Treatment of Narcissistic Personality Disorders.* New York: International Universities Press.

Lampl-de Groot, J. (1946), The preoedipal phase in the development of the male child. *The Psychoanalytic Study of the Child,* 2:75–112. New York: International Universities Press.

Lothane, Z. (1992), *In Defense of Schreber: Soul Murder and Psychiatry.* Hillsdale, NJ: Analytic Press.

Mahler, M. S. (1965), On the significance of the normal separation-individuation phase: With reference to research in symbiotic child psychosis. In: *Drives, Affects, Behavior,* Vol. 2, ed. M. Schur. New York: International Universities Press, pp. 161–169.

——— Pine, F., & Bergman, A. (1975), *The Psychological Birth of the Human Infant.* New York: Basic Books.

Meissner, W. (1978), *The Paranoid Process.* New York: Jason Aronson.

——— (1990), Paranoid process and homosexuality. In: *The Homosexualities: Reality, Fantasy and the Arts,* ed. C. W. Socarides & V. D. Volkan. Madison, CT: International Universities Press, pp. 79–100.

Ovesey, L. (1969), *Homosexuality and Pseudohomosexuality.* New York: Science House.

Rado, S. (1949), An adaptational view of sexual behavior. In: *The Psychoanalysis of Behavior: Collected Papers of Sandor Rado,* Vol. 1, rev. ed. New York: Grune & Stratton, 1956, pp. 186–213.

Rosenfeld, H. (1949), Remarks on the relation of male homosexuality to paranoia, paranoid anxiety and narcissism. *Internat. J. Psycho-Anal.*, 30:36–47.

Sandler, J. (1960), On the concept of the superego. *The Psychoanalytic Study of the Child,* 15:128–162. New York: International Universities Press.

Socarides, C. W. (1960), The development of a fetishistic perversion: The contribution of preoedipal phase conflict. *J. Amer. Psychoanal. Assn.*, 8:281–311.

——— (1968), *The Overt Homosexual.* New York: Grune & Stratton, 1987.

——— (1978), *Homosexuality.* New York: Jason Aronson.

——— (1980), Perverse symptoms and the manifest dream of perversion. In: *Preoedipal Origin and the Psychoanalytic Theory of Sexual Perversions.* New York: International Universities Press, 1988.

——— (1985), Depression in perversion: With special reference to the function of erotic experience in sexual perversion. In: *Depressive States and Their Treatment,* ed. V. D. Volkan. Hillsdale, NJ: Analytic Press, pp. 317–334.

——— (1988), *The Preoedipal Origin and Psychoanalytic Theory of Sexual Perversions.* Madison, CT: International Universities Press.

——— (1991), Form and function in sexual perversion: A contribution to the problem of "choice" of perversion. In: *Beyond the Symbiotic Orbit: Advances in Separation-Individuation—Essays in Honor of Selma Kramer,* ed. S. Akhtar & H. Parens. Hillsdale, NJ: Analytic Press.

——— (1995), *Homosexuality: A Freedom Too Far.* Phoenix, AZ: Margrave Books.

Stoller, R. J. (1964), A contribution to the study of gender identity. *Internat. J. Psycho-Anal.*, 45:220–226.

——— (1967), Gender identity and a biological force. *Psychoanal. Forum,* 2:318–338.

——— (1968), *Sex and Gender.* New York: Science House.

van der Leeuw, P. J. (1958), The preoedipal phase of the male. *The Psychoanalytic Study of the Child,* 13:352–374. New York: International Universities Press.

9

The Oedipus Complex and the "Third Position"

JUDY GAMMELGAARD, Dr. Phil.

A Shift in Emphasis to a Preoedipal Stage of Development

In many ways the Oedipus complex was central to Freud's theoretical speculations. Around this idea, he gathered the threads from the theories on psychic structures, personality development, infantile sexuality, the unconscious, and repression. Infantile sexuality culminates in the Oedipus complex, its dissolution being a precondition for a mature nonincestuous love life. It is also a precondition for a self-responsible, autonomous individual.

It is not strange that Freud made the Oedipus complex the nucleus of psychoanalysis—its "shibboleth," as he called it with a biblical turn of phrase. Clinical observations and theoretical reflections on the significance of the preoedipal period in more recent years, however, have pushed the center of gravity from the "nuclear complex" toward its infantile preconditions. This has led to a considerable extension of insight into the early mother–child relationship, the individuation–separation problem in self development, and, not least, it has expanded our knowledge of the girl's psychosexual development.

With the Kleinian school, the emphasis on the nature of the Oedipus complex has shifted to a much earlier phase, focusing on the depressive position and the development of the child's ability to relate to a whole object. It is my contention that such a shift, despite its merits, has to some extent toned down, hiding somehow from sight what in Freud's thinking was closely linked to the Oedipus complex and its dissolution. Infantile sexuality culminates in the Oedipus complex's triangular field, repeating itself with the emergence of puberty so that the psychosexual development traverses the two-phased course Freud defined with the term *nachträglich* or deferred action.

Freud's Oedipus Complex

In the discussion of the classical Oedipus complex that follows, I have chosen to focus on two psychological conditions: the oedipal triangulation of emotional relations and the two-phased course of sexuality, meaning the return of the repressed. To begin with, regarding the mythological and literary sources of Freud's term "Oedipus Complex," I do not share the view, formulated by some scholars and psychoanalysts, that Freud's theory and Sophocles' two tragedies *Oedipus Rex* and *Oedipus at Colonus,* have in common only the name of the tragic hero. On the contrary there exist many readings of the classical texts which may serve as inspiration for psychoanalytic reflection. I will try to take advantage of this inventiveness to show how Freud's classical Oedipus complex and its place in personality development match Sophocles' dramatic recreation of the Oedipus myth in both tragedies.

The psychological basis for Freud's Oedipus theory is convincingly expressed in his essay, "A Short Account of Psycho-Analysis" (1924a).

> And now, as a third point, psychoanalysis has shown us, to our growing astonishment, the enormously important part played by what is known as the "Oedipus complex"—that is, the emotional relation

> of a child to its two parents—in the mental life of human beings. Our astonishment diminishes when we realize that the Oedipus complex is the psychical correlate of two fundamental biological facts: the long period of the human child's dependence, and the remarkable way in which its sexual life reaches a first climax in the third to fifth years of life, and then, after a period of inhibition, sets in again at puberty [p. 208].

The first of the two "biological facts" cited by Freud refers to an important hypothesis in his *Three Essays on Sexuality* (1905), namely that infantile sexuality emerges and develops along with the instincts of self-preservation. By necessity, satisfaction of these instincts occurs in relation to the nursing person. Freud reasoned that satisfying the instincts of self-preservation is bound to create sexual tensions around the implicated body zones as a by-product. These tensions are the core of the sexual partial instincts demanding their independent satisfaction from earliest childhood. It is natural for emerging sexual partial instincts and instincts of self-preservation to choose the same object. The early partial objects gradually gather into a psychic image of the mother, who then becomes the child's first whole sexual object. Thus they establish the basic emotional relation in the Oedipus complex, that is, the emotional relationship to the mother. At the same time, a fundamental difficulty standing in the way for the little boy's successful dissolution of the Oedipus complex is suggested. Behind the phallic love for the mother, who then, in a primitive genital sense, is the love object, stands the image of the preoedipal nursing and narcissistically confirming mother.

Though many analysts rightfully have pointed out the problems preventing the little girl's development concerning the object change (Brunswick, 1940; Chasseguet-Smirgel, 1975), there are only few references to the difficulty experienced by the boy in the process of his separation from the preoedipal mother while developing his phallic desire toward the oedipal mother. This difficulty explains the clinical observation that behind the adult male's sexual object choice lurks the image of a narcissistically confirming and at the same time omnipotent preoedipal mother.

A male patient of mine had an apparently active sexual life, but complained that his wife did not care to participate in what he himself described as his "perverse" fantasies. These fantasies clearly had a remarkable infantile character, reminding one of small children's earliest sexual curiosity and explorations. It was as if this man, behind an apparently genital facade, deployed a phallic form of sexuality where complete satisfaction was of a narcissistic character. Regression to such pregenital, phallic fantasies can remind one of what Janine Chasseguet-Smirgel (1975) has discussed in her studies about perversions as an idealization of pregenital sexuality in the boy. In my patient this regression was created by the loss of the mother, who took her own life when he was a 12-year-old, and an incomplete projection of the ego ideal onto the father, who appeared to be an extremely rigid and neurotic person.

Even with a successful dissolution of the Oedipus complex, one may suppose that behind a man's genital satisfaction there are phallic wishes of domination and control of the object linked with narcissistic fears and gratifications from the preoedipal phases of development. I shall return to this double mother image in my discussion of Oedipus' incestuous relation to Jocasta.

Phallic Sexuality and the Oedipus Complex

More than twenty years after introducing the concept of the Oedipus complex, Freud (1923) advanced the idea of the phallic phase or the infantile genital organization, when the genitals become dominating, with masturbation the most important source of pleasure. In so doing, he linked the phallic phase with the Oedipus complex in the boy's development.

This intimate linking of phallic sexuality with the Oedipus complex is, as far as I can see, quite decisive for the significance Freud attached to the other "biological fact" of his theory: the psychosexual development's two-phased course. The phallic sexuality is inscribed into the psyche in two places, or as Freud (1882–1904) put it in his correspondence with Fliess, a "re-arrangement," a "re-transcription" of the phallic sexuality is taking place with genital maturity in puberty.

In placing the Oedipus complex in transition from the paranoid–schizoid position to the depressive position, as done by the

Kleinian school, the phallic element of the Oedipus complex is, so far as I can see, toned down. It is difficult to understand how, out of a small child's partial instincts and partial objects, a mature human being with genital pleasure aimed at a whole object can develop at all.

The Oedipal Triangle

Clinical observation of the preoedipal phase over a number of years has, generally speaking, diminished the interest of the two phases in the psychosexual development, including the fate of the Oedipus complex and its dissolution over time.

Despite divergences on the question of placing the Oedipus complex in the psychosexual development, most analysts agree in using Freud's triangle as a model for the child's emotional relations to his parents. With its three persons and three relations, the oedipal triangle is almost geometric. That is how Freud described it, when he first formally discussed the Oedipus myth in *The Interpretation of Dreams* (1900):

> In my experience, which is already extensive, the chief part in the mental lives of all children who later become psycho-neurotics is played by their parents. Being in love with the one parent and hating the other are among the essential constituents of the stock of psychical impulses which is formed at that time and which is of such importance in determining the symptoms of the later neurosis. It is not my belief, however, that psycho-neurotics differ sharply in this respect from other human beings who remain normal—that they are able, that is, to create something absolutely new and peculiar to themselves. It is far more probable—and this is confirmed by occasional observations on normal children—that they are only distinguished by exhibiting on a magnified scale feelings of love and hatred to their parents which occur less obviously and less intensely in the minds of most children.
>
> This discovery is confirmed by a legend that has come down to us from classical antiquity: a legend whose profound and universal power to move can only be understood if the hypothesis I have put forward in regard to the psychology of children has an equally universal validity. What I have in mind is the legend of King Oedipus and Sophocles' drama which bears his name [pp. 260–261].

The discussion of Oedipus in the same text is focused on the tragedy's *phobos* (fear) and *eleos* (pity). In Oedipus we recognize our own fate.

> But, more fortunate than he, we have meanwhile succeeded, in so far as we have not become psycho-neurotics, in detaching our sexual impulses from our mothers and in forgetting our jealousy of our fathers. Here is one in whom these primeval wishes of our childhood have been fulfilled, and we shrink back from him with the whole force of the repression by which those wishes have since that time been held down within us. While the poet, as he unravels the past, brings to light the guilt of Oedipus, he is at the same time compelling us to recognize our own inner minds, in which those same impulses, though suppressed, are still to be found. . . . Like Oedipus, we live in ignorance of these wishes, repugnant to morality, which have been forced upon us by Nature, and after their revelation we may all of us well seek to close our eyes to the scenes of our childhood [pp. 262–263].

Freud's remark about closing our eyes will be argued later in a discussion about tragic self-recognition, and we shall see the eye metaphor as a central trope in Sophocles' tragedy *Oedipus Rex*.

The oedipal triangle is presented in different versions. Since Karl Abraham (1927), theories of psychosexual development have included the hypothesis of a transition from partial to total object. According to Klein (1945), the Oedipus complex begins with a relation to the partial object before it develops into the well-known Oedipus complex as the child relates itself to his parents now perceived as two whole objects. However, the Oedipus complex includes also the fantasies of earliest childhood about the relation between breast and penis and the primal scene. To the child, the gradual acknowledgment of the parents' mutual sexual relationship means the necessary loss of privileged access to the mother. Ronald Britton (1989) has suggested that the reworking of the Oedipus complex and the depressive position are two sides of the same coin. With Winnicott's idea of the transitional object, Thomas Ogden (1992) defined the triangle as a triangulation between two persons: mother and child and the father image in mother, while later oedipal drama places the father as an external object.

The "Third Position" and Self-Consciousness

Ronald Britton (1995) has added an important observation to the oedipal triangle in pointing out the implications of the child being at once part of a relation and an observer of the relation between the parents. This double relation gives the child the opportunity to observe what Britton has called the "third position."

> The closure of the oedipal triangle by the recognition of the link joining the parents provides a limiting boundary for the internal world. It creates what I call a "triangular space," i.e., a space bounded by the three persons of the oedipal situation and all their potential relationships. It includes, therefore, the possibility of being a participant in a relationship and observed by a third person as well. . . . This provides us with a capacity for seeing ourselves in interaction with others and for entertaining our own point of view whilst retaining our own, for reflecting on ourselves whilst being ourselves [p. 1].

Therefore, the "third position" of the oedipal triangle is synonymous with the origin of self-consciousness. The penetration of self-consciousness is linked to the child's experience of the primal scene. Britton has illustrated this process through an acute observation of Jean-Paul Sartre's in his *Being and Nothingness* (1943):

> Let us imagine that moved by jealousy, curiosity, or vice I have just glued my ear to the door and looked through the keyhole. I am alone and on the level of a non-thetic self-consciousness. This means first of all, that . . . I am a pure consciousness of things. . . . Behind that door a spectacle is presented as "to be seen," a conversation as "to be heard."
>
> But all of a sudden I hear footsteps in the hall. Someone is looking at me! What does this mean?. . .
>
> First of all, I now exist as myself for my unreflective consciousness. It is this irruption of the self which has most often been described: I see myself because somebody sees me [cited in Britton, 1995, p. 1].

It seems reasonable to draw a parallel to Søren Kierkegaard's (1901–1904) description of the self as a relation which relates to itself. To be myself means a third position from where I see myself as a relation. The eruption of the self as a relation that is relating itself has implications for knowledge. As Britton (1996) again put it: "the awareness that the individual believes something and not simply that he knows something is dependent on the self-awareness which depends on the existence of the triangular space and therefore on the tolerance of the Oedipus situation" (p. 4).

The question of knowledge as opposed to belief is essential in Sophocles' tragedy. This is shown in the dialogue between Oedipus, who sees but does not know, and Apollo's priest, Teiresias, who knows but does not see.

In the understanding of Sartre and Kierkegaard as well as Britton, this third position is, however, not understandable within the geometrical triangle. It is, if anything, the third in the Hegelian sense. Which raises the question whether the geometrical triangle is not too static to be able to hold what Britton has called the "third position." I propose that we add yet another dimension—the dimension of time. This is necessary if we want to add the origin of self-realization to the libidinal and hostile emotions of the oedipal structure. Is not self-recognition a precondition for the development of an autonomous individual with the capacity of entering nonincestuous and competing relations or, in other words, with the dissolution of the Oedipus complex over time?

Sartre (cited in Britton [1995]) continues his reflection on the origin of the self as a destruction of the unreflecting self-consciousness. "The other looks at me and as such he holds the secret of my being, he knows what I am. Thus the profound meaning of my being is outside of me, imprisoned in an absence. . . . The other's look as the necessary condition of my objectivity is the destruction of all objectivity for me" (p. 1).

This could be the heading of Sophocles' two tragedies about Oedipus. The tragedy of Oedipus' fate is that he has not extricated himself from the oedipal triangle. Sophocles' dramatic genius consists in showing that only the destruction of the apparent objective identity with which King Oedipus understands himself and the recognition as deferred action *(nachträglich)* about who he is and what he has sinned against, enables him to take responsibility and find himself by acknowledging his parents.

As Paul Ricoeur (1974) has suggested, one can interpret the tragedy of *Oedipus Rex* in two different ways. One can go behind and understand Oedipus' fate in the light of the infantile complex. The play touches us, writes Freud, because therein we see our own deeply buried infantile desires and anxieties come true.

In his "Oedipus Without the Complex," Jean-Pierre Vernant (1972) has argued that there is no suggestion of Oedipus being prompted in his acts by unconscious incestuous or murderous motives in Sophocles' text. His infantile motives exist as a concealed precondition enveloped in the triangular no-man's land between Corinth, Delphi, and Thebes. In this land, Oedipus, temporarily nameless, as Charles Segal (1994) has put it, travels around, murders his father, and marries his mother. It is true that, on the Sophoclean text's immediate level, Oedipus does everything to avoid the fate Apollo prophesizes will be his. Still, as Segal points out, the unconscious appears in metaphoric and metonymic drifts of the language. In Oedipus' mention of Merope, Jocasta, Polybus, and Laïus, the linguistic processes unveil how the unconscious is displaced into the language. In verse 775 of *Oedipus Rex,* he tells Jocasta his story and makes it clear that Polybus is his father, Merope his mother. Nevertheless, soon anxiety penetrates the apparent natural and confident statement when Oedipus slowly understands that he might be the murderer—that behind Polybus is Laïus. In the messenger scene, Merope's name becomes an animated mother figure. We see this in Oedipus' anxious answer to Jocasta, "Agreed; but while *she* lives, I am not safe" (verse 988) and in the Corinthian messenger's apparently harmless and simple question: "But pray, sir, who is the woman whom you still fear?" (verse 989). As Segal (1994) points out again, this is a game of words on the contrast among the three female figures: the woman Oedipus believes to be his mother, the unknown mother—the object of his fear—and Jocasta. The people in the audience know the truth. They experience how these images disintegrate and how the dreaded incestuous relationship gradually is realized as Oedipus' relationship to Jocasta.

The Dialectic between Self-knowledge and Ignorance

Freud abandoned the traditional explanation of Sophocles' tragedy, seeing it as a disastrous game between divine power and the futile effort of an individual to escape his fate. Terence Cave (1988) has called Freud's interpretation imperialistic in the sense that the parricide and incest are proclaimed to be the effect of that universal recognition, which this classical masterpiece any time will cause in any audience. It is also imperialistic in the sense that Freud, in the principles of poetical composition, recognizes the fundamental principles of the psychoanalytical process. In this last statement, we will find the other psychoanalytical possibility of interpreting Sophocles. "The action of the play consists in nothing other than the process of revealing, with cunning delays and ever-mounting excitement—a process that can be likened to the work of a psychoanalysis—that Oedipus himself is the murderer of Laïus, but further that he is the son of the murdered man and of Jocasta" (Freud, 1900, pp. 261–262).

Only indirectly is Sophocles' tragedy about parricide and incest. It is not about the child Oedipus but about the adult King Oedipus. However, the incestuous and murderous acts mentioned earlier are preconditions for plot as the *pathos,* which sets the tragedy's action in motion.

Sophocles has chosen to let the myth of his tragedy take place solely in the process through which the adult Oedipus painfully understands himself, a process which, like a psychoanalytical course, takes place as deferred action *(nachträglich).* Oedipus' *hamartia* (error) does not mean that he, in inflamed anger or because of a hot temper, kills an old man, but because he does not know himself, he sees without understanding. The tragedy's central theme is the contradiction between seeing blindness and blind seeing, between the duplicity of knowledge and ignorance. Its *peripeteia* (reversal) and *anagnorisis* (recognition) consist in the total destruction of the apparently unambiguous and objective identity so characteristic of King Oedipus—the wise man who once solved the enigma of the Sphinx. The gradual destruction of intellectual *hubris* culminates in Oedipus' self-blinding. This symbolizes the tragic self-recognition which acknowledges that the dialectic between knowledge and ignorance is unstable and that sight can be blinded.

Sophocles' tragedy shows that Oedipus, to escape imprisonment from the triangular field of childhood, must accept the painful task of acknowledging himself. *Pathei mathos,* to experience through suffering, as Aeschylus has put it in his tragedy, *Agamemnon.* Self-recognition is not a result but a process of interminable character. It is presumably this process that Freud (1924b) hesitantly suggests in his study "The Dissolution of the Oedipus Complex," and primarily in his "Analysis Terminable and Interminable" (Freud, 1937).

Ever since Hegel (1920) the question of guilt has been a central theme in the interpretation of *Oedipus Rex* and *Oedipus at Colonus.* To interpret the two tragedies as the atonement and punishment Oedipus must endure because of his intellectual arrogance, or as an expression of an ultimate conflict, would be too superficial as a psychoanalytical interpretation, giving the superego too much credit. We consider it obvious that parricide involves guilt and the demand for atonement and punishment.

As Loewald (1979) has stated, parricide is psychologically necessary for the emancipation of an autonomous and responsible individual. Seen in this light, the repression of the Oedipus complex can be an unconscious strategy to avoid murder, a means to preserve the libidinal parental relations. Parricide, according to Loewald, is committed in a double movement where aspects of the oedipal relations are transformed into the superego and other aspects to new forms of object relations separated from incestuous and murderous reminiscences. By taking responsibility and engaging in nonincestuous relations we kill by necessity our parents. To harbor guilt instead of wanting punishment means, in this light, a form of atonement or reparation; which Hegel saw in the aging ex-king of *Oedipus at Colonus* and which the Kleinians describe as the mourning process of the depressive position. Incest is, as Loewald again has it, the other side of parricide, the insulting character of incest lying in the sexual substance it bestows to the preoedipal mother–child relationship.

The Resolution of the Oedipus Complex and Adult Sexuality

Apparently the boy is confronted with a developmental psychological task in separating himself from the double mother image as a precondition for developing a mature love and a genital desire. In the myth and tragedy, Oedipus has not wrenched free of the oedipal desire toward his mother. As Jean-Joseph Goux (1993) observes, the Oedipus myth is an anomaly when compared to the typical myth of the hero, who must obtain his royal power by finding his bride and committing matricide as symbolized by the figure of the dragon, the serpent, or the monster. A bloody murder must be executed in order for the hero to liberate the young woman who will be his bride. In the Oedipus myth the hero commits parricide, not matricide, and he finds his bride in his mother. In short, Oedipus does not perform the violent separation from the mother image, which is the precondition for finding a mature love object. And, as Peter Rudnytsky (1987) has observed, while the theory of the Oedipus complex mandates that the man will choose his love object in his mother's image, the hero, transforming simile into identity, marries the woman who is his mother. Oedipus, in other words, lacks "the saving difference brought about by time" (p. 274).

Oedipus' conquest of the archaic mother symbol does not take place in murder but in words. Implicitly in Sophocles and explicitly in Hegel, Oedipus is the prototypical philosopher, the constitution of individuality and intellectuality. Oedipus gains his victory over the Sphinx without help, without preliminary steps, in a single word.

Nietzsche (1871) has expressed this eloquently. Oedipus' victory over the Sphinx is a homage to the Apollonian, to the clear thought and to a form of knowledge which, however, is fragile, because it arouses the antagonistic Dionysian forces. In solving the enigma of the Sphinx, Oedipus commits intellectual *hubris*, challenges nature, to which the parricide and incest bear witness. The conclusion of these reflections is that, because Oedipus has not committed the compulsory symbolical matricide, he keeps himself within the oedipal triangle and at the end prepares the way for killing the real mother.

Sophocles' tragedy shows that for Oedipus to escape the triangular field, he must take on the tragic self-recognition described in the tragedy as a movement from seeing blindness to blind seeing. As the play opens, Oedipus announces the unknown killer's punishment in order to purify his city from the plague. By doing this he ignores the possibility that he himself might be the killer. John Steiner (1985) has discussed Oedipus and Jocasta's turning a blind eye to the facts pointing at Oedipus himself, while André Green (1969) has suggested the metaphor of "one eye too many." They both agreed that Sophocles' tragedy is about seeing without understanding, to close your eyes to the truth about yourself, as Freud put it. It is remarkable that an external event, a breakthrough from reality into the relationship between Jocasta and Oedipus, sets the self-recognition in motion. First, it is the plague; then, at the height of reversal, the Corinthian messenger. When the external reality breaks through the defense of blindness, it augurs the return of repression. Freud (1919) has suggested for this the term *uncanny (das Unheimlich),* which, in its duplicity of benign and sinister, fits well the case of Oedipus, who is not at home with himself. The appearance of the uncanny in relation to the gradually exposed self-recognition shows that the tragic is related to our recognizing *nachträglich.*

In Sophocles' recreation of the myth, the recognition continues as a gradual destruction of the individuality, as Nietzsche would say, of the *autarch* (despotic) consciousness which is convinced that nothing exits outside conscious and certain knowledge. When Oedipus commands that Laïus' murderer be found and punished, it is the King who is talking. Nevertheless, it is an ignorant person's talk. Opposite him stands Teiresias, the blind seer. Teiresias represents, as Ricoeur (1974) has suggested, compelling truth; Oedipus, on the other hand, only the *hubris* of truth. Teiresias also represents the breakthrough of reality, which in this context consists of the necessary submission to more clear-sighted consciousness. This, however, insults the narcissistic ego, which does not readily submit to alien consciousness. Oedipus' anger towards Teiresias is a witness to such an insult.

Oedipus' self-blinding is self-punishment, the necessary consequence of acts done in blindness. However, the self-blinding must also be seen in relation to Teiresias, who is blind but seeing, and

Oedipus who sees but is blind. Yet not just turning a blind eye. He is blind in his understanding. He will remain so not only until he has recognized his birth and the extent of his actions, but until he has taken responsibility for his anger, his self-punishment, and the parricide as preconditions for escaping the oedipal triangle. Such a process is of an interminable character—it proceeds over time. It is the two-phased course of sexual life and the fact that only as adults do we pass moral judgment on our incestuous and murderous infantile impulses, which makes self-recognition a process taking place *nacthträglich.* Only by stepping out of the triangle and connecting ourselves to a new reality, a clearer consciousness, can we dissolve the guilt linked to the infantile Oedipus complex. And thus, from *Oedipus Rex* we arrive at *Oedipus at Colonus,* the play Sophocles wrote some twenty years later at the end of his own long and creative life course.

References

Abraham, K. (1927), *Selected Papers,* trans. D. Bryan & A. Strachey. London: Hogarth Press.

Britton, R. (1989), The missing link—Parental sexuality in the Oedipus complex. In: *The Oedipus Complex Today,* ed. R. Britton, M. Feldman, & E. O'Shaughnessy. London: Karnac Books.

——— (1995), Second thoughts on the third position. Typescript.

——— (1996), Psychic development and psychic repression. Typescript.

Brunswick, R. Mack (1940), The preoedipal phase of the libido development. In: *The Psycho-Analytic Reader,* ed. R. Fliess. London: Hogarth Press, 1950, pp. 231–253.

Cave, T. (1988), *Recognitions. A Study in Poetics.* Oxford: Clarendon Press.

Chasseguet-Smirgel, J. (1975), *Das Ich-Ideal.* Frankfurt-am-Main, Germany: Suhrkamp Verlag.

Freud, S. (1887–1902), *The Origins of Psychoanalysis. Letters to Wilhelm Fliess, Drafts and Notes: 1887–1902,* ed. M. Bonaparte, A. Freud, & E. Kris. New York: Basic Books, 1954.

——— (1900), The Interpretation of Dreams. *Standard Edition,* 4 & 5. London: Hogarth Press, 1953.

——— (1905), Three Essays on the Theory of Sexuality. *Standard Edi-Tion,* 7:123–243. London: Hogarth Press, 1953.

——— (1919), The "uncanny." *Standard Edition,* 17:217–252. London: Hogarth Press, 1955.

——— (1923), The infantile genital organisation: An interpolation into the theory of sexuality. *Standard Edition,* 19:139–145. London: Hogarth Press, 1961.

——— (1924a), A Short Account of Psycho-Analysis. *Standard Edition,* 19. London: Hogarth Press, 1961.

——— (1924b), The dissolution of the Oedipus complex. *Standard Edition,* 19:171–179. London: Hogarth Press, 1961.

——— (1937), Analysis terminable and interminable. *Standard Edition,* 23:209–253. London: Hogarth Press, 1964.

Goux, J.-J. (1993), *Oedipus, Philosopher.* Stanford, CA: Stanford University Press.

Green, A. (1969), *The Tragic Effect. The Oedipus Complex in Tragedy.* Cambridge, U.K.: Cambridge University Press, 1979.

Hegel, G. W. F. (1920), Dramatic action and character. In: *On Tragedy,* ed. , trans. A. Paolucci & H. Paolucci. Westport, CT: Greenwood Press, 1962, pp. 97–163.

Kierkegaard, S. (1901–1906), Sickness unto death. In: *Complete Works,* Vol. 15. Copenhagen: Gyldendal, pp. 65–181.

Klein, M. (1945), The Oedipus complex in the light of early anxieties. In: *The Writings,* Vol. 1. London: Karnac/Institute of Psycho-Analysis, 1992.

Loewald, H. (1979), The waning of the Oedipus complex. In: *Papers on Psychoanalysis,* ed. H. Loewald. New Haven, CT: Yale University Press, 1980.

Nietzsche, F. W. (1871), *Die Geburt der Tragedie aus dem Geiste der Musik.* Frankfurt am Main, Germany: Insel Verlag, 1987.

Ogden, T. (1992), *The Primitive Edge of Experience.* London: Karnac Books.

Ricoeur, P. (1974), Consciousness and the unconscious. In: *Conflict of Interpretations,* ed. P. Ricoeur. Evanston, IL: Northwestern University Press.

Rudnytsky, P. (1987), *Freud and Oedipus.* New York: Columbia University Press.

Sartre, J.-P. (1943), *Being and Nothingness.* London: Routledge, 1995.

Segal, C. (1994), Sophocles' Oedipus Tyrannus. Freud, language and the unconscious. In: *Freud and Forbidden Knowledge,* ed. P. Rudnytsky & H. E. Spitz. New York: New York University Press,

Sophocles, *The Theban Plays,* trans. E. F. Watling. Harmondsworth, U.K.: Penguin Books, 1947.

Steiner, J. (1985), Turning a blind eye: The cover up for Oedipus. *Internat. Rev. Psycho-Anal.,* 12:161–172.

Vernant, J.-P. (1972), Oedipus without the complex. In: *Myth and Tragedy in Ancient Greece,* ed. J.-P. Vernant & P. Vidal-Naquet. New York: Zone Books, 1988.

10

Oedipus and the Search for Reality

CHARLES HANLY, Ph.D.

Sophocles' *Oedipus Rex* achieves its magnificent formal realization of Aristotle's *(Poetics)* three unities of time, place, and action by including a dramatic enquiry into the history of Oedipus within the play. Thebes has been overtaken by a plague. The Delphic oracle has identified its cause. The murderer of Laïus, the former King of Thebes, lives unpunished in the city. Oedipus, moved by the vainglory of having saved Thebes from the Sphinx, is determined to discover the identity of the regicide.

Tragedy and History

What view of historical discovery and knowledge is imbedded in Oedipus' history as it unfolds in the play? From the soothsayer Teiresias, Oedipus first hears that it is he who pollutes Thebes by having killed Laïus who was his father; it is he who is now married to his mother. Oedipus, buoyed up by his own reputation as a solver of riddles and by his belief that he is the son of Polybus,

King of Corinth, repudiates Teiresias and accuses him of conspiring with Creon to deprive him of his throne. At Teiresias' mention of the Pythia's oracle brought by Creon from Delphi, Oedipus quickly fastens upon a story to explain how Teiresias could make these accusations. Teiresias is party to a conspiracy with Creon to bring him down. This story provides a coherent explanation consistent with Oedipus' belief that he is the son of Polybus, with his wish to repudiate Teiresias' accusations, and to protect his throne. For all of its coherence, Oedipus' explanation is a cruelly false self-deception.

The testimony of the messenger from Corinth and the Theban shepherd, his memory of having killed an old man in a carriage at the meeting of three roads, and the evidence of his own ankles and name, eventually force upon Oedipus the awful realization that Teiresias had told him the truth. It was he who had killed Laïus, who was his father. Oedipus has found the answer to the question posed by the oracle. The effect of this knowledge on Jocasta and Oedipus leaves no room to doubt that they believe that now the truth is known. This is not just a coherent story, one of a number of possible coherent stories. It is a story that recounts what actually happened. Dismayed as the Chorus is by Oedipus' self-punishment, it takes the reality of the crimes to be beyond the least shadow of a doubt when it says to Oedipus:

Twice-tormented; in the spirit, and in the flesh,
Would you had never lived to read the riddle [p. 63]

and to us:

And none can be called happy until that day when he carries
His happiness down to the grave in peace [p. 68].

Despite its theology, realism informs Sophocles' tragedy.

Psychic Reality: The Universality of the Oedipus Complex

Sophocles builds the character of Oedipus around the core of a truth seeking that is both his greatest weakness *(hubris)* and his greatest strength. His search for truth led him to his downfall as surely as his piety led him into parricide and incest. Sophocles portrays the profound struggle with narcissism in which Oedipus engages in order to discover his true identity (Grunberger, 1971). Oedipus refuses Jocasta's repeated plea to forget. Still believing that, if he is not the son of Polybus, he must be of lowly origin, Sophocles has him passionately affirm, "I cannot leave the truth unknown" (p. 55). Oedipus' question, "Who killed Laïus?" gradually becomes the question, "Who am I?" To introduce sophistical caveats about memory and knowledge of the past, to redefine truth as social construction or subjective perspective could be a way of forgetting, a way of seeing without knowing the terror of helpless guilt. It could be to refuse an affective identification with Oedipus and to avoid the catharsis that Aristotle *(Poetics)* considered essential to a deeply civilized life.

Scholars and psychoanalysts have often commented on the unintended and unavoidable nature of the crimes of Oedipus. He is the plaything of the gods. He is provoked into killing Laïus by Laïus himself without knowing that he is killing his father. Indeed, he finds himself at the place where three roads meet because he had exiled himself from Corinth in order not to kill the man he believed to be his father. But the Greek poets tied responsibility to agency even though the agent, in this case Oedipus, was led inexorably to commit the culpable acts. Similarly, the Calvinists did not consider a sinner any less sinful because his sinning had been preordained. Sophocles provides Oedipus with every possible extenuating circumstance. Yet the poet has Oedipus unhesitatingly take upon himself, and accept as his own, the fate the gods had planned for him that they might make good the curse laid upon Laïus by Pelops for his having kidnapped and raped his son Chrysippus. It is only his blinding that Oedipus expressly claims as the work of his own hand and not Apollo's. While attributing his fate to the gods, Oedipus accepts it as his own. How are we to understand Sophocles' apparently contradictory attitude to causality when Oedipus says to the Chorus,

Apollo
Has laid this agony upon me;
Not by his hand; I did it [p. 62]?

Hanging between what is forced upon him and what he is responsible for, "it" is left undefined. This rhetorical ambiguity allows the audience to associate the "it" with its own oedipal desires while hearing the "it" as Oedipus' incest and parricide. Oedipus' life was not one he had asked for or sought after; it was laid upon him. Oedipus' attitude is at the heart of an authentic human response to the Oedipus complex.

Jocasta ridicules Oedipus for his unabated anxiety about incest even after he had been assured by the messenger from Corinth that Polybus has died a natural death,

Nor need this mother marrying frighten you;
any a man has dreamt as much.
Such things must be forgotten,
if life is to be endured [p. 58].

For Oedipus there is no comfort in being one of many when the many have only dreamed what he may have done. But the audience may wonder, identifying with the many that have only dreamed of "mother marrying," whether Apollo has made an instrument of Oedipus by contriving for him a fate that is the fulfillment of his dreams.

As it seeks to come to terms with "who Oedipus is" and "what he has done," the Chorus asks,

When the same bosom enfolded the son and the father,
Could not the engendering clay have shouted aloud
its indignation? [p. 59].

Despite its piety, the Chorus expresses its anxious incredulity that the mother could not have identified her son or the son his mother. When Oedipus, the truth seeker, was offered marriage to the aging Jocasta, widow of recently murdered Laïus, the audience may wonder why Oedipus forgot his doubts about his parentage that took him from Corinth to Delphi; the old man he had killed on the road from Delphi to Thebes; and, thus, failed to enquire whether Jocasta was the mother and Laïus the father the dread oracle had spoken of?

Woven into the animistic beliefs of the text there appear to be some indications that Sophocles was approaching a poetic understanding of an unconscious psychic reality. However, the play concerns an actual parricide and incest, historical and not psychic reality. The conflict does not occur so much within Oedipus as between Oedipus and Apollo in Oedipus' efforts to escape from the oracle he received at Delphi. Apollo's influence upon the action of the play facilitates defenses in the spectators that allow them, through insight generating identification and catharsis, to gain a sense of desires of their own through the experience of the dramatic actions of the play. Moreover, there is a disguised truth about the Oedipus complex in Sophocles' animism. Apollo's influence upon Oedipus' actions is to animism what the constitutional genesis of the Oedipus complex is to psychoanalysis.

The Ancient Greek Quest for Psychic Reality

Sophocles' *Oedipus Rex* is evidence and measure of a remarkable transformation of individual psychic life from the Homeric age to the fifth century B.C., a transition from projection to repression (Hanly, 1988). Homer's Agamemnon, trying to persuade Achilles to rejoin the battle at Troy, solemnly informs Achilles that it was not he, Agamemnon, who had given him offense:

> It was Zeus and Fate and the Fury who walks in the dark
> that blinded my judgement that day at the meeting . . .
> What could I do? At such moments there is a Power that takes
> complete command, Ate, the eldest daughter of Zeus,
> who blinds us all, accursed spirit that she is . . . [*Iliad,* p. 356].

Agamemnon's animistic experience of himself and his world allows him to sincerely scapegoat Ate and direct Achilles' animus away from himself and against her. In contrast, Sophocles' Oedipus, who also believes in the gods and their oracles, does not avail himself of Agamemnon's excuse. The gods had sealed a terrible fate for him; yet he acknowledged it as his own doing. In one sense, Oedipus is the antithesis of Sartre's existential man who creates and recreates himself and his destiny by his uncaused choices of action. Buried in the Sophoclean vision is the idea of a nature and history that causes the individual's destiny. Yet, in another sense, Oedipus, like the existentialist, is what he does. He has commited parricide, therefore he is guilty of parricide; that the parricide was arranged by Apollo provides no excuse. But the agency of the gods remains. Human nature remains to that extent bifurcated and ignornant of itself. The world is experienced as being divided into two realms: of man and of the gods.

Plato's Socrates, like Sophocles' Jocasta, turned to the evidence of dreams in his effort to understand the nature of desire. Dreams, Socrates said, reveal "that a terrible, fierce, and lawless class of desires exists in every man, even in those of us who have every appearance of being decent people" *(Republic,* IX, 572). What, according to Plato, makes up this class of desires at work in everyone? In dreams, desire "does not shrink from attempting incestual intercourse with a mother or with any man or god or beast. It is ready for any deed of blood, and there is no unhallowed food it will not eat" *(Republic,* IX, 571). From the perspective of Plato's or Freud's psychological insight, Oedipus had motives at work in himself, without the gods, that made his guilt and suffering more powerful than mere error could have done. Plato had taken the final step of reducing the machinations of the gods to human desire. Heraclitus expressed the same insight when he said, "man's character is his daimon (personal destiny)" (Heraclitus, fragment 51). Plato could not complete the task of reduction, however; he needed to preserve the gods to underwrite morality. It was left to other thinkers, among them Hume, Feuerbach, and Freud, to complete the task, which was facilitated by a reduction of the anxiety that fed the narcissism of ancient man—an anxiety heightened by the real threats to survival to which ancient people were exposed.

These reflections on the struggle with the Oedipus complex by the ancient Greeks, and their evolving awareness of its place in human nature, raise the question about the role of the Oedipus complex in the capacity for reality testing in self-knowledge and in knowledge generally. In his greatest work, Sophocles portrays Oedipus in a hubristic search after the identity of a murderer who turns out to be himself. Was his portrait of Oedipus a way of holding up a mirror in which he and his contemporaries could catch an image of themselves? Did the image have to be distorted to be seen at all by presenting Oedipus as the victim of a destiny preordained by the gods and occasioned by the wrongdoing of the father?

The Oedipus Complex and Self-awareness

Sophocles' *Oedipus Rex* is no less grounded in the piety of ancient Greece than are Shakespeare's tragedies grounded in Elizabethan Christian belief. Further, Sophoclean and Shakespearean theater cannot be deeply appreciated without a sympathetic identification with the experience of life and the world organized by these beliefs. The same is true of our efforts as analysts to grasp in imagination the experience of our patients, including their experience of ourselves as well as of our interpretations. But Sophocles' and Shakespeare's characters and their actions go beyond the relativities of cultures, and the idiosyncracies of individuals, to express, in and through these relativities and idiosyncracies, persistent, fundamental forces at work in human nature no less in modern than in ancient times. Sophocles' image of the psyche as having a destiny ordained by the gods is a good symbolic equivalent for the inescapable ways in which drive development and family life combine to shape the individual life. Sophocles' image of the power of the gods is also a good symbolic equivalent for the inescapability of the Oedipus complex—an inescapability that makes the Oedipus complex and the manner of its resolution a universal determinant of the fates of individuals.

The Oedipus Complex and Rationality

The resolution of the Oedipus complex contributes in a fundamental way to the psychological foundation of human rationality: the capacity for reality-bound observation of self, others, and nature. Knowledge requires two things: a subject equipped with a capacity to know, and an object capable of being known. Knowledge presupposes a measure of objectivity in the philosophical sense. In order to know an object, the knowing human subject must not distort his perceptions, images, and thoughts about the object with his own nature or, if he does, he must be able to become aware that he does and how he does. Such a critical awareness is at the origins of the Copernican revolution in astronomy and the Freudian revolution in psychology. This awareness is not infallible or beyond question, but it is often sufficient for a genuine, if limited, knowledge of self, others, and nature. Negation and differentiation are essential to knowledge. Adequate trial identifications of the analyst with a patient are rooted in the recognition that the patient is the other, the not-me, whose life experiences are his or her own whether similar to or different from the analyst's experiences. Here we come upon the process of subject–object differentiation which is no less basic to individual human development than it is to the development of science and culture. Stated differently, we come upon the natural history of the reality principle as an organizer of psychic processes brought into existence by the exigencies of life. I want to briefly consider three stages of this history.

As Freud (1895) pointed out, at the origin of human rationality is the differentiation between the memory image of the satisfying object and the object that satisfies. The image of the satisfying object, despite its hallucinatory vividness, does not satisfy. The infant psyche is obliged by need to seek the object that does satisfy. This first dawning of subject–object, inside–outside, self–other differentiation gives rise to the use of an image to indicate an object, to the intentional organization, and to the beginnings of symbolization in psychic life. This first intentionality is inherent in the infant's substitution of his thumb, or other object, for the breast to which the substitute object refers. Soon images and then words come to refer beyond themselves to objects and self. The reality of self would probably be most poignantly experienced as need, need gratification and the memory of the experience of satisfaction, and external reality as the object that satisfies—the breast and its accompanying attachment aspects of the mother. A first rudimentary experience of truth and time might arise as the agreement between the memory of satisfaction (what was) and the experience of satisfaction (what is);

hence, also Freud's (1895) statement that the experience of satisfaction is the first organizer of a sense of social responsibility. Such a development is complicated by disturbances of reality testing, as in Klein's idea of the paranoid–schizoid position with its distorting projections and introjections, and by the narcissistic projections which defend the vulnerable infantile ego from experiencing its precariousness (Hanly, 1992).

A second stage is reached when the child is able to identify with and to use a parent as an auxiliary ego or self-object. By means of this special aspect of the anaclitic bond, the child is able to avail himself of the superior reality and value testing functions of his parents. We can see, at once, the extent to which the differentiation between child and parent has occurred and is still incomplete. The dominant anxiety on which the anaclitic tie depends is shame, the fear of the loss of the love of the object and anxiety about survival. The experience of self and objects organized by this anaclitic bond provides the child with the capacity to contrast his own experience of the object with the parental experience. The parent's experience is granted authority (Hanly, 1996) by the child's dependent identificatory tie. This relation allows the child to develop a capacity to criticize his own perceptions and images of objects in the light of parental perceptions of the objects as well as against the objects themselves. A first stage of cognitive, surrogate self-criticism is set in motion, which applies no less to his experience of himself than to his experience of objects. If a child is afraid of the dark and knows that his father is not, he remains afraid but reassured. There is posed for him a question about the source of his fear within himself; he is challenged to find an experience of the dark on his own that is akin to his father's. He begins to experience the difference between appearance and reality. He realizes that his experience of what is in the dark does not correspond with what is in the dark. He takes his father's experience as indicative of the dark as it really is. All of this presupposes good enough parenting and good enough endowment.

Interwoven with this development is the triangulation of the oedipal situation. Klein (1928) suggested a strong link between the viscissitudes of the oedipal situation and cognitive development. Britton (1989) has elaborated the contribution of the oedipal situation to the expansion of the awareness of self and other.

In what follows, I shall use the term *oedipal situation* to refer to the triangulation of awareness in the oral and anal stages and the *Oedipus complex* to refer to the triangulation of awareness in the phallic organization of boys and the clitoral–vaginal organization of girls. The use of such terms identifies the triangularity which the preoedipal situation has in common with the Oedipus complex proper, while retaining the special place of the latter as the *terminus ad quem* of early childhood psychosexual and ego development.

The early triangulation of the oedipal situation provides the child with the experience of being in a relationship with one parent while being observed by the other.[1] The child's needy possessiveness makes him elated, contented, or anxious at being the object of parental observation, depending on the intensity and history of his needs and the approval or disapproval that invests the parent's observation of him. The child also becomes an observer of the parental relationship and especially the primal scene in reality or in imagination. But for the purposes of our argument, it is the experience of being observed in a relationship that is crucial. Given that the observer functions for the child as an auxiliary ego, a potential arises for a discrepancy between the nature and value of the relationship as the child experiences it and as his other parent experiences it. A grade within the ego first arises from within this early object relationship. A child is able to experience himself as objectified in his relationship with one parent by being observed by the other. He is liberated from the adhesive, unreflective, unknowing, "innocence" of his engagement with one parent by seeing himself through the eyes of another with approval or disapproval, with pleasure or envy. An enriched potential for critical self-awareness is slowly put in place and grows with the expanded horizon caused by this triangulation. There is no reason to think that the oedipal situation is the only contributor to this development of the capacity for self-knowledge and self-evaluation. It is, however, usually and naturally the most important contributor because of the depth of the

[1]Along with the satisfaction of desire comes the desire for the repetition of the satisfaction of the need when it arises again, and, hence, the desire to possess the gratifying object. Plato in his *Symposium* recognized the fundamental nature of this instinctual formation when he defined love as the desire for the permanent possession of the beautiful.

child's anaclitic ties to his parents and because these ties are deeply invested with the child's libidinal and aggressive wants, impulses and fears.

The Emergence of Rationality

The resolution of the Oedipus complex brings this development of self-criticism and self-knowledge to a new stage which can serve as the foundation of further maturation. The ancient Athenians laid down the psychological foundations of mature civilized life by cultivating an individual psyche that could tolerate and accept its own conflicts (Hanly, 1992). Freud (1923) enabled us to understand the processes of identification that bear the burden of the resolution of the conflicts of the Oedipus complex. The strengthening of the identification with the parents brings about a stable development in the child of the self-observing function which, during the period of the parent as surrogate ego in the oedipal situation, was still given over to the parents. The child begins to be able to evaluate himself where before he could only be finally evaluated by his parents. Even what his parents do not know of his wrongdoing can now hurt his estimation of himself. Whereas before, the parent's perceptions and ideas about an object could constitute its reality, now the object has its own reality to be known or not known. The burden and pride for the child of perceiving and thinking for himself are gradually assumed. And, most importantly, perceiving and thinking is now equipped with a capacity for self-reflection, the capacity, that is, to question and test the reliability of one's own perceptions of and thoughts about self and objects in order to make them better agree with their reality. The reality principle has come of age in the psychic life of the child. A measure of objectivity about self and objects has become possible. It was to this measure of objectivity that the ancient Greeks contributed so much in many fields and, especially, in their tragedies and philosophy to the cultivation and understanding of psychic reality.

I say "a measure of objectivity" and "possible" for a number of reasons. A 6- or 7-year-old child has by no means mastered the complex affective and intellectual tasks required to achieve such objectivity as human perception and thought, at its best, can achieve. We know how deeply compromised by delusions, illusions, and projections, experience and thought can be. There is no evidence that anyone is completely free of such compromises in one sector or another of their experience. And to know that a strongly motivated belief is an illusion does not remove it, so long as the need to believe continues, any more than our knowing that the enlargement of the sun at the horizon corresponds to no change in the sun itself alters our perception of it. That the human capacity for objectivity is real, is evidenced by the edifice of scientific knowledge and the amelioration of life that it has made possible. But the capacity for critical self-reflection remains intrinsically fallible. Critical self-reflection is not the philosopher's stone, the infallible test of truth, that Descartes hoped it might be when, in the *Meditations,* he embarked on his attempt at systematic doubt. A psychoanalytic meditation on *Oedipus Rex* reveals a search for the reality of psychic life even at its darkest. Inherent in this search are the connected questions concerning agency, causality, and responsibility. Who is the agent and who is responsible? Apollo or Oedipus? But if Sophocles in his struggle to represent the catastrophe of parricide and incest, could only catch a glimpse of its motives in the distorting lens of animistic beliefs, how confident can we be that our own ideas about psychic reality are sound?

Subjectivisim and Objectivism

Some contemporary psychoanalysts associate objectivism or realism with authoritarianism, dogmatism, rigidity, claims to certainty, absolutism, and the insensitive imposition of the analyst's preconceptions on the patient. By contrast, subjectivism or idealism, is often thought to be liberal, open, adaptive, modest, satisfied with probabilities, and sensitively respectful of the patient. Subjectivism, which began as a reflection on the obstacles to an analytic understanding of the patient's life, has ended by claiming that objectivity is impossible and that its pursuit is dangerous. But contemporary epistemologists, philosophers of science, and others who hold that objectivity is possible would be unable to recognize themselves in the descriptions of their position implied by the assertions and claims of psychoanalytic subjectivists. The realist's assumption that each person is an individual with a nature and a life of his or her own, similar and different from our own, against which we are obliged to test our perceptions and understanding, implies neither authoritarianism, dogmatism, nor rigidity. On the contrary, the realist assumption demands that every interpretation must be carefully and patiently tested before confidence can be placed even in its probability.

The intelligibility of the psychic life of human beings, including our own, depends upon the causalities of sexuality, aggression, defenses, and object relations that give each psychic life its character, boundaries, stability, and direction despite its illusiveness, disguises, dissemblings, avoidances, variability, and inventiveness. Psychic causality is not fundamentally different from the efficient causality of nature generally except that, because of consciousness, it gives rise to the twin subjective illusions of teleology and free will (Spinoza, 1677). It is because determinate wishes are formed within ourselves, caused by our needs (drives) that we have an individual, yet shared, conative nature that gives us agency, purpose, and boundaries. Otherwise, psychic life would have only a passive chameleon existence dominated by its environment. But neither do the drives insulate us from objects to form a Leibnizian monadic (Leibniz, 1714) existence. Sexuality and aggression cause object seeking because the best they can do, on their own, is to give rise to memories or phantasies of satisfaction, which do not satisfactorily diminish the force of primary needs. Objects thus come to exert a profound causal influence of their own on psychic life.

Psychoanalytic claims to knowledge depend upon this psychic agency, rooted in primary needs, that forms the motivational core of the subjectivity of the individual life. Psychoanalysis is itself an object relationship in which the analyst occupies a position of great influence over the patient. The charge against psychoanalysis has been and remains that it cannot lay claim to objectivity because the analyst only observes the consequences of the suggestive influence of his interpretations upon the patient.

The influence of the analyst upon the analysand consequent upon interpretation and the transference, on the one hand, and the influence of the patient on the analyst consequent upon the countertransference, on the other, are inevitable. But are they either all-determining or beyond recognition and correction? Independently of any suggestive influence of the analyst upon the patient, the unconscious sexual and aggression laden memories and fantasies that bring about dreams and symptoms are at work as the agency of the patient's psyche. The very same forces are at work in clinical processes of free association.

> A young woman patient dreamed that she was walking by a lake which became increasingly storm tossed with great breakers rolling in upon the beach. She was frightened by a large, green crocodilelike monster in the dark, churning water. To the analyst's surprise and the patient's initial confusion, she associated the monster of her dream to the green, crocodile insignia of a line of sportswear. Then she recalled having recently had lunch with a woman friend who was wearing a T-shirt bearing the crocodile insignia. The association still appeared to be incongruent with the storm imagery and the affect of the dream. Further associations revealed the patient's submerged anger at her friend for having sought to ingratiate herself with the patient's mother by showing off her superiority. My patient was envious of her friend because she had landed a man, which my patient had not been able to do, but her envy was embroiled in a conflicting sexual competitiveness with her friend for possession of the mother. Only much later did the biting and phallic meanings of the dream emerge.

In this case, the manifest content of the dream did not seem to owe anything to the analyst's influence. Freud (1917, pp. 243–496) had pointed out that even when the manifest content of a patient's dream is greatly influenced by the analyst, this influence does not extend to the motives at work in the latent dream where its meaning resides in the spontaneous needs and wishes of the individual's own subjectivity, that is, in the individual's own agency. The work of analysis requires us to find our way through our own and the patient's resistances and disguises to the wishes and anxieties actually at work in the patient's life. As difficult as this work can be, it is made feasible by the motivational influence of libidinal and aggressive memories and phantasies at work in the patient's life. It is by facilitating the forward movement of the organizations of sexuality, narcissism, and aggression into mature forms of internal and external relationship, that neuroses are resolved. Among other constants that render psychic reality intelligible is the inevitability of the Oedipus complex.

Oedipus and the Issue of Responsibility

Psychic determinism has been supposed by some philosophers and psychoanalysts to be incompatible with responsibility. If objectivity depends on psychic determinism, are we not committed to a stoic fatalism which likens the human condition to the predicament of a captive chained by the neck to the victor's war chariot? He may go with dignity or he may struggle against his chains and be dragged, but go he must. Can man defy the gods as Oedipus tried to do? Must defiance always fail? Are we constrained, as the Stoics believed we were, to be able to live, as best we can, only by learning to know and to live according to the laws of our nature and of nature?

Let us return to Sophocles' vision of the human condition as expressed in the play Freud took as model for his theory. His hero's fate was unavoidable. It was contrived by the gods. Oedipus' efforts to avoid his fate only sealed it. He killed his father and married his mother unknowingly. At the end, he says to his children that he did not see or know what he did when he became their father. Nevertheless, he identifies with his fate, accepts it as his own, and accepts responsibility for it. Responsibility does not require free will; psychic determinism and responsibility are compatible (Hanly, 1979; Alford, 1992). In this obscure way, the ancient Greeks acknowledged the gods' wishes for them as their own. Psychoanalysis, in the footsteps of Shakespeare, has replaced the gods in Sophocles' vision with desire, trauma, and character. But the core of the Sophoclean idea of responsibility remains at the core of psychoanalysis. Freud (1900) pointed out that "there seems to be no justification for people's reluctance in accepting responsibility for the immorality of their dreams" (p. 620). The same applies to the wants that animate our psychic lives. They are not our doing; yet we have no justifiable alternative but to accept responsibility for the love and hate the Oedipus complex arouses in us. Although there is no justice in this, for nature is neither just nor unjust, we can only manage to be just, as Plato in his *Republic* and Aristotle in his *Poetics* long ago made clear, by accepting these desires as our own. And even though it be unjust, for justice and injustice do apply to human relations, to be made to suffer psychic trauma during the helplessness of childhood, one has to assume responsibility for the consequences of the trauma in one's character, motives, and actions, if one is to do anything constructive about them. In saying this, I am not in the least suggesting that individuals unconsciously bring trauma upon themselves or that analysts should not help patients to understand the difference between what has been done to them, what they have done, and what they only wanted to do. These differences must be taken into account in adequate analytic work (Hanly, 1986a). Psychoanalysis has pushed back a little the frontiers of that about which the only realistic attitude is fatalism. The Oedipus complex is inevitable. There is no parenting that is good enough to avoid it. Its resolution, on the other hand, depends partly on the force of its demands and partly on the objects and the object relations the oedipal child has available to him or her to mitigate the conflicts it generates. When good enough parenting and genetic good fortune are not available psychoanalysis may accomplish the psychosexual and aggressive maturation which the natural family could not provide.

Instinct Mastery, Adult Sexuality, and the Oedipus Complex

If the mastery of the oedipal demands lays down a cornerstone of human cognitive and moral rationality, rationality must have deep roots in libido and in the instinctual unconscious. Down through the centuries, *Oedipus Rex* has reminded mankind that there is no greater catastrophe than to be led into parricide and incest by the same gods who prohibit these acts. These conflicting attributes of the gods of ancient Greek religion contain a hidden truth—the dynamic relation between human conscience and human instinct life. In Plato, as in modern man, fear of the gods has given way to fear of the instincts and the guilt provoked by actions instincts motivate. *Oedipus Rex* continues to stir up and then chastise the unbound, primary process impulses and phantasies that do not know themselves to be wishes and not deeds.

The horrifying spectacle of the self-punishments of Jocasta and Oedipus strengthen the unconscious identifications that form the nucleus of conscience and, in consequence, the responsibility assumed for one's own impulse life. To borrow the imagery of ancient Greek legend and religion, when psychoanalysis neglects or discounts libido in the lives of men and women in theory or therapy, it runs the risks of Hippolitus' failure to give Aphrodite her due. But how does one give Aphrodite her due without becoming a plaything of the gods?

Plato was the advocate of ascetic privation as the best method for instinct mastery. Plato had the homosexual's disdain for, and fear of heterosexual love. In the *Symposium* and *Phaedrus,* the sublimation of homosexual love aimed at transcending physical love altogether. Plato believed that parricidal and incestuous appetites would dwindle so long as they were not stimulated from without. Consequently, he advocated that the men and women of the intellectual, moral and military elite of his ideal state should be deprived of family life and nurtured in "rearing pens" where they would be cared for by the men and women of their parental generation without children being able to identify their parents or parents their children. He also believed it necessary to completely censor all of the great literature of his time including *Oedipus Rex.* The asceticism advocated by Plato to moralize adult sexuality consisted of a resignation sustained by severe privations and transcending sublimations in the pursuit of psychic harmony.

Aristotle *(Poetics)* appears not to have been subject to the moral terror that oedipal impulses aroused in Plato. He articulated his understanding of the need for great literature and theater in his idea of the cathartic function of tragedy. Aristotle considered *Oedipus Rex* to be an example of what is best in tragedy in its form and content. Catharsis involves pity and fear: in the case of Oedipus, pity for his suffering and fear of what he has done and what has befallen him. I would add that these emotions surely imply a degree of identification with Oedipus. If so, the identification which brings about a purgation of pity and fear, as Aristotle said, may also achieve something more, a reduction in the force of unconscious parricidal and incestuous wishes implicated in the identification. The catharsis of great theater and literature can sustain resignation by promoting psychic harmony by means of vicarious gratification and punishment.

Psychoanalysis has uncovered the inadequacies of asceticism and catharsis. Plato did not understand how deeply connected are moral ideals, virtues, imperatives, and affects with libido and aggression or with what ingenuity their regressed, perverse forms can insinuate themselves into reason's citadel. The ascetic impoverishment of sexuality as a solution of oedipal problems is a poor alternative to their resolution. Catharsis is much to be preferred to asceticism, but its effectiveness is limited to reprieves from such incestuous and parricidal wishes as are retained despite their predominant resolution. However, catharsis as a need of adult sexuality should not be underestimated because oedipal wishes are retained and may undergo regressive intensification as a result of inevitable or untoward life events.

Unless one accepts Freud's death instinct, psychoanalysis is committed by the primacy of the pleasure principle and the pathogenic potential of repressed drives to the view that the mastery of instinct life and the psychic harmony it brings are best achieved through gratification in adult sexuality. Freud (1895) had early rooted the psychoanalytic notion of psychic harmony in the homeostasis of the pleasure principle. The mastery of instinct by means of self-imposed privation, even with its accompanying substitute narcissistic gratifications of elational self-righteousness, is a poor alternative to mastery of instinct life by means of the gratification of instinctual demands (Freud, 1908, 1930). Adult sexuality is assigned a crucial role in the achievement of instinct mastery. But if the Oedipus complex is as universal and dangerous as we have supposed, gratification of instinctual demands as a preferred means of instinct control has obvious limits.

The Oedipus complex consists of two quintessential libidinal and aggressive wants that cannot be mastered by satisfaction and which become painfully unwanted. The Oedipus complex imposes a precarious yet fundamental and crucially important developmental task. It may end in asceticism or perversion either because of earlier fixating traumata or because of flaws in the relations with whose objects strengthened identifications have to be made. But the institution of growth promoting sublimations sufficient to defer genital gratification, a temporary asceticism or perversity, is all that seems to be intrinsically required, unless constitutional (genetic) factors or historical misfortunes (trauma) intervene. The resolution of the Oedipus complex provides for the return in adult life to the mastery of libidal impulses through gratification. The Oedipus complex complicates but does not finally compromise the fundamental hedonism of human nature.

As troublesome as the Oedipus complex is, we may like to think that mature sexuality owes little to it, to the Oedipus complex as such, while allowing that it owes a great deal to its resolution and to the onset of puberty. But the Oedipus complex helps to bring about a concentration of the pleasures of the infantile sexual organization in genital foreplay. It motivates substitute forms of satisfaction through sublimation for sexual and aggressive demands that escape this concentration. It contributes to the formation of ideals which order libidinal pleasures according to internalized parental images which can eventually be tested. If all else fails, it submits to the asceticism of duty for duty's sake (moral categorical imperatives) that can spare humiliation and console with moral narcissism. But, perhaps, the greatest contribution of the resolution of the Oedipus complex is the unification of the tenderness of aim-inhibited affection with the force of genital desire in mature sexuality. It is some consolation for the travail or tragedy caused by oedipal desires in our lives that the relationships and psychic processes that lead to the resolution of the conflicts they generate should stabilize the capacities for self-observation and self-criticism essential to both morality and reason along with the capacity for genital love.

And if the Oedipus complex seems to offer no advantages to adult sexuality that puberty could not better and more easily provide on its own, its resolution does provide adult narcissitic libido with an organization and with functions that are indispensable to civilized life: the capacity for self-observation and self-criticism in the search for objectivity about oneself, others, and the world grounded in the awareness that this capacity is itself subject to conscious and unconscious motives that can compromise or enhance its work; the capacity for an adult sexuality that is aggressively passionate while being tender, considerate, and substantially uncompromised by infantile sexual demands; the capacity to take responsibility for one's own instinct life and the shadows cast by abandoned object relations.

References

Alford, F. (1992), *The Psychoanalytic Theory of Greek Tragedy.* New Haven, CT: Yale University Press.

Aristotle, *Poetics,* trans. G. M. A. Grube. Library of the Liberal Arts. Indianapolis & New York: Bobbs-Merrill, 1958.

——— *Politics.* In: *Introduction to Aristotle,* ed. R. McKeon. New York: Modern Library, 1947, pp. 546–617.

Britton, R. (1989), The missing link: Parental sexuality in the Oedipus complex. In: *The Oedipus Complex Today,* ed. J. Steiner. London: Karnac Books.

Freud, S. (1895), Project for a Scientific Psychology. *Standard Edition,* 1:281–391. London: Hogarth Press, 1966.

——— (1900), The Interpretation of Dreams. *Standard Edition,* 5. London: Hogarth Press, 1953.

——— (1908), "Civilized" sexual morality and modern nervous illness. *Standard Edition,* 9:177–204. London: Hogarth Press, 1959.

——— (1917), Introductory Lectures on Psycho-Analysis. *Standard Edition,* 16. London: Hogarth Press, 1963.

——— (1923), The Ego and the Id. *Standard Edition,* 19:1–66. London: Hogarth Press, 1961.

——— (1930), Civilization and Its Discontents. *Standard Edition,* 21:57–145. London: Hogarth Press, 1961.

Grunberger, B. (1971), *Narcissism: Psychoanalytic Essays,* trans. J. S. Diamanti. New York: International Universities Press, 1979.

Hanly, C. (1979), *Existentialism and Psychoanalysis.* New York: International Universities Press.

——— (1986a), Review of J. M. Masson, *The Assault on Truth: Freud's Suspension of the Seduction Theory. Internat. J. Psycho-Anal.,* 67:517–519.

——— (1986b), Lear and his daughters. In: *The Problem of Truth in Applied Psychoanalysis.* New York: Guilford Press, 1992.

——— (1988), From animism to rationalism. In: *The Problem of Truth in Applied Psychoanalysis.* New York: Guilford Press, 1992.

——— (1992), On narcissistic defenses. *The Psychoanalytic Study of the Child,* 47:139–158. New Haven, CT: Yale University Press.

——— (1996), Reflections on feminine and masculine authority: A developmental perspective. *Psychoanal. Quart.*, 65:84–101.

Homer, *Iliad,* trans. E. V. Rieu. Harmondsworth, U.K.: Penguin Books, 1950.

Klein, M. (1928), Early stages of the Oedipus conflict. *Internat. J. Psycho-Anal.*, 9:167–180.

Leibniz, G. W. H. (1714), Monadology. In: *Leibniz Selections,* ed. P. Wiener. New York: Scribner's Sons, 1951.

Plato, *Republic,* trans. B. Jowett. New York: Liberal Arts Press, 1948.

——— *Symposium,* trans. W. C. Helmbold & W. G. Rabinowitz. New York: Bobbs-Merrill, 1956.

——— *Phaedrus,* trans. W. B. Helmbold & W. G. Rabinowitz. New York: Library of the Liberal Arts, 1956.

Sophocles, *Oedipus Rex.* In: *Sophocles: The Theban Tragedies,* trans. E. F. Watling. Harmondsworth, U.K.: Penguin Books, 1947.

Spinoza, B. (1677), Ethics. In: *Spinoza Selections,* ed. J. Wild. New York: Scribner, 1930.

11

Matricide and the Oedipus Complex

HAROLD P. BLUM, M.D.

Traditional Psychoanalysis and Matricide

Through myths, historical example, and clinical illustration, I will hereby explore universal matricidal fantasy and propose a more balanced view of unconscious murderous conflicts with respect to both parents. The Oedipus complex has a preoedipal foundation, being negative as well as positive, matricidal as well as parricidal. Matricidal fantasy is ubiquitous, and has universal significance. Particular illustrations in the text, however, generally refer to men. Although the focus is on men, it is important to note that matricidal fantasy is ubiquitous in women as well as in men.

The formulation of the Oedipus complex by Freud has always included the boy's hostility to his male rival, father, with fantasies of murdering him and marrying mother. The converse, although little emphasized, was postulated for women. Freud repeatedly and specifically dealt with parricide. He began by attributing his own magnum opus, *The Interpretation of Dreams* (Freud, 1900), to his guilty reaction to the death of his father. Finally, in one of his last psychoanalytic writings, *Moses and Monotheism,* Freud (1939) proposed that Moses had been murdered by the primal horde, a parricide, and that the Christian crucifixion of the son was punishment for parricide. There is little exploration of matricidal fantasy in Freud's writings, the term *matricide* being missing from the index of the *Standard Edition.*

Contrasting with the vast literature on parricidal jealousy and rivalry, psychoanalytic writings lack a systematic exposition of matricidal feeling and fantasy. Hostility toward the mother may have been displaced quite regularly onto the father or split off from the "good mother" (Klein, 1946). Murderous displacements onto wives, daughters, sisters, and nursemaids have also been hardly considered. Mothers and motherhood have been idealized, and the father is the representation not only of reality, but of prohibition and punishment.

Although only the prohibition of parricide and incest has been identified as critical for superego development, the prohibition of matricide is similarly related to civilization and morality. Freud (1913) proposed that guilt and remorse were consequent to the murder of the father by the primal horde of sons. This proposition did not consider female guilt or the relationship of guilt to matricide. The issue of matricide did not entirely escape Freud; there were sporadic references to it in the form of death wishes against the mother in, for example, *The Interpretation of Dreams* (Freud, 1900), "Dreams and Telepathy" (Freud, 1922), and "Femininity" (Freud, 1933).

Discussing typical dreams, Freud (1900) described a young woman who had a special aversion to her mother, hitting and abusing her whenever she was near, while at the same time being docile and affectionate toward a much older sister. This woman had many dreams of the death of her mother:

> [A]t one time she would be attending an old woman's funeral, at another she and her sister would be sitting at table dressed in mourning . . . hysterical phobias developed. The most tormenting of these was the fear that something might have happened to her mother. She was obliged to hurry home, wherever she might be, to convince herself that her mother was still alive. . . . When a normal state was still more firmly established, it led to the production of her exaggerated worry about her mother as an hysterical counter-reaction and

> defensive phenomenon. In view of this it is no longer hard to understand why hysterical girls are so often attached to their mothers with such exaggerated affection [Freud, 1900, pp. 259–260].

This was followed immediately by Freud's discussion of a young man unable to go out into the street, tortured by the fear that he would kill everyone he met. Analysis showed that the basis of his obsession was an impulse to murder his severe father. This symmetrical discussion of matricidal and parricidal fantasies did not resume, however, until Freud (1923) first described the complete Oedipus complex:

> Closer study usually discloses the more complete Oedipus complex, which is two-fold, positive and negative, and is due to the bisexuality originally present in children: that is to say, a boy has not merely an ambivalent attitude towards his father and an affectionate object-choice towards his mother, but at the same time he also behaves like a girl and displays . . . a corresponding jealousy and hostility towards his mother [p. 33].

Though the great father complex had dominated Freud's case histories, mothers were gradually given greater attention. Pointing to her own mother, Dora's cousin stated, "You can't think how I hate that person!, and when she is dead I shall marry daddy" (Freud, 1905, p. 57). But Dora's hatred of her own mother did not emerge in her three months of treatment. In the Rat-Man Case (Freud, 1909), Freud emphasized the Rat-Man's parricidal fantasies. However, he also referred to matricidal fantasy when discussing the Rat-Man's suicidal impulses. Freud (1909, p. 187) stated:

> While he was working he was overcome by a longing for his absent lady, and he thought of the cause of her absence. And now there came over him something which if had been a normal man would probably have been some kind of feeling of annoyance with her grandmother: why must the old woman get ill just at the very moment when I'm longing for her so frightfully? We must suppose that something similar but far more intense passed through our patient's mind—an unconscious fit of rage which could combine with his longing and find expression in the exclamation: "Oh, I should like to go

> and kill that old woman for robbing me of my love!'' Thereupon followed the command: ''Kill yourself, as punishment for the savage and murderous passions!'' [p. 187].

Mack Brunswick (1928) interpreted the Wolf Man's fantasies of murdering Freud and herself in terms of killing both parents. She emphasized the Wolf Man's feminine identification with mother and repressed homosexual conflict in paranoia. In a later article Freud (1933) observed, ''We discovered the fear of being murdered or poisoned, which may later form the core of the paranoia illness already present in this pre-Oedipus period in relation to the mother'' (p. 120).

The toddler's projection of aggression, experiences of hate and rage in response to maternal limits, separation, and imposed frustrations, inevitable disappointments of maternal love and care, and threats of castration and punishment by the mother (e.g., the mother of Little Hans), also were not elaborated in relation to matricide. Impulses to ''bite the hand that feeds'' and kill the nurturer were deeply repressed. The preoedipal devouring and engulfing mother; the phallic castrating and vengeful mother; the seductive, destructive mother were all noted in the pioneer literature, but the preoedipal maternal representations and their relationship to the matricidal oedipal conflict remained very much in the background.

Preoedipal Issues and Ego Fragility

It is, of course, now apparent that the preoedipal, murderous hostility to the mother figures prominently in fantasies and acts of suicide and homicide. In the act of suicide, the murder of the self-mother with unconscious guilt and the fantasied merging with the primary object are often considered to be critically important issues. Atonement, which derives from being ''at one,'' was not connected to the restoration of mother–infant unity or to the emergence of guilt and reparation connected to matricidal fantasy. In borderline patients, severe addictions, and perversions, current clinical evidence points toward preoedipal disturbances in the mother–infant relationship, not excluding factors of endowment and later life experience. Borderline adults have usually been very disturbed children (Weil, 1956; Blum, 1974). Ego weakness combined with excessive aggression (Kernberg, 1975), narcissistic rage (Kohut, 1968), and infantile murderous fantasies are commonly noted. In addition to roots in preoedipal aggression, infantile sadomasochism, and excessive unpleasure and frustration, hate and murderous fantasies are stimulated by the entire process of separation-individuation. Both separation and merger become dangers. Incest horrifies not only because of oedipal guilt, but also on account of the regressive desire, yet dreaded wish to return to the womb. If rage and hate are not tamed, there is danger of splitting of the representational world (Mahler, Pine, and Bergman, 1975), analogous to the Kleinian split of the "all good and all bad object" in the first year of life (Klein, 1946). The object of murderous rage and the murderous object whom the paranoid fears is a narcissistic object, an incompletely differentiated self-object. The hate is often projected onto father figures so that the assassin, for example, may pursue the father figure with hateful and vindictive violence. The oedipal defeat of the father figure affirms masculinity and protects the self and mother from infantile aggression. Despite manifest oedipal conflict, it is the latent preoedipal murderous rage which has infiltrated an extremely fragile and distorted oedipal constellation. In such cases, the oedipal object is both idealized and devalued; castration anxiety is fused with separation anxiety, and there is insufficient love and self and object constancy for full oedipal engagement and resolution (Blum, 1994).

Matricide in Myth and Literature

I shall first turn to applied psychoanalysis, for it is in this area that matricide was confronted in the early literature, rather than in the clinical sphere. Myth, literature, and history have commonly portrayed matricidal fantasy. Accounts of the lives of the saints regularly depicted the murder of idealized mother figures and their martyrdom. The burning of witches represented a displaced matricidal enactment, destroying the devalued, dangerous, incestuous mother figures, the "bad objects." History is not only replete with regicides, but with the matricidal elimination of queen mothers as well. Even in the applied analytic literature, however, the murder of the mother has been often interpreted as a defense against or punishment for incestuous love. The matricidal narratives are often forced into the mold of parricidal fantasy, with matricide explained as manifest content and disguise for underlying parricidal fantasy.

In this connection, it is of interest that Freud overlooked the matricidal myth of Orestes. The Oedipus myth openly referred to the son's incestuous relationship to the mother, but not to the matricide which is manifest in the Orestes myth. Though artfully disguised, matricidal fantasy can be uncovered in the oedipal myth as well. In Greek mythology, Orestes was the son of Agamemnon and Clytemnestra. His mother's lover, Aegistus, conspired with Orestes' mother, and they murdered his father. Orestes was secretly removed and protected by his sister, Electra. Orestes was ordered by Apollo to avenge his father (like Hamlet), when he reached manhood. Orestes, colluding with Electra, killed his mother, Clytemnestra, and her lover, Aegistus. Orestes was then pursued by retaliating female goddesses, the Furies. First seeking refuge at Delphi, he went to Athens to plead his case before an all-male jury that rendered an equally divided verdict. Athena, a female childless judge who was not born or raised by a mother, and was not a mother, cast a deciding vote for acquittal. The Furies were appeased and newly worshipped as kindly goddesses, referred to as Eumenides. In the Orestes myth, the matricide was justified and undisguised, unlike the parricide in the Oedipus myth (Green, 1975). Perhaps the lack of disguise rendered it of less interest to analysts. The fantasy of overt murder of the mother succumbs to similar repression as parricide, but it seems that the theme of parricide far more readily returns from the repressed.

The murderous attitudes of fathers and sons was also approached in Freud's (1900, 1928) analysis of Hamlet and of Dostoevsky. Dostoevsky's father was actually murdered when the author was 18. In "Dostoevski and Parricide," Freud (1928) elucidated parricidal conflict with its constellation of guilt and tragic self-punitive patterns.

In choosing *The Brothers Karamazov* for his study of oedipal parricide, Freud did not simultaneously consider the complementary novel, *Crime and Punishment.* The latter narrates the murder by a young man of an old woman and her younger sister. The murdered women have been interpreted as representing the young murderer's own mother and sister. *Crime and Punishment* has been interpreted as a classic story of matricide (Kanzer, 1948; Florance, 1955). Kanzer (1948) stressed matricide in the murders of other women in Dostoevsky's stories, but also interpreted the dual murders as concurrent matricide and parricide. Considering the dual murders of both parents in the paired novels, *The Brothers Karamazov* and *Crime and Punishment,* an old murder trial rhyme is relevant: "Lizzie Borden took an ax / And gave her mother forty whacks; When she saw what she had done / She gave her father forty-one!"

Lower (1969) further explored the overdetermined murders in *Crime and Punishment* and proposed that Raskolnikov destroyed his own feminine submissive strivings in killing "the worthless woman." The murder was a disguised sexual attack on the mother and a murder of his own castrated feminine self. Analyzing the literary dreams of Raskolnikov-Dostoevsky, he concluded that the old woman unconsciously represented the dead father, so that the ax murder of the mother was manifest content for the latent theme of parricide. The ax murder of the old woman represented destruction of the feminine self and father, but not a previously matricidal enactment. The manifest matricide was interpreted as Dostoevsky's attempt to resolve parricidal conflict. Marinov (1990) described both themes of matricide and parricide in Dostoevsky and split representations of the mother figure as virgin and prostitute, castrated and phallic.

The oedipal myth is overdetermined, with multiple levels of interpretation. In the Oedipus myth, two mother figures, the Sphinx and Jocasta, kill themselves, both suicides being instigated by the oedipal son. The Greeks condemned Jocasta, because, being old enough to be Oedipus' mother when she met and married him, she did not know her own son. Failing to recognize her child, Jocasta bore the greater guilt and responsibility for committing incest.

In the oedipal myth, Laïus, the father of Oedipus, had been cursed because of his homosexual rape of young Chrysippus, Laïus being regarded as the first mortal to have engaged in such "unnatural love." The curse-prophecy by an Oracle was that Laïus should not have children. If he disobeyed, the child would kill him and also bring a sequence of misfortunes to his house and land. Oedipus was similarly warned by an Oracle that he was fated to kill his father and marry his mother, and it is for that reason that he resolved never to return to Corinth, the home of his presumed parents. On his way to Thebes, he encountered Laïus where three roads meet and, without conscious awareness, killed his biological father. Further en route, he encountered the Sphinx, a winged monster, half woman, half lion. At the gates of Thebes, she, the Sphinx, posed riddles to those who would pass, and devoured or otherwise destroyed those who could not solve these riddles. There were actually two riddles, always presented identically: what being walks sometimes on two feet, sometimes on three, sometimes on four, and is weakest when it has most? Who are the two sisters who give birth to one another? The answers were, man and then, day and night. Only Oedipus had been able to solve both riddles, causing the Sphinx to leap off a cliff and self-destruct. The grateful Thebans offered Oedipus their kingdom and the hand of their widowed queen, Jocasta.

While Laïus was accused of having invented pederasty, no such invention was cited for heterosexual relations. Heterosexual relations in these myths were not the subjects of accusation and required no explanation of origin. Both homosexual and heterosexual relations between parents and son were proscribed. Actually, the Oedipus myth does not begin with parental love. Laïus has earlier on committed pederasty, and the myth overtly represents Laïus' attempt to kill his son. He anticipated that his son would kill him. Projection of murderous jealousy justified a preemptive strike against the infant. Jocasta colluded with Laïus in the abandonment of her infant son Oedipus.

It would be particularly relevant here to consider the Sphinx as primarily a mother figure. The Sphinx may or may not be truly leonid, and the hindquarters may be in possession of male genitalia, making her a phallic woman. It has been suggested that the wings may have represented a bird's flight, the ability to appear, disappear, and reappear, representing the preoedipal omnipotent mother of separation and reunion. In the Oedipus myth, the Sphinx represents the filicidal mother, the parent who harbors murderous impulses toward the child or represents the projection of the child's infantile omnipotence and murderous fantasies onto the parent. Considering that deeply disturbed mothers may act out such impulses, it is significant that Freud never relinquished the importance of actual trauma. He reported cases of incestuous seduction and assumed that in primeval times parents actually castrated their sons long before the symbolic, token castration of circumcision. At the same time, he did not discuss the child's vengeful fantasy of murdering the mother who in fantasy and reality wished to murder her child.

Matricide forced into the mold of parricide characterized early pioneer papers on Oedipus and the Sphinx (Reik, 1920). While matricide was often recast into the mold of incest and parricide, few authors suggested that the murder of either parent could defend against murderous impulses toward the other parent. Matricide was often recast into the mold of incest and parricide. The murder of the mother figure by the aggressor-father wielding an ax or sword was treated as a disguise for rape and incest. Incest was then a more significant issue than matricide. In the vernacular, a "mother fucker" was a lesser evil than a mother murderer. The lack of more serious attention to matricide also had elements of a group analytic countertransference with identification with authority and transference to theory (Rangell, 1982).

As in the complementary pair of Dostoevsky's great novels, with their respective representations of parricide and matricide, Oedipus commits the murder first of his father and then, symbolically, of his mother. On his tragic trajectory, he first battles with Laïus and then with the Sphinx. His unconscious fantasies are projected onto fate, the forces of destiny. However, it is the capacity of Oedipus to relentlessly question, to pursue his own frightening game of "truth and consequences," and to persist despite resistances to solving the deepest and darkest riddles of life that strongly contribute to making him a tragic hero. He proceeds to solve a murder mystery in which he is the culprit. The Oedipus myth unfolds as an analytic process (Freud, 1900) with disguise and defense alternating with insight and new integration. The role of the Sphinx may also be compared to the nature of the unconscious. Unraveling her riddles lead to the discovery of his origins and identity, the Oedipus complex, and the mysteries of the female genitals—the primal scene, pregnancy, birth, and death. While the Sphinx and her surrogate, Jocasta, kill themselves, they can be seen as symbolically murdered consequent to incest.

When parental oedipal fantasies are enacted, the child is also enraged at the parent who perpetrates incest trauma. The parents' sexual abuse of the child is simultaneously an act of hateful violence and a massive narcissistic mortification. Incest has a long prehistory, and there is usually evidence of preoedipal parental dysfunction. This may be discerned in the Oedipus myth in the parental abandonment and neglect of Oedipus and their lack of recognition and empathy (Blum, 1996). Oedipus returns to, actively and passively, murder the biological father and, indirectly, the mother who nearly murdered him. In the myth he would have died had he not been found by the shepherd in a fantasy of rebirth and adoption similar to the story of Moses. The binding and piercing of his feet, similar to the crucifixion of Jesus, give rise to his name "Oedipus" or swollen foot. Swollen also refers to symbolic erection so that the very name condenses potency and castration, crime and punishment.

However, the pierced "birthmarked" feet of Oedipus (Rosner, 1977) also represent the crippling effects of child abuse (Rascovsky and Rascovsky, 1968). Oedipus was scarred and nearly crippled by his parents, Jocasta colluding with Laïus in his postpartum abandonment at only 3 days of age. The Sphinx represents a destructive mother, the mother who had almost killed him. Oedipus' realization of his mother's murderous impulses toward him and his relinquishing his idealization of Jocasta are a turning point in the drama. Jocasta will suffer the same fate as the Sphinx whom Oedipus has driven to suicide. Oedipus wards off unconscious fantasy even as he answers the questions of the Sphinx and asks questions of Jocasta (Sophocles, 425 B.C.). These questions are reminiscent of the questions children ask parents about their origins and the "facts of life." Oedipus has to defend not only against awareness of his own oedipal impulses but the infanticidal impulses of his parents. Although it is Laïus who tears his son, Oedipus, from the arms of his nurse and leaves him to die without killing him outright, thus avoiding direct guilt, the mother of Oedipus is complicit and her lack of protection is implicit. Fears of abusing children are among the most common presenting problems which bring mothers to mental health clinics (Anthony and Benedek, 1970). Moreover, actual abandonment and infanticide have been perpetrated by mothers more often than many societies are ready to acknowledge. Such maternal aggression and hostility is found to impact on her child.

Cognitive combat through presenting and penetrating secrets or riddles is presumed to have been a much later intellectual sublimation than real battle. The fantasied physical-sexual has been transformed to riddles (Reik, 1920), but the sublimation is unsuccessful since murder of child or mother inevitably ensues. Why should failure to solve the riddle lead the Sphinx to devour the Thebans one by one? Why should solving the riddle lead to the destruction of the monster Sphinx and the award of the City of Thebes and its queen? Oedipus demonstrates his intellectual and symbolic sexual potency in solving the riddles. Solving a riddle may be regarded as an attempt at insight and mastery. Oedipus' encounter with, and indirect killing of, the Sphinx may be regarded as a matricidal repetition of his previous killing of his father. Matricide is inextricably linked to the consummation of incest with his mother. But Oedipus has a propensity for murder borne of hate and rage, embodied in the preoedipal mother–infant relationship and consolidated in oedipal conflict and fantasy. The angry, hot tempered youth who kills all but one of those in the chariot which had run over his foot must have been reminded of the infantile injury to his foot. Despite the warning of the oracle, he kills a man old enough to be his father. The murder of his father derives from and condenses the earlier rage of his infancy against the mother who was "so hard" that she might have left him to die, to be abandoned, or perchance to be adopted. It is the earlier injuries to her son which also paved the way for the guilt and self-destruction of Jocasta. Son and mother are blind to the fact that Oedipus is the age of her son and that she is the age of his mother. Oedipus is compelled to attain self-knowledge and to discover his own identity and impulses. Jocasta overlooked his swollen, scarred feet, his "birthmarks." She defended against recognition, knowing exactly how her child's feet were mutilated after his birth. She had to have known her own son, and yet she is a mother who does not know who her child is, despite physical knowing and possession. She bears the guilt of incest superimposed on the earlier guilt of the postpartum mother with infanticidal impulses. Oedipus confronts the filicidal mother who destroys her children, first in the Sphinx, again in Jocasta. (As in actual cases of sexual abuse of children, it is the parents who are primarily culpable even though the child inevitably blames him- or herself and takes on the guilt of the parents. This, of course, does not mean that the child is not responsible for his own sexual and aggressive impulses. The abused child's drives and dependency, however, have been exploited by pathological, abusive parents.)

In the oedipal myth and Greek drama, at a much earlier period of civilization, the unconscious conflicts are much more overt and less disguised than in the Elizabethan dramas of Shakespeare or, even later, in the novels of Doesoevsky and of our time. What is also striking in the earlier drama is that the oedipal wishes break through repression and are enacted. The very enactment of incest and parenticide appears to be closely connected with the traumatic experience of Oedipus. Identifying with the aggressor, Oedipus inflicts and reenacts the traumatic experiences which are part of the history of so many individuals and of so many peoples. Oedipus is the universal man with the universal schematic Oedipus complex, distilled from the innumerable variations on universal unconscious themes. Yet the myth, which has psychological, social, and anthropological dimensions, points also to the importance of the intergenerational transmission of trauma.

The Delphic oracle, an omniscient mother with both dangerous and protective qualities, has warned Oedipus of the fate which awaits him. He leaves the home of his adoptive parents even though he has been taunted by a drunk that he is not the biological son of his assumed parents. Laïus has been cursed for his enactments, his descendants are cursed, foreshadowing repetitive acting out. The trauma of incest and infanticide, sexual and aggressive child abuse, is repeated through the generations in vicious cycles associated with shame, guilt, punishment, and self-punishment. The generations are also conflated and confused, and "sisters give birth to each other." The boundaries between the generations are breached, as is the recognition of reality and morality which regulates the intergenerational relationships

(Chasseguet-Smirgel, 1984). In the cycles of such unremitting conflict of and through the generations, Oedipus has to solve the great riddle of being unconsciously bisexual and bigenerational. This can only be done with insight into his negative matricidal Oedipus complex as well as his positive parricidal complex. Oedipus must be able to confront ultimately the horror of murderous impulses against his mother and his father, coupled with homosexual love of his father and the fear of his own femininity. His oedipal development has been influenced by his preoedipal rage against the preoedipal mother. He must also confront the infanticidal mother who destroys her own offspring. The Sphinx and Jocasta, mothers who acted on wishes for their children's death, kill themselves. There are many legends and novels that deal with child murder. Medea and Andromeda are mothers who are overtly murderous, in addition to the wicked witches and evil stepmothers who "merit" their own murder. A fuller explanation of the transmission of intergenerational trauma would take into account the interweaving of the Oedipus myth with other myths, such as that of Tantalus (Bergmann, 1992).

Devereux (1953) considered the murderous wishes of parents toward children and introduced the concept of the "Laïus complex" and the "Jocasta complex." There is an important constellation of filicidal attitudes in the Laïus complex (Ross, 1982), and the father's hostility antedates and intensifies the son's oedipal conflicts. Yet, it is the infantile conflicts of the father which are activated in his antagonistic relationship with his son. The jealousy that many fathers feel toward their sons for the mother's (wife's) love is a reactivation of the oedipal and preoedipal conflicts of the father. The Laïus and Jocasta complexes are basically later editions of the parental Oedipus complex, and these conflicts are regressively reactivated in parenthood.

Side-by-side with maternal incestuous fantasy and behavior, the mother's hostility, rivalry, and envy of her child have very important developmental consequences. Oedipus had reason to fear and hate his mother because of her collusion in his infantile abandonment and castrating mutilation, her destructive seduction, and her failure to set limits for herself and her son. Latent matricidal feelings of Oedipus are displaced onto the Sphinx and are more deeply repressed than his parricidal hostility or cravings for parental love (Kanzer, 1948). Parenthetically, the deeper repression of matricidal fantasy probably colored Freud's self-analysis and his analysis of the Oedipus myth. Freud's smoking addiction, his travel phobia, his separation and death anxiety, and his discomfort with fantasies of oceanic reunion all point to his preoedipal fears of separation and merger. One may conjecture unconscious rage and destructive impulses toward his bereaved mother who had lost her baby, his brother, and then produced one sibling rival after another, may have been split off from the primary love object and displaced onto nursemaids. Hostility toward the mother was displaced onto the father (Blum, 1996).

Case Illustration

Conflict over matricidal fantasies of great clinical significance gradually became evident in the case of Mr. S, a merchant with overt bisexual fantasies. Massive defenses were employed to protect the maternal object and the self from murderous impulses. Mr. S sought treatment because of feelings of anxiety and depression. He was seemingly content in his marriage and business and enjoyed his child. He wanted help in dealing with his own dissatisfactions, as well as to relieve the pressure from his wife to be more assertive. Mr. S's conscious goals were the improvement of his marriage, greater self-assertiveness, less inhibition of aggression, and assurance of impulse control. The recommendation for analysis was accepted with outer passive compliance.

Mr. S gradually revealed that although he loved his wife, his fantasy life was predominantly homosexual. He had had some homosexual experiences during adolescence, but he had never had any homosexual contact after college and his marriage. He thought of himself as a kindly and caring person who generally got along well with people superficially. He did not wish to harm his marital, social, or business relationships. He passively avoided angry confrontation and was timid, distant, and uninvolved. When challenged, he would withdraw into sullen silence or attempts at appeasement. This was also initially true in the analytic relationship. In the transference, the analyst was initially an idealized parent, approving, tolerant, protective, and empathic, so very different from his chronically complaining, self-centered mother and distant, workaholic father.

He secretly masturbated, usually with homosexual fantasy, occasionally augmented by pictures of nude male youths. He had not been "one of the guys," had not sought competitive sports, and had not shared his contemporaries' impassioned heterosexual adolescent pursuits. Yet he was not effeminate and did not care for girls' clothes, games, and interests. Living a heterosexual life, he was also attracted to youthful males with just the right color hair and what he fantasied as the "perfect penis." The penis was almost given the characteristics of a person; the youth's general features were not very important, provided that the genitals were not small or deformed. His own penis was regarded as defective, even though it was anatomically and functionally normal. He could satisfy both himself and his wife in their sexual relationship.

The determinants of Mr. S's conscious bisexuality choice are very complex, and I shall only emphasize what is relevant to this presentation. He was probably constitutionally endowed with tendencies toward passivity. His sense of defect was related to his primary identification with his long-suffering mother. His hatred of his mother was partially consequent to her withdrawal and her angry, self-centered preoccupation. Identifying with his mother as aggressor contributed to his adoption of profound passive–aggressive attitudes. His mother's behavior was characterized by excessive distance and emotional withdrawal, as well as seductive behavior. His father did not offer a buffering or supportive relationship vis-à-vis his mother and was insufficiently present as an alternate love object. Relative parental neglect and detachment had led him to feel almost like a waif or an orphan. In analysis, he slowly recognized his narcissistic investment in his own thoughts, feelings, and body and particularly in his own genitals. Profoundly disappointed in his cravings for maternal love, he loved the idealized youthful representation of himself as he wished his mother loved him (Freud, 1910). However, this was also a defensive, regressive retreat from his incestuous attachment to his mother. He wanted to penetrate and possess her and was simultaneously afraid of her seductively dominating and castrating him. To defend against castration, he fantasied a phallic mother but also retained an unconscious fantasy of the dangerous, faithless female. The bilateral detachment of mother and son was later paralleled by episodic detachment from his wife.

An underlying murderous rage against his wife was originally displaced from the mother–child conflict. As the analysis proceeded, the rage and hate behind his passivity emerged more clearly in his fantasy life. A fellatio fantasy conveying his frustrated wish for nurturance was followed by undisguised fantasies of explosive rage. He dreamt of atomic explosions destroying whole families, although he might also survive with his own child. He was the villain having murdered in his fantasy several members of a family. He had dreamt that he murdered the mother of a male friend to whom he had been homosexually attracted. He could unconsciously commit matricide and eliminate his own feminine self. He now fantasied eliminating his staff and his analyst. He would invite punishment and banishment for his forbidden wishes. Mr. S struggled against the recognition of his matricidal fantasy but increasingly recognized its origins in his childhood rage at his mother and wishes for her disappearance. It was much easier for him to think than to feel, to understand matricidal thoughts than to feel murderous rage and hatred toward his analyst-mother. His incestuous love was actually more superficial than his infantile hate. He was deeply guilty about his wishes to both unite with his mother and to destroy her. These fantasies were similar to those of Oedipus, both uniting with and destroying Jocasta and the Sphinx. Mr. S's fantasies were codetermined by superego development, but were also a source of shame, guilt, and self-denigration. His childhood pseudoindependence had been a struggle against these fearful wishes for both union and separation, based also upon an identification with his distant father. His oedipal victory over his distant father only increased the dangers with his mother.

Though Mr. S loved his wife consciously, to some extent his relationship had been an unconscious disguise and a facade of heterosexual normality. Marriage and parenthood denied and suppressed his unconscious matricidal and feminine wishes. These wishes were another source of his guilt toward his wife and his fear of maternal talion wrath. His destructive wishes toward his wife and child derived from the destructive wishes toward his mother and the sibling born after him. His oedipal love of his mother was infiltrated with hatefully murderous feelings so that he simultaneously destroyed her and identified with her, possessing and repairing her. He fantasied returning to the idealized, perfect parent with the perfect nurturing and reassuring breast-penis. The fantasy of living in a world devoid of women was, in part, a disguise for having eliminated his mother. In an inverted or negative oedipal compromise, he was jealous of rivals and turned to father figures and idealized self-objects. Furthermore, if he withdrew from women, he could defend against his horrifying incestuous and murderous impulses while protecting his separation and individuation. The homosexual fantasies thus defended against very deep-seated fears of destruction of the mother and of the self (Socarides, 1988). It provided magical power for dealing with an omnipotently dangerous narcissistic and incestuous object at the same time that his feminine identification threatened his manhood and self-esteem. He defended against murderous aggression toward both parents. In his case, however, he was particularly disturbed by the unconscious fantasy of matricide and the related unconscious maternal identification.

It is significant that Mr. S's jealousy and rage toward the mother figure was heightened after fatherhood. His unconscious jealous rage of his wife's attention to the infant reactivated his murderous rage against his mother and his siblings. Extraordinary ambivalence threatened object constancy, contributed to bisexual attachments and avoidance, and impeded oedipal conflict resolution.

Conclusion

Matricide is a universal fantasy, a core conflict in certain cases, although often more deeply repressed than other conflicts. Matricidal fantasy will emerge in analysis if there is sufficient development of negative maternal transference and attention to derivatives of matricidal fantasy in the patient's external life. Matricidal fantasy regularly appears in fairytales, plays, and nightmares of childhood. Because of the prolonged helplessness of the infant and dependence on maternal love, protection, and nurturance, defenses against matricidal impulses are particularly powerful. This may be one source of the idealization of motherhood, and such idealization culturally reinforces defenses against destructive impulses. Conversely, such impulses and defenses contribute to contemptuous denigration of women. In case of wife battering and assaults on pregnant women, matricidal urges are often thinly disguised. Wives are often particularly assaulted when they are pregnant, and in the Holocaust pregnant women were quickly selected for dual murder. Sometimes matricidal fantasies are displaced onto parricidal fantasies. The murder of the father is regarded as a macho conquest and a lesser evil than "mother" murder. The father is killed as a substitute for the mother, as an oedipal rival for her love and nurturance and as the father who failed to protect the child against the dangerous preoedipal mother.

Because of projection, introjection, and fluid primary identifications, a matricidal transference relationship may be particularly difficult to clarify and reconstruct. The splitting of representations protects the primary maternal love object from murderous urges. For a common example, the wife-mother is loved and the mother-in-law is hated. Protracted idealization may be punctuated by intermittent, hostile, destructive attitudes inside and/or outside the analytic transference relationship. The analysis of particularly negative maternal transference is never easy. Perhaps it surfaces more readily with female analysts. Whether countertransference problems are greater in an analyst of a particular gender or match is questionable because of universal bisexuality and variable capacities for analytic work (Blum and Blum, 1986). Daughters and sons, both, have deep-seated matricidal impulses. And ambivalence is part of all love relationships.

An analysis that reaches sufficient depth will inevitably encounter the forbidden fantasy of matricide and the complementary fantasy of maternal hatred and murder of the child. Matricide is a very important, often overlooked component of oedipal fantasy, fueled by preoedipal aggression and hate. The internalization of the prohibition of matricide contributes to the development of moral values and ego ideals, being essential to the child's socialization.

References

Anthony, E., & Benedek, T. (1970), *Parenthood.* Boston: Little Brown.

Bergmann, M. (1992), *In the Shadow of Moloch.* New York: Columbia University Press.

Blum, H. (1974), The borderline childhood of the Wolf Man. *J. Amer. Psychoanal. Assn.,* 22:721–742.

——— (1994), Paranoid betrayal and jealousy. In: *Paranoia: New Psychoanalytic Perspectives,* ed. J. Oldham & S. Bone. New York: International Universities Press, pp. 97–114.

——— (1996), The Irma dream: Self-analysis and self-supervision. *J. Amer. Psychoanal. Assn.,* 44:511–532.

——— Blum, E. (1986), Reflections on transference and countertransference in the treatment of women. In: *Between Analyst and Patient,* ed. H. Meyers. Hillsdale, NJ: Analytic Press, 1985, pp. 177–192.

Brunswick, R. Mack (1928), A supplement to Freud's "History of an infantile neurosis." In: *The Wolf-Man by the Wolf-Man,* ed. M. Gardiner. New York: Basic Books, 1971, pp. 263–307.

Chasseguet-Smirgel, J. (1984), *Creativity and Perversion.* New York: Norton.

Devereux, G. (1953), Why Oedipus killed Laius. *Internat. J. Psychoanal.,* 34:132–141.

Florance, E. (1955), The neurosis of Raskolnikov: A study of incest and murder. *Arch. Crisn. Psychodynamics,* 1:344–396.

Freud, S. (1900), The Interpretation of Dreams. *Standard Edition,* 4 & 5. London: Hogarth Press, 1953.

——— (1905), Fragment of an Analysis of a Case of Hysteria. *Standard Edition,* 7:1–122. London: Hogarth Press, 1953.

——— (1909), Notes upon a case of obsessional neurosis. *Standard Edition,* 10:151–249. London: Hogarth Press, 1955.

——— (1910), Leonardo Da Vinci and a Memory of His Childhood. *Standard Edition,* 11:58–137. London: Hogarth Press, 1957.

——— (1913), Totem and Taboo. *Standard Edition,* 13:1–161. London: Hogarth Press, 1955.

——— (1922), Dreams and telepathy. *Standard Edition,* 18:195–220. London: Hogarth Press, 1955.

——— (1923), The Ego and the Id. *Standard Edition,* 19:1–59. London: Hogarth Press, 1961.

——— (1928), Dostoevsky and parricide. *Standard Edition,* 21:173–194. London: Hogarth Press, 1961.

——— (1933), New Introductory Lectures on Psycho-Analysis. *Standard Edition,* 22:1–182. London: Hogarth Press, 1964.

——— (1939), Moses and Monotheism. *Standard Edition,* 23:1–137. London: Hogarth Press, 1964.

Green, A. (1975), Orestes and Oedipus. *Internat. Rev. Psychoanal.,* 2:355–366.

Kanzer, M. (1948), Dostoevsky's matricidal impulses. *Psychoanal. Rev.,* 35:115–125.

Kernberg, O. (1975), *Borderline Conditions and Pathological Narcissism.* New York: Aronson.

Klein, M. (1946), Notes on some schizoid mechanisms. *Internat. J. Psycho-Anal.,* 21:125–153.

Kohut, H. (1968), The psychoanalytic treatment of narcissistic personality disorders: Outline of a systematic approach. *The Psychoanalytic Study of the Child,* 23:86–113. New York: International Universities Press.

Lower, R. (1969), On Raskolnikov's dreams in Dostoevsky's Crime and Punishment. *J. Amer. Psychoanal. Assn.,* 17:728–742.

Mahler, M., Pine, F., & Bergman, A. (1975), *The Psychological Birth of the Human Infant.* New York: Basic Books.

Marinov, V. (1990), *Figures du crime chez Dostoievski.* Paris: Presses Universitaires de France.

Rangell, L. (1982), Transference to theory. *Ann. Psychoanal.,* 10:29–56.

Rascovsky, A., & Rascovsky, M. (1968), On the genesis of acting out and psychopathic behavior in Sophocles' Oedipus: Notes on filicide. In: *The Oedipus Papers,* ed. G. Pollock & J. Ross. New York: International Universities Press, 1988, pp. 169–178.

Reik, T. (1920), Oedipus and the Sphinx. In: *Dogma and Compulsion: Psychoanalytic Studies of Religion and Myth.* New York: International Universities Press, 1951, pp. 289–332.

Rosner, H. (1977), Oedipus and his cradle scars. In: *The Oedipus Papers,* ed. G. Pollock & J. Ross. New York: International Universities Press, 1988, pp. 203–222.

Ross, J. (1982), Oedipus revisited: Laius and the "Laius complex." *The Psychoanalytic Study of the Child,* 37:169–200. New Haven, CT: Yale University Press.

Socarides, C. (1988), *The Preoedipal Origin and Psychoanalytic Therapy of Sexual Perversions.* New York: International Universities Press.

Sophocles, *The Oedipus Cycle,* trans. D. Fitts & R. Fitzgerald. New York: Harcourt, Brace & World, 1969.

Weil, A. (1956), Some evidences of deviational development in infancy and early childhood. *The Psychoanalytic Study of the Child,* 8:271–287. New York: International Universities Press.

12

The Oedipus Complex as a Lifelong Developmental Process: A Psychoanalytic Reading of Sophocles' Trachiniae

MICHAEL PARSONS, M.D.

This work has three aims: to discuss something theoretically and clinically important to do with oedipal relationships; to understand more deeply one of the tragedies of Sophocles; to show that the distinction between psychoanalysis proper and applied psychoanalysis is not at all a clear one, and that if we take less notice of it we may liberate and enrich our thinking.

The End-Point of the Oedipus Complex

Freud (1924) wrote a paper which he called *Der Untergang des Oedipuscomplexes.* Strachey's footnote (Freud, 1924, p. 173) on

Acknowledgment. Easterling's edition of *Trachiniae,* although specifically referred to only once, has been invaluable to me throughout this paper. Quotations are from the translation by Jameson (1957) in THE COMPLETE GREEK TRAGEDIES, edited by Grene & Lattimore and reprinted with permission of The University of Chicago Press.

the translation of this title as "The Dissolution of the Oedipus Complex" debates whether "dissolution" is too strong a word, but notes also that in *The Ego and the Id* (1923) Freud had written of the "demolition" of the Oedipus complex. In the 1924 paper itself, Freud speaks unequivocally of the "destruction" and "abolition" of the complex. This occurs, he says, under the threat of castration, as a result of which "The object cathexes are given up and replaced by identifications" (p. 176). That is to say, the infant (male, for present purposes) gives up the desire for certain relationships, a sexual one with his mother and one of superiority to his father, and replaces this by internalizing the too powerful father and identifying with him and his prohibition of incest. This theory is classical and familiar, of course; what I want to underline is that, according to it, oedipal striving and conflict disappears as the desire for oedipal relationships is given up.

Puberty needs a mention as being a stage, after the Oedipus complex is supposed to have dissolved, which can restimulate, as part of normal development, the fantasies of the oedipal period. Four years before "The Dissolution of the Oedipus Complex," Freud (1905, p. 226) added a footnote to this effect to the section on puberty in the *Three Essays on the Theory of Sexuality*. But this is an extension of the same developmental task, still linked to a particular developmental stage. Once puberty is safely negotiated, conflict based on the oedipal triangle should, as described above, be over and done with.

Elements of the Oedipus complex may persist into adult life, and possibly do so to some extent in everyone. But its failure to dissolve in the normal way is, according to Freud, the most important element in neurosis. The more that oedipal elements persist into adulthood, the more vulnerable that person is to neurotic pathology, because what should have been left behind for good has not been.

Kleinian views of the Oedipus complex (Britton, Feldman, and O'Shaughnessy, 1989) differ significantly from Freud's, but it is still seen as a developmental phase which should arrive at a successful conclusion. That successful conclusion involves the child's becoming able to sustain the idea of the parents as two individuals who engage in a happy and creative intercourse from which he is excluded. For this to happen, primitive anxieties of the paranoid–schizoid position have to be overcome. These anxieties may turn either or both parents into dangerous, destructive objects. They may produce the fantasy of a combined parental object, which serves to deny the notion of intercourse between two separate people. If intercourse does get seen as something good, exclusion from it may be unbearable, so the parental intercourse has to become an object of attack. As these fantasies and anxieties are worked through, however, and the depressive position is reached, the exclusion becomes bearable and the parental intercourse can become something to be grateful for. Temporary regressions are always possible, but overall this position becomes stable and consolidated.

Trachiniae and Oedipus

I offer now a reading of Sophocles' tragedy *Trachiniae,* to show that this is an incomplete account of the place of oedipal relationships and conflict in human life. The vicissitudes of normal adult life do involve object relationships based on the oedipal triangle, and involve us in the conflicts of that triangularity. It is wrong to think of such oedipally charged object relationships as being superseded and left behind in childhood. Furthermore, puberty is not just a postscript. Adult life continues to have its developmental landmarks, which provoke their own specific forms of conflict based on the oedipal triangle. Handling our oedipal conflicts is, in fact, a lifelong developmental task and a continuing part of progress toward a fulfilling old age.

Analysts regularly use psychoanalytic ideas to try and understand literature better. But this encounter with a 2500-year-old play forcibly illustrates that the traffic goes in both directions. If we approach a work of literature with respect, meeting it on its own terms, and attending to the details of what the author wrote, we do not just understand the work better, but it can shed new light for us on our own psychoanalytic ideas.

Of the seven surviving tragedies by Sophocles, *Trachiniae* or *The Women of Trachis* is probably the least known and studied. Its themes and dramatic construction are rather baffling. There is a mysterious quality to it. It is hard to see why it is put together in the way it is. It gives a sense of something unknown going on, not only in the characters but in the mind of the author as well.

The play deals with the return home of Heracles and his death when his wife Deianira gives him the robe to wear which she has poisoned with the blood of the centaur Nessus. Heracles was one of the great heroes and his story was well known. But he usually appeared on the stage as a comic figure, and the theme of this play is sufficiently out-of-the-way for tragedy for us to wonder what it was that moved Sophocles to write about it.

Despite what psychoanalysts might think, Sophocles did not write *Oedipus Tyrannus* in order to illustrate the Oedipus complex, but because the theme aroused an intense artistic response in him. If this theme meant so much to him as a dramatist, we might expect it to appear elsewhere in his work. It does turn out to play an important part in the *Trachiniae,* and other parallels between *Oedipus Tyrannus* and *Trachiniae* are worth noting too. Both deal with the shift from ignorance to knowledge, brought about by the gradual but relentless revelation of an oracle's real meaning. As a result a great leader of his people is ruined and his wife commits suicide. Some of the apparent difficulties in the *Trachiniae* do become clearer when we see that Sophocles is again pursuing themes we have come to call "oedipal," but from a particular angle specific to this play.

Summary of the Play

The action takes place in front of the house in Trachis of Heracles and his wife Deianira. In the prologue, Deianira describes her marriage to Heracles. He defeated her other suitor, the river god Achelous, whom she describes in monstrous, inhuman terms. Heracles, the son of Zeus and a mortal woman, Alcmena, is constantly absent on his labors. He has now been away for fifteen months and nobody knows where he is. The nurse suggests sending Hyllus, the son of Deianira and Heracles, to look for him; but Hyllus turns out to have just heard that he is in Euboea, campaigning against the city of Oechalia, ruled by Eurytus. Deianira is startled; Heracles left her a prophecy about Oechalia that he would either die there or spend the rest of his life in peace.

The Chorus enters. They are young women of Trachis (hence the name of the play; Greek tragedies regularly taking their title from the identity of the Chorus). They comfort Deianira in her worry about Heracles' long absence and encourage her to be optimistic.

A messenger arrives with the news that Heracles is alive and victorious, followed by the herald Lichas escorting a group of captive women. Lichas explains the events of Heracles' absence. He was humiliated in an argument with Eurytus and killed Eurytus' son Iphitus in revenge. He spent a period in slavery to the Lydian Queen Omphale to expiate this and then came back to sack Eurytus' city, Oechalia. This is the expedition he is now returning from. Deianira notices a particularly beautiful and dignified woman among the captives. Lichas is evasive when she inquires about her identity.

When Lichas and the captives go indoors, the messenger tells Deianira that Lichas has been lying. The true reason for Heracles' conquest of Oechalia was not revenge. He has fallen in love with Eurytus' daughter Iole and Eurytus refused to give her to him. That is why he sacked the city and, sure enough, the captive woman whom Deianira had noticed is Iole herself whom Heracles is bringing home, not as a slave, but to be his new wife. Lichas reappears and, when confronted, confirms that this is the truth.

Deianira says she has a love-charm to use on Heracles. On the day of her wedding the centaur Nessus made a sexual assault on her while ferrying her across a river. Heracles shot him with an arrow dipped in the bile of the Hydra. The dying Nessus told Deianira that his blood, mixed with the Hydra's poison, would act as a love charm to stop Heracles ever desiring another woman more than her. She asks the chorus's advice and with some misgiving decides to use the magic. She gives Lichas a robe, dipped in the Centaur's blood, for Heracles to wear when he makes his sacrifice of thanksgiving for victory.

Deianira then finds that the wool which she used to smear the charm onto Heracles' robe, once exposed to the sun, has shrivelled up and crumbled to dust. Perhaps the charm is actually a poison. She asks herself why, after all, the centaur who was dying because of her should have shown her a kindness. She says that if she is responsible for the poison that killed Nessus also killing

Heracles, she will die too. Hyllus now arrives and tells how the robe, in the heat of the sacrificial fire, fastened itself around Heracles and began eating into his flesh. He attacks Deianira with furious hatred, denouncing her for murdering his father. She goes silently into the house.

The Chorus now understands the prophecy; it is death which brings Heracles rest from his labors. They lament Deianira's mistake and sympathize with her anguish. All this, they say, is the work of Aphrodite.

The Nurse comes out and decribes how Deianira, distraught, rushed through the house, finally stabbing herself with a sword on her marriage bed. Hyllus, learning that his mother had sent Heracles the poison unwittingly, is consumed with guilt at having driven her to suicide, and the Nurse describes him embracing his mother's body in passionate grief.

Now Heracles is borne in on a litter. He has spasms of unbearable pain. He asks Hyllus to end his suffering by killing him and wishes death for Deianira who did this to him. He demands that Hyllus bring her to him so that he can kill her in revenge. Hyllus tells him she has killed herself already and explains that she thought Nessus' blood was a love charm. Heracles sees that another prophecy has been fulfilled; Zeus had told him he could only be killed by someone who was already dead, and this is what Nessus has done. He makes Hyllus swear to fulfill his final commands. The first is to build a funeral pyre and burn him on it. His second command is that Hyllus should marry Iole. Hyllus is horrified at both commands, but consents. The funeral procession departs.

The Chorus closes the play saying that among all these terrible happenings "there is nothing which is not Zeus."

Structure and Characters of the Play

The focus of the play is the relationship between Deianira and Heracles. The action springs from conflicts within that relationship and Deianira's attempt to repair it: a tragically mistaken attempt which leads to the deaths of both of them. It is remarkable, then, that these two characters, whose relationship is the central issue of the play, never meet on stage. This has sometimes been seen as a dramatic fault, a weakness in the play; but that is surely a mistake. The overwhelming sense of the effect these two people have on each other binds the play together. The tragic unpredictability of human fortune, and the significance of the past and its effect in the present, give the play a thematic consistency which highlights the two chief characters' failure to meet each other and makes it powerfully dramatic.

The most important link between them, however, and the most important element in binding the two parts of the play together, is their son Hyllus. He is the person who plays an essential role in both parts of it by his relationship, first, to his mother and then to his father. Moreover his relation to each is about the other. In the first part his relation to his mother revolves around his absent father; and in the second part his relation to his father is concerned with his dead mother's guilt or innocence.

So although the play is undoubtedly the story of a conflictual relationship between two people, its structure ensures that this two-person relationship can only be seen in the context of a triangular relationship which embraces it. We shall see, moreover, that there is a set of triangular relationships, evident or implied, which runs through the play. The play shows that, powerful and dominant as a two-person sexual relationship may appear to be, it can only be understood or properly worked out by the lovers themselves in terms of triangular relationships between the generations.

Deianira strongly arouses our sympathy, while Heracles is a thoroughly unsympathetic character. We hear throughout the play of his greatness and his victories—and the Greeks did, indeed, celebrate him as the greatest of their legendary heroes. But the raw physicality with which Sophocles imbues these references makes us see Heracles as a man whose life revolved around violence. He is a brutal character. In the first description the audience gets of Heracles while we are actually looking at him, he is referred to as "savage-minded" (line 975). We see what this means when he demands that Hyllus shall bring Deianira, whom he does not yet know is dead, to him so that he can kill her with his own hands (line 1109). Heracles cruelly insists that Hyllus personally force his mother out of the house, so he can see whether Hyllus is more pained by his father's agony or by watching his mother be killed (lines 1066–1069). When Hyllus finally manages to tell Heracles that Deianira was trying to put a love charm on him because of Iole, and has committed suicide out of grief and guilt, Heracles makes no comment on this. There is no word of sorrow, no compassion or forgiveness for Deianira. He makes no further reference to her at all, but goes on about his own death and the prophesy about it which has now become clear. His callous egocentricity stands out. When he emphasizes the savage, violent, unapproachable natures of the monsters he has killed (lines 1090ff.) we cannot help thinking that although he is their enemy and has made the country safe from them, his nature is the same as theirs. The Chorus remembers his victory over Achelous in terms which minimize any difference between them, and the savagery which they share is contrasted with the gentle nature of Deianira.

> Then there was thudding of fists and clang of bows
> and confusion of bulls' horns;
> and there was contorted grappling,
> and there were deadly blows from butting heads
> and groaning on both sides.
> But the tender girl with the lovely eyes sat far from them on a hillside,
> waiting for the one who would be her husband.
> So the struggle raged, as I have told it:
> but the bride over whom they fought
> awaited the end pitiably [lines 517–528].

Deianira is horrified by Achelous and wants Heracles to win and save her from him. But she seems frightened of the violence of whichever suitor will win and claim her. This passage echoes Deianira's description of herself, while awaiting the outcome of the fight, as "stricken with fear lest her beauty should bring pain to her" (line 25).

This emphasis on the savagery of Heracles goes unmitigated. By the end of the play there is still no sign of any moral shift in him or development of his character. As we have seen, his attitude to Deianira does not change. When he gives Hyllus instructions about the funeral pyre on Mt. Oeta and his marriage to Iole there is no explanation, no indication that this comes from some new understanding that Heracles has arrived at. There is no Aeschylean *"pathei mathos,"* no learning through suffering. Moreover, Sophocles did have the option of ennobling Heracles at the end, because the popular myth was that Zeus lifted him up from the blazing pyre to live on Olympus with Hebe as his bride. Sophocles mentions this story in another of his plays, the *Philoctetes* (lines 727–729). So the reference to some kind of transformation in Heracles' nature was there for the making, and Sophocles' avoidance of it must be deliberate.

Aggression and Sexuality

One theme of the play, then, is the interaction between two aspects of mankind; the untamed primitive savagery which Heracles embodies, and the ordered culture and civilized sensibility represented by Deianira. Freud viewed civilization as being in constant tension with the archaic force of the drives, trying to put their power to constructive use at the same time as finding the constraints needed to control their potential for damage. We can see Deianira's hope of containing the raw ferocity of Heracles, which is like a force of nature, within the restraints of domestic life, as a clear reflection of exactly this struggle. That Heracles' essential nature remains unchanged to the end corresponds to the fact that the drives themselves cannot be modified. All we can do is strive for the best kinds of sublimation, defense, or compromise formation so that they become constructive not destructive. This is what Deianira, like all of us, is trying to do; but her own unconscious savagery gets the upper hand and brings about the tragedy.

Sexuality, above all, is the arena where this struggle is played out. And however else we may understand this play, there is no doubt that it is a tragedy of sexual passion. When Deianira leaves the stage to kill herself, the Chorus says of the catastrophe that it is the work of Aphrodite (lines 860–861). The Chorus says specifically that Achelous and Heracles fought because of sexual desire for Deianira and Aphrodite was both referee and victor of the contest (lines 497, 514–516). It is as Heracles' sexual partner that Deianira fears Iole will replace her. She says the two of them will be under the same blanket awaiting Heracles' embrace (lines 539–540). She may retain the status of wife, but she fears Heracles will be called "the younger woman's man" (lines 550–551). And when she prepares to kill herself, her language is full of sexual connotations (lines 920–922).

So the action of the play is driven by sex. But Deianira's desire for Heracles is not straightforward. Nessus' story about his poisoned blood being a love charm is, given the situation, so implausible that the audience must wonder why on earth she believed him. When the wool has shrivelled, but the deadly gift is already on its way, she herself asks,

From what possible motive, in return for what,
could the dying beast have shown me kindness, when he
was dying because of me? No, he beguiled me,
only to destroy the man who shot him. But I
have come to understand now when it is too late [lines 707–711].

Some such awareness was trying to express itself in the form of anxiety before she sent the robe. She asked the Chorus if they think she is acting rashly; if so she will stop (lines 586–587). But the Chorus is typically noncommittal and she goes ahead. Her act in sending Heracles the robe contains both her love for him and her hostility towards him. She was too reasonable in trying to deny her rage and hostility, saying there is no point in fighting against Love:

For he rules even the gods as he pleases, and
he rules me—why not another woman like me?
You see that I would be altogether mad
to blame my husband because he suffers from this sickness,
or that woman. She has been guilty of nothing shameful,
and she has done no harm to me [lines 443–448].

Just now I mentioned Deianira's unconscious savagery. If she had been more conscious of the conflict between love and fury in her feelings towards Heracles, she might have avoided acting out the unconscious murderous impulse.

These conflicted feelings, however, are not simply because of Heracles' relationship with Iole. There are plenty of indications in the play that sexuality is problematical in itself. Just after speaking with such acceptance, in the passage I quoted, Deianira refers to Heracles' feelings for Iole as a *nosos,* a sickness (line 445). This reference becomes more and more important as the play goes on. When Hyllus describes Heracles' agony in the robe, he refers to him as *tou men nosountos,* "having a *nosos*" (line 784). The Chorus takes up the word, saying Heracles has *nosos* spread throughout him (line 852). When the Nurse tells of Deianira's death, the Chorus asks what *nosos* killed her (line 882). When Heracles is on stage, *nosos* is used several times for his condition (lines 981, 1013, 1115), most notably by Heracles himself in his final words (line 1260). His physical *nosos* reflects the emotional *nosos* which brought it about. At the onset of Heracles' agony, Hyllus says his reaction was to curse Deianira's *dyspareunon lectron* (line 791), "her bed with its evil intercourse." Heracles at that moment was not cursing her jealous revenge but the nature of their sexuality together.

Deianira's words at the beginning of the play, when she sets the scene by telling how she married Heracles, are very interesting. She says that she experienced *nymphion oknon algiston* (lines 7–8), "the most agonizing fear of marriage," more so than any other of the women where she lived. *Algistos,* which Sophocles uses to describe her fearfulness, has the specific meaning of "painful." It can refer to physical or mental pain, but fear of what will happen to her body cannot be absent from her use of the word in this context. Her fear was of Achelous, because of his monstrous appearances as a bull, a serpent, and a man with a bull's face from which torrents of water pour forth. The phallic imagery in this, of course, is striking. She prayed for death rather than have to be his sexual partner, and she was full of relief that Heracles won her instead. We have already noticed the similarities, though, between Heracles and Achelous, and that Deianira seems terrified of the contest as a whole. Sophocles has her speak quite clearly of her fear of marriage in general before she goes on to explain about Achelous; and when she says that Heracles' victory was a good outcome she immediately adds "Or was it?" (line 27).

In fact this exclamation beautifully highlights the conflict that sexuality arouses in her. So far we have been shown her fear of its primitive, uncontrollable power. But what she means by "Or was it a good outcome?" is that since marrying Heracles she has had endless worry about him, and also for herself and their children, because he is always away and she does not know what is happening to him. She specifically says the fears come at night and it is being Heracles' bed partner that exposes her to them. But what she is talking about now is not fear of Heracles' sexuality, but fear of losing him. These themes are repeated after the Chorus enters, when Deianira addresses them pointedly as young, unmarried women. Being still virgins, she says, they cannot understand her nighttime concerns about her husband and children (lines 142–152). After her speech, the Messenger brings the news that Heracles is alive and victorious and the Chorus sings an ode of jubilation and thanksgiving. The language of this song, however, has a certain irony. The Chorus calls for cries of joy within the house because it is *mellonymphos* (line 207), "ready for marriage." The audience must suppose that this refers to the reunion of Heracles and Deianira. But the coming union of Heracles and Iole, which so far we have not heard about, is also being ironically foreshadowed. The element *nymph* in *mellonymphos* is, of course, the same root as in *nympheia,* the word Deianira used in telling of her agonizing fear of marriage. So the return of Heracles, which is something Deianira welcomes, also brings back to mind the primitive sexuality she is so afraid of. The Chorus gives thanks to Apollo and Dionysos and also, significantly, to Artemis and *geitonas te nymphas* (line 215), the "neighboring nymphs." *Nymphe* has the two meanings of "nature spirit" and "young bride," and here, of course, it means the former. But this comes only seven lines after *mellonymphos,* and to repeat the same word root, this time in conjunction with Artemis, the virgin goddess, must reemphasize the tension between virginity and sexuality.

A Set of Triangles

I have said that the structure of the play is unified by the figure of Hyllus, whose relationship to each of his parents is crucial. But the situation only allows him to relate to them separately; the bridge between them, which he could represent, fails. If the sexual relationship between Deianira and Heracles was to be successfully worked out, it needed to be seen not simply in two-person terms, but in a triangular context. It is this theme of triangularity in the play which I now want to explore.

The play opens with a mother and son at home together and the father absent. Sophocles makes the point deliberately, and implicitly underlines the importance of the missing father–son relationship. In her opening speech Deianira says (lines 31–35),

We have had children now, whom he sees at times,
like a farmer working an outlying field,
who sees it only when he sows and when he reaps.
This has been his life, that only brings him home
to send him out again, to serve some man or other.

The image of crops growing conveys vividly the growth and development of children and how Heracles has not been part of that for Hyllus. When the Chorus enters and encourages Deianira about Heracles' safety, they remember that he is the son of Zeus and say, optimistically, that Zeus would not be careless of his children (line 140).

This is the first of many references throughout the play emphasizing the father–son relationship between Zeus and Heracles. Coming so soon after Deianira's comment on Heracles' lack of involvement with his own son it has an ironic twist. We know that Zeus will not save his son but allow him to die in agony. Indeed, the play ends with the mysterious words, "There is nothing of this which is not Zeus" (line 1278). These references at the beginning to parent–child, and particularly father–son, relationships are setting out one of the main themes of the play.

Sophocles shows us the destructiveness that comes about when the various relationships and emotional tensions of the family triangle, mother-father-child, are not worked through. At the end of the play, in the midst of the tragedy, and for all Heracles' unchanging arrogance, I think Sophocles allows one bit of movement which shows us the direction that such working through would need to take.

We must not import our late twentieth-century ways of thinking into the play. The Greek husband and father, let alone the Greek legendary hero, was not meant to be a New Man, always at home to take the children to school and practicing for the Augean Stables by taking his turn at washing the dishes. We must stick to what is in the text, seen in terms of its own time. But the text that Sophocles wrote does show a concern with the same pattern of conflict in triangular family relationships that emerged so famously in *Oedipus Tyrannus*. And if this was a continuing preoccupation for him as a dramatist, it may be that, like Freud, Sophocles sensed its fundamental importance in human nature.

Hyllus has grown up with his mother, his father being effectively absent. The implications of this are not spelled out, but we have a clue to the sexualization it leads to between mother and son, and the destructiveness caused when that replaces the sexuality that should have been there between the parents. I have already mentioned that when Hyllus denounces his mother for murdering his father, he describes how Heracles cursed his and Deianira's sexuality together. When Hyllus implicitly agrees with Heracles, he is cursing his own parents' sexuality. When Deianira leaves the stage, he says with savage irony (lines 819–820),

And the delight
she gave my father, may she find the same herself.

When he finds his mother's dead body, however, he is stricken with grief and guilt, thinking he has driven her to suicide. Sophocles has the Nurse describe the way he embraces her body in terms that would suit a lover. He falls upon her lips and presses his side up against her side (lines 938–939). Sophocles word order, *pleurothen pleuran pareis,* brings their two bodies close up against each other. This is all the more striking given Deianira's last words, reported by the Nurse a few lines earlier. Before killing herself on her marriage bed she says,

O my bed, O my bridal chamber, farewell
now forever, for never again will you take me
to lie as a wife between these sheets of yours [lines 920–922].

Through this whole passage Sophocles gives Deianira a vocabulary with deliberately sexual overtones. The Greek words emphasize that it is specifically her intercourse with Heracles that she is saying goodbye to. And then a few lines later we have her son embracing her dead body on the marriage bed, like a lover.

The cumulative effect of these passages is to indicate that, if the parental intercourse is seen as destructive or is not happening at all, this lets it be replaced by a false sexualization of the mother–son relationship. In Hyllus' denunciation of Deianira, he makes much play of being a proper son to his father. In the first stanza of their ode immediately after Deianira's final exit, the Chorus sings of Heracles as Zeus' very own son, using the rare and emphatic word *autopais* (line 826). Hyllus, however, has no way of being a true son to his father. Heracles has not sustained a proper sexual relationship with his wife. By not being a husband in this way, he has not been a father either, because it means he has left his son exposed to the sexualization of his relationship with his mother. The only way offered to Hyllus to stand up for his father as a true son to him means cursing his mother and pushing her toward her suicide. That is the tragedy of his situation.

Deianira and Heracles could not sustain their side of a triangle. We have noted the indications of Deianira's conflicts over sex. Heracles' part in the failure is represented by his chronic absence and also, of course, his choice of Iole instead of Deianira. This is not simply a matter of preferring one woman to another. Deianira makes a point of the age difference between her and Iole (line 551), and it is important to recognize that Heracles has chosen a woman who belongs to his son's generation. When we think of oedipal conflict, we most commonly think of the upward conflict, the child's desire and jealousy directed toward its parents. But there is also the downward conflict which belongs to the parents. As children reach maturity, the father is jealous of his son and the mother of her daughter, and they may desire the women and the men who would be appropriate partners for their children, but no longer for themselves. These desires in the parents also represent, of course, their incestuous desires toward their own children of the opposite sex, which have to be given up. Just as the child has to give up its unrealizable desire for one parent and its jealousy of the other, so parents have the later developmental task of relinquishing to their children the desire that is now unrealizable, and giving up the jealousy of the son or daughter who *can* realize it. This is the only way for their sexuality to continue developing as they age with a new maturity of its own. The reason Heracles could not sustain the relationship with Deianira, keeping that side of the triangle alive and being the father Hyllus needed him to be, is that he could not give up his desire for a woman who belonged to his son's generation rather than his own.

In the Deianira–Heracles–Hyllus triangle, the failure of the Deianira–Heracles bond lets an inappropriate Deianira–Hyllus pairing develop, and prevents a normal father–son relationship. It means the bond between Heracles and Hyllus can only be a destructive one. This is particularly clear where Heracles makes the sadistic demand I have already drawn attention to, that Hyllus should bring his mother out and watch his father kill her. He prefaces this with,

> O my son, now truly be my true born son
> and pay no more respect to the name of mother [lines 1064–1065].

Being a true-born son has come to mean helping his father kill his mother.

Alongside this there is the Deianira–Heracles–Iole triangle. In this case the failure of the Deianira–Heracles pairing is linked to an inappropriate pairing between Heracles and Iole. Hyllus was not called on to give up his inappropriate oedipal attachment to his mother because his father did not play his proper role. This second triangle shows why. Heracles himself was unable to give up an inappropriate inverted oedipal attachment. Iole, being a generation younger, would be a suitable partner for his son, but Heracles refuses his proper bond with Deianira and insists on having Iole for himself.

The competitive element in this inverted oedipal conflict comes out in another triangle, one that is only implied in the play, but important for our theme. This is the Heracles–Iole–Iphitus triangle. When Lichas is giving Deianira his first version of why Heracles sacked Oechalia, he tells the story of how the enmity arose between Heracles and Eurytus, who had been friends (lines 262ff). Heracles was defeated in an archery contest by the sons of Eurytus. It was in revenge for this that Heracles killed Eurytus' son Iphitus, and attacked Oechalia. Then we learn the missing element in the story, which is Heracles' love for and abduction of Iole. Heracles had thus been faced with a couple in the younger generation: a brother–sister couple, the children of his friend. And his reaction is to kill the young man who is superior to him and steal the woman. We can read this as a displaced representation of an older man's jealousy of his own son and rivalrous desire for the younger woman. It is very clear at this point, as I indicated just now, that Iole represents someone who might have been his own daughter. This Heracles–Iole–Iphitus triangle is an exact reflection, upside down, of the son's desire to kill his father and marry his mother. The insistence of Heracles on having Iole for himself is driven by his wish to deny castration anxiety—not the castration anxiety of the small child, but the version of it which presents itself in later life.

Resolving (Or Not) the Inverted Oedipus Complex

In the long scene which ends the play there is a shift in the quality of the relationship between Heracles and Hyllus. This is related to developments within another triangle, this time between Heracles, Hyllus, and Iole. The theme of the father–son relationship is emphasized throughout the scene. While Heracles is still asleep the Old Man who brings him in has three lines telling Hyllus he must help his father, and his very first words are "O child of this man!" (line 1018). Hyllus replies in three exactly balanced lines, saying he will help Heracles but cannot release him from his pain, ending, "that is what Zeus ordains" (line 1022). The reference to Zeus as Heracles' father is clear. Heracles wakes up and his first words are, "My child!" (line 1022). In his agony, he impulsively begs Hyllus to kill him with his sword. Then comes his speech with the passage I have commented on, telling Hyllus, as a true-born son, to help in killing his mother. Hyllus explains his mother's mistake and Heracles understands the prophecy about his death at the hands of someone already dead.

At this point the shift begins. Heracles calls on Hyllus to follow the instructions he will give, and specifically invokes the father–son relationship (lines 1177–1178):

On your own, agree to act with me; discover
yourself the finest rule—obedience to your father.

When he makes Hyllus swear it is "by the head of Zeus who begot me" (line 1185), bringing the two father–son relationships into explicit apposition. The first thing he binds Hyllus to do is to see to his death on the funeral pyre, and take an active part in it. This is no longer, however, an impulsive wish born from the agony caused by "your godless mother" (lines 1034–1040). It has become a solemn ritual which Hyllus must perform with dignity and no tears "if you are my son" (line 1201). His second duty is to marry Iole.

Hyllus is naturally horrified by both demands; readers and commentators have likewise found them hard to interpret. But I think we can make some sense of them after all. The Heracles–Iole–Hyllus triangle is an undisplaced version of the Heracles–Iole–Iphitus triangle. In making Hyllus marry Iole, Heracles is restoring the natural situation. The father gives up his rivalry and acknowledges that the younger woman belongs to his son, not himself. The father who can do this, accepting the implications of his aging, would be able to go on developing the relationship with his wife and become a true father to his son. This exactly matches how the son, acknowledging that his mother does belong to his father, becomes free to find a woman of his own outside the family and develop a new relationship with his father based on that. Both father and son have to accept the way in which the son really is superseding his father. This is symbolized by Hyllus' participation in his father's death, specifically in his role as son, and by Heracles' declaration that Iole must belong to Hyllus instead of himself.

In view of all this, it is fascinating to note that one of the ancient commentators on the play quotes an obscure variant of the story which has Heracles asking Eurytus for Iole on Hyllus' behalf, not his own! (Easterling, 1982, p. 17).

None of this changes the fact that this play is a tragedy. Deianira is dead and Heracles is going to his death. Far from developing, that relationship has been destroyed. I am not giving the play some falsely optimistic, upbeat ending. Nor am I implying a moral development in the character of Heracles. His arrogant, unforgiving nature remains to the end. His compelling Hyllus to marry Iole *is* horrifying. It allows the young man no choices of his own and the nearest Heracles gets to giving a reason seems self-regarding and narcissistic:

No other man but you must ever
have her who has lain with me at my side [lines 1225–1226].

But this is not primarily a play about individual character. If it were, Sophocles would surely have given us a face-to-face confrontation between Deianira and Heracles instead of deliberately avoiding it. The characters are certainly there; but Sophocles can explore themes which permeate the play and which the language and the action express, without having to tie them too closely to individual personalities.

All Sexual Relationships are Triangular

It is clear by now that *Trachiniae* does show Sophocles' continuing interest in the theme that underlies *Oedipus Tyrannus,* but his exploration of it here is on a broader front. Every two-person sexual relationship implies triangular relationships as well, both up and down the generations. The conflicts these produce, and the understanding needed for their resolution, permeate the play and make it resonate for all of us.

The relevance of this for the psychoanalytic theory of the Oedipus complex is, I hope, equally clear. Of course the boy has to give up his desire to possess his mother, and the girl her father. The identifications which allow them to do this are formative elements in their psychic structure, and failure of this to happen leaves them psychologically vulnerable. All of that is true. The mistake is to think that this marks the completion of a developmental task, instead of the beginning of a lifelong process of dealing with the triangularity inherent in all sexual relationships.

Clinical Material

A supervisee reported the following from a session with a patient who is a single woman living alone with her 18-year-old son. The patient said her son had asked for a cigarette in a graceless sort of way. She had replied "Eighteen years old, and you still don't know how to ask for something so that you'll get it!" The tone showed that this was not a lesson in manners but distinctly flirtatious. She said that her son had then asked for a cigarette so nicely that she couldn't refuse him. The therapist said, "He seduced you!" The patient replied, "Yes he did, didn't he?" with obvious pleasure.

As well as the son's oedipal interaction with his mother, this episode shows the mother being caught up in an oedipal involvement of her own with her son. The lack of a husband and father, who should be the third point of a triangle, seems to be causing a problem not just for the son, but also for his mother in working through the oedipal situation.

In this connection, a colleague told me of a male patient who had been adopted. When, in his early twenties, he had sought out his biological mother, this developed into a sexual relationship between them. My colleague told me he had heard of other examples of the same situation, where the mother got caught up in a physical enactment of oedipal sexuality which there had been no opportunity for herself as well as for the son, to work through normally.

Finally, some material from a session with a patient in later life: He is a successful man, well respected in the financial world. He is married, for the second time, to a woman of about the same age as himself; he has a son from each marriage. This marriage has been, by and large, a happy one in spite of intermittent interest in other women. The sexual relationship with his wife is satisfying to both of them, but he sometimes feels it lacks a really deep level of fulfillment. He is liable to talk in a derogatory way about himself as an old man who is "past it" and cannot hope to have any sexual or creative drive left.

The analysis is well advanced and this material shows the patient becoming able to grapple with what the last scene, in particular, of *Trachiniae* refers to.

He was speaking about his sons. They have a rich network of relationships; one is successful in the business world and the other is doing well in his profession. His pleasure in them was obvious, but he was talking rather intensely, as though he needed to convince me of it. Then he mentioned a conference he is going to where he is not sure how his contribution will be received. He hoped he would impress the colleague, a woman, who had invited him. I picked up the worry about whether what he had to offer was really wanted and said that, alongside his pleasure in his sons' success, he might also feel competitive with them. He told me a colleague had recently asked him for some technical advice outside his own specialty. He had suddenly realized that one of his sons had better access to the necessary information than he did, and referred the colleague to his son. He told me this with a kind of rueful pride. Next he talked about the holiday he and his wife were planning, and then said again that he was nervous about the conference. The woman who has invited him is attractive, single, and some years younger than he. He had a sexual feeling about her but was quite clear that he did not want an affair with her. This left him confused about what it would be like between them. I said I thought he was trying to give up an automatic kind of sexuality, which again had an element of competitiveness with his sons. This was difficult, because giving that up meant recognizing that he could not compete with them, and he did not know what sort of sexual feeling of his own he would be left with. But it might be the only way to discover whatever feelings of a different sort were possible between him and his wife. This made him thoughtful and after a while he said, with some relief, that of course the woman had not invited him for a sexual adventure but for what he did have to offer, which was his expertise in what the conference was about.

The overall connection between this material and the themes of *Trachiniae* should be clear enough. But I want to focus on something about the woman at the conference. The patient is trying to sort out whether he sees her sexually as an alternative to his wife, and it would be easy to think in terms of a horizontal triangle of the two women and himself. But to analyze his confusion, what matters is a different triangle, a vertical one, which is not so obvious at first sight. This has himself at one point, his sons at another, and at the third a fantasized woman, the Iole character, whose role is to confirm that he is still as young and potent as ever he was. There was no connection in reality between his sons and the woman at the conference. But the unconscious, late-life, downward-directed oedipal fantasy was of winning out against his sons in rivalry for the affections of the Iole figure, whom the woman at the conference represents. Before he can properly develop his relationship with his own wife, that fantasy has to be given up. He needs to acknowledge, as he did recognize with the other colleague's request, that there is a woman whose needs are going to be met by his son and not himself.

Returning to the three aims I set out at the beginning: I hope I have provoked some fresh thinking about the Oedipus complex, and to have opened our eyes further to the riches of Sophocles. I also hope to have shown that what might look like a piece of applied psychoanalysis can be as practically relevant and helpful as any clinical paper.

References

Britton, R., Feldman, F., & O'Shaughnessy, E. (1989), *The Oedipus Complex Today: Clinical Implications.* London: Karnac Books.

Easterling, P. E., Ed. (1982), *Sophocles' Trachiniae.* Cambridge, U.K.: Cambridge University Press.

Freud, S. (1905), Three Essays on the Theory of Sexuality. *Standard Edition,* 7:123–243. London: Hogarth Press, 1953.

——— (1923), The Ego and the Id. *Standard Edition,* 19:1–59. London: Hogarth Press, 1961.

——— (1924), The dissolution of the Oedipus complex. *Standard Edition,* 19:171–179. London: Hogarth Press, 1961.

Sophocles, *The Women of Trachis,* trans. & intro., M. Jameson. Chicago: University of Chicago Press, 1957.

13

Prohibition and Transience

OSAMU KITAYAMA, M.D.

Transience in Sexuality

The Japanese word *Arigatou,* being almost equivalent to "thank you" in English, literally means "difficult to exist." This shows how important it is in Japan to appreciate the general difficulty of existence inherent in the transience of things. In everyday life, the concept of transience is symbolized by objects of nature, such as cherry blossoms, which are often associated with birth and death (Figure 13.1). The traditional *Ukiyoe* pictures show how a positive sense of transience develops into forms of popular entertainment such as flower arrangement, moon-viewing (Figure 13.2); and fireworks (Figure 13.3).

The word *Ukiyoe* means "picture of the floating world": *Uki* is "floating"; *yo* is "world," and *e* is "picture." Furthermore, the word *uki* ambiguously means "sorrowful," and the word *ukiyo* is equivalent to that of "transitory world." It is often said that the floating world exists phenomenologically between life and death; topographically between reality and fantasy.

Figure 13.1: Artist—Isoda Koryusai (New Otani Art Museum, Tokyo, Japan, Otani Collection)

Almost all physical excitement is transitory and the positive sense of transience is very important in determining adult sexual behavior, because sensual experiences involved in sexual play and

Figure 13.2: Artist—Utagawa Toyohiro (Museum of Fine Arts, Springfield, Illinois, Raymond A. Bidwell Collection)

intercourse are typically transient. I shall focus my discussion on the two areas of behavior for which the term *sexual* is used: the search for erotic pleasure, and the development of a relationship between sexual partners. On the whole, cultural factors and historical traditions have a role to play. Therefore, I would like to utilize cultural material from Japanese mythology and popular pictures in order to illustrate visually the capacity to appreciate the sense of transience and its development.

Freud taught us that parents have the greatest possible influence on their children's sexual development, that sexual desire and gratification have their origins in infancy, and that adult sexuality can be traced back to events that occur in infancy. In fact, sexual intercourse and a mother–infant relationship are two distinctive themes of *Ukiyoe* pictures. They sometimes show adult sexual intercourse superimposed on the mother–boy relationship (Figure 13.4). And the sense of transience as well as excitement have something in common in these pictures.

Figure 13.3: Artist—Kobayaski Kiyochika (Private Collection)

It is obvious to the viewer that the excitement illustrated in these pictures will fade away sooner or later. They are so theatrical and colorful that they give a certain feeling of unreality and the sense of an impending disillusionment.

Maternal Disillusioning

The concept of transience should be a product of maturation because it develops over time. So I am going to trace it back to the world of infancy.

Winnicott (1953, 1971) was keenly interested in the topographic question of psychic reality versus external reality. His idea of transitional objects and the intermediate area of experience not only challenges the dichotomy of inner and outer reality, but also asks us to tolerate the paradox and not to challenge whether it belongs to an inner or an outer reality. According to him, the ordinary devoted mother places the breast where and when the

Figure 13.4: Artist—Gofutei Sadatora (Kumon Publishing Co. Ltd., and Kumon Children's Research Institute, Osaka, Japan)

baby needs it. In this way, she permits the illusion that it is the baby's need which has created the breast. In addition, good enough mothering should also include well-dosed failure of need gratification, as illusion is almost always associated with an ensuing or concurrent process of disillusionment. I think that this dual nature of illusion, that is, illusion and the subsequent disillusionment, is what makes for the transitionality of transitional objects. Their transience serves mainly the function of representing both the presence and absence of the maternal object in a two-way process: not only "Fort/Da," which Freud (1920) saw in his grandson's game, but also "Da/Fort" (p. 15).

We know that the process of graduated disillusionment following illusion is necessary for normal development to occur. But do we know how such a process takes place? And what is the role of the mother in this process?

In order to answer these questions, I have surveyed some ten thousand *Ukiyoe* pictures, sorting out about two hundred, which show mother–infant interactions. Most of these pictures—woodcut prints—were produced about two hundred years ago, when scientific developmental psychology did not exist. In more than one-third of my sample mother and infant are pictured together sharing objects such as toys and fish, transitional objects in a broader sense. These pictures are, I think, interesting not only because of their bridging objects, but also because of their depicting joint attention from a point of view of developmental psychology (Bruner, 1975; see Figure 13.5). This repetitive pattern (Figure 13.6) of "viewing together" (Kitayama, 1995) or "parallel looking" (Freeman, 1995, personal communication) could be motivated by a strong urge for emotional ties, accompanied by separation anxiety.

The (transitional) object is put between mother and infant, acting as a bridge to both sides and being shared by both. This side-by-side sharing takes place mostly visually. The visually shared or bridging objects are pieces of candy, paper windmills, goldfish, and other small "floating" objects. Through this sharing, an illusory tie or a metaphorical bridge is created and sustained. It is usually mothers who share the objects with their children. But there are father figures as well (Figure 13.7), when the children in the pictures appear to be older, but then the objects may not be "floating."

In fact, some of the objects appear to be floating away in a distance (Figure 13.8). For example, fireflies both connect a

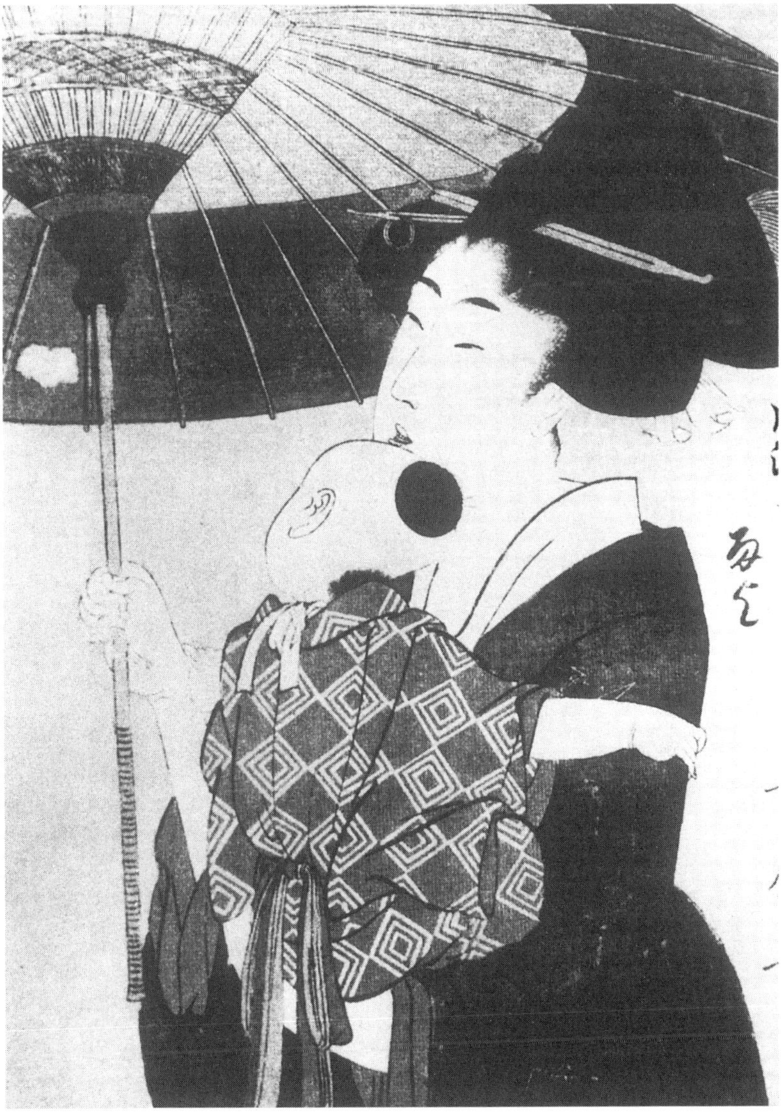

Figure 13.5: Artist—Kitagwa Utamaro (Musées royaux d'Art et d'Histoire, Brussels, Belgium)

mother figure and an infant and keep them apart by appearing and disappearing. There may be a moment of disillusionment from the illusory tie between them. In Figure 13.9 a mother and

Figure 13.6: Artist—Tamagawa Shucho (Kanagawa Prefectual Museum of Cultural History, Yokohama, Japan)

her boy are playing together with soap bubbles. Clearly the artist is illustrating the mother's role in disillusioning her child by putting between the two of them a space which is filled with bubbles whose existence is very momentary or transitory. At a closer look,

Figure 13.7: Artist—Ichikawa Kansai (Katsushika Hokusai Museum of Art, Tsuwano, Japan)

Figure 13.8: Artist—Utagawa Toyokuni (Kumon Publishing Co., Ltd., and Kumon Children's Research Institute, Osaka, Japan)

Figure 13.9: Artist—Suzuki Harunobu (Kimiko and Jhon Powers Collection, Carbondale, Illinois)

Figure 13.10: Artist—Isoda Koryusai (New Otani Art Museum, Tokyo, Japan, Otani Collection)

one can see the bubbles, just disappearing and leaving an empty space. This transitory process involves not only space; it is also experienced in terms of time. The snow rabbit in Figure 13.10 melts quietly within hours.

"She Died for Us"

Freeman (1995, personal communication)[1] once pointed out to me that I am using the two English concepts, "transition" and "transience," interchangeably. In fact, I use one Japanese word *utsuroi* to mean both concepts, "transition" and transience."

In the transitional process of disillusionment, the mother may be experienced as rejecting or betraying the child, something that is depressing and painful to the child. But the possibly traumatic consequences of such maternal disillusionment may not be readily observable, as a mother substitute may alleviate them (Kitayama, 1991, 1994).

In investigating Japanese myths and folktales, I have found a plot of marriage, of breaking a prohibition against *looking* and of disillusionment (Kitayama, 1985), which may portray the tragic outcome of a sexually determined relationship between a man and a woman. Most of the heroes in these myths show a marked incapacity to experience the ugly[2] mixture of the incompatible mother figures in the transitional passage from an undifferentiated to a separate state of being.

The main plot of this tragic story develops as follows:

1. Marriage: *Izanagi,* a paternal deity, and *Izanami,* a maternal deity, descended, to an island, where they gave birth to the islands as well as the deities of Japan.
2. Death of *Izanami:* She finally bore the fire deity, who, in the process of being born, burned *Izanami's* genitals, causing her to die.
3. Prohibition against *looking: Isanagi* followed her to the land of the dead, where he asked her to return. She replied, "Pray do not look at me."

[1]D. Freeman, making an analytical study of Japanese mythology, has pointed out that "Mythology can serve as the royal road to an understanding of the shared developmental experiences . . . common to members of a culture" (1981, p. 337).

[2]The word *ugly* appears in the story which follows the sentence. This indigestion of the Kleinian depressive object is discussed in my previous papers.

4. Breaking the prohibition: Her absence was so long that he impatiently followed her, only to see her corpse, riddled with maggots and roaring thunder deities, and he fled in fear.
5. Revenge: Ashamed and angry, she dispatched ugly females to attack him and also went after him herself.
6. Separation: In order to stop her, he sealed the pass to the land of the dead, and then he pronounced the fomula of divorce.

This myth, like other folktales, can be interpreted on various levels. On a sexual level, the prohibition against looking is intended to forbid the dependent person from seeing the painful death of his partner who died after giving birth to the land of the Japanese people.

Acute Disillusionment

One can find the same theme in many Japanese folktales. The typical plot of marriage, breaking a prohibition, and separation can be found in *The Crane Wife,* one of the most popular Japanese legends. An outline of this tragic tale follows:

1. A young man rescues an injured crane.
2. A beautiful woman visits him. They get married and live happily. She is highly productive and benevolent. For example, she is very good at weaving precious cloth. She looks thinner and becomes sick after working hard in response to his demands. In contrast, he becomes rich by selling the cloth she makes, and demands more from her.
3. She prohibits the hero from looking at her when she is weaving. He cannot, however, help but break the prohibition against *looking,* suddenly discovering that she is a wounded crane. She is wounded because she weaves cloth made out of her own feathers.
4. The young man is frightened; she feels ashamed, and then flies away (Figure 13.11). They separate in the end.

The symbolism of weaving in *The Crane Wife* is related to sexuality. Weaving used to be a requisite of becoming a wife and could be thought of as a part of female sexual and generative functions.

Figure 13.11 (From: *Tsuni No Ongaeshi* by Shinya Takahashi. Tokyo: Popurasha, 1991)

The Taboo to Be Broken in Time

The heroine visits spontaneously and falls in love with the male protagonist, who appears to be a passive, innocent man. She is

Figure 13.12 [From: *Tsuru No Ongaeshi* (Yaoshi: Mikih House, 1988)] by Daihachi Ohta.

very maternal, and as I have shown in previous publications (Kitayama, 1985, 1991, 1994, 1995) the hero can be seen as her "baby" attached to the maternal heroine.[3]

What is then the heroine's secret? What does the hero see there to be disillusioned? Of course, one has to take into consideration the principles of desexualization and overdetermination. The woman's secret is usually hidden from the readers of the tale, and her injury or death is rarely illustrated openly as in Figure 13.12. This should stimulate the imagination rather than fix ideas: usually myths and folktales are narrated without pictures. One may interpret the secret injury and bleeding, illustrated in this

[3]In Japan there are also many tales of marriage between a human wife and an animal-husband, which also end up in the wife's expelling the animal-husband. The animal-husband is usually described as a monkey, which the human wife rejects or tries to kill. Actually, in comparison with foreign tales of this type, there is a marked incidence of rejection of the animal spouse in Japanese tales. In Western tales like "The Princess and the Frog" and "Beauty and the Beast" the animal usually changes into a human in the end through the miracle or magic of love, by which the disgust toward unacceptable facts seems to be isolated.

picture, as "female castration," resulting in a serious difference between men and women. One has to remember that the maternal deity in the myth dies from having her genitals burned in childbirth. On another level, the injured crane-wife weaving precious cloth in the picture represents very figuratively a parturient mother with her legs spread wide apart giving birth to a baby who is injured in the middle (his genitals).[4] But one sees blood coming out from her chest as she is sacrificing her own feathers. This may signify "breastectomy" of the mother. Therefore, the secret disclosed in the end may be interpreted as the mother having been injured by her devotion to the hero, by her inexhaustible breast-feeding in response to his greedy demand.

In spite of its catastrophic consequences, the prohibition against *looking* is nearly always broken by the hero as the story develops. This maternal prohibition concerning a two-person relationship is a taboo "to be broken in time," as opposed to the oedipal incest taboo, the paternal prohibition in a triangular relationship, which is a prohibition "to be kept" (Kitayama, 1985). The maternal prohibition against looking becomes so relative as to be broken, while the incest taboo is absolute.[5]

Here I will refer to the Greek tragedy *Oedipus Rex* for a brief comparison. Toward the end of Sophocles' play, queen-mother Jocasta, who knows the truth, prohibits Oedipus from looking into the incestuous fact, saying, "Yet do not do it. I implore you, do not do it." But Oedipus says, "I must, I cannot leave the truth unknown." Then he is confronted with the prohibited incestuous fact. The mother kills herself; the son blinds himself at having brought about the loss of his mother. This catastrophic development is very similar to the tragic consequence of the Japanese

[4]It was not unusual in the old days for a woman to be seriously injured and become very sick or even die at the time of delivery, so that the legend of the injured mother reflects an external reality of those times.

[5]Heisaku Kosawa, known as "the father of Japanese psychoanalysis," developed his theory of the "Ajase complex" from stories found in Buddhist scripture (Kosawa, 1931). In Kosawa's version of the Ajase story, Prince Ajase tried to kill his mother because he became disillusioned when he learned that she had attempted to kill him by giving birth to him. Feeling guilty, Ajase then developed a skin disease. Kosawa contrasted his theory with the Oedipus complex, as the "Ajase complex" centered on the theme of matricide or maternal conflict. I think that acute disillusionment from the idealized mother played an important role in generating Ajase's matricidal wish.

stories developing around the maternal prohibition against looking as I described it above.[6]

The finest form of discovery *(anagnorisis)* is one attended by reversals *(peripeteia)* like that which goes with the discovery in the Oedipus story, as Aristotle points out in his *Poetics*. In the Japanese tragedies of prohibition and its breaking, the discovery is most effective when it coincides with the reversal. Thus in a Christian illustration of a pelican-mother, one may unconsciously see the injured mother or the dead mother behind this devoted mother, the reversal figure; although one will consciously think, "Christ died for us." According to the Japanese plot, the bird-mother may fly away soon, so that her existence becomes transient.

Valuable and Transient

Finally, I would like to point out that some *Ukiyoe* artists deal with infantile sexuality and adult sexuality interchangeably or in parallel (see Figure 13.13). Judging from her dress and hairstyle one can tell that the mother in some pictures is also a courtesan entertaining her guest.

In fact, the mother looking after her child and making love to her husband can happen at the same time or alternatively, not exclusively, as parents and baby in the nuclear family of Japan usually sleep together side by side in the same room. In the middle of making love, the parents sometimes have to keep their sexual intercourse from the child's attention by playing together with the child, so that they do not become sexually exclusive if everything goes well. People often remember these efforts made by the parents as a matter of laughter when they grow up.

Thus we have seen how the Japanese mother does her best to render the early oedipal situation "peaceful." She tries to make the preoedipal and the oedipal relationship coexist. She often succeeds, but this valuable coexistence could be unstable. As a traumatic consequence of abrupt confrontation with mother's fragility, we have many clinical cases which center on a serious

---

[6]In Greek mythology, Orpheus broke the prohibition against looking and lost Eurydice (informed by P. Hartocollis).

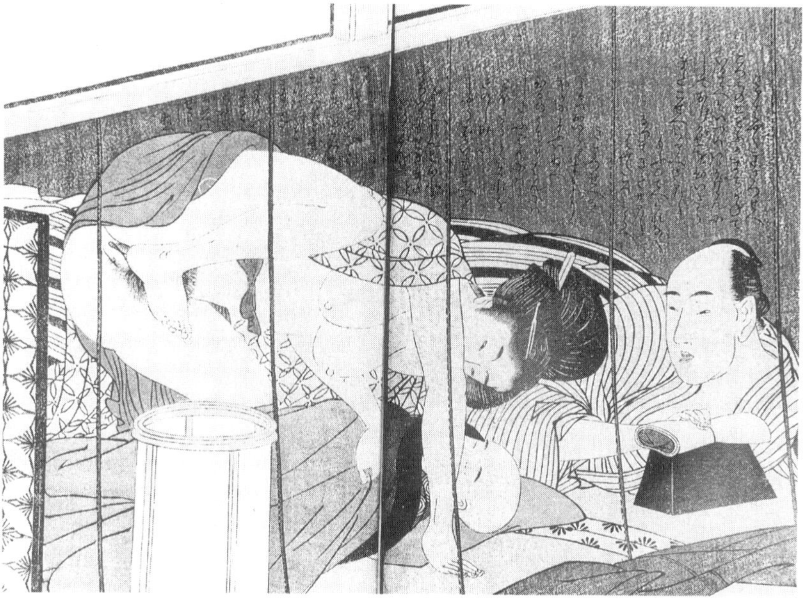

Figure 13.13: Artist—Kitagwa Utamaro (Private Collection)

sense of debt, which is called *on* in Japanese, and the obligation for reparation. In analyzing the conflict which may find expression in the patient's transference and repeated acting out of masochistic or suicidal behavior, one may discover a conscious or unconscious pathological accumulation of debt or guilt toward the benevolent mother.

As Freud (1916) said, "Transience value is scarcity value in time. Limitation in the possibility of an enjoyment raises the value of the enjoyment" (p. 305). The phenomenon of transience also develops into a more mature concept in Japanese art as *mononoaware,* literally meaning "pathos of things and beings." It tends to focus on the impermanence of things and the fragility of beings, and one is supposed to have a capacity to appreciate it, to feel grateful for it. It is floating, like the soap bubbles of the picture. With the help of artists, one may be able to catch a glimpse of the transient moment when the bubbles are gone.

References

Aristotle (1927), *The Poetics,* trans. W. Hamilton Fyfe. London: William Heinemann, 1960.

Bruner, J. (1975), The capacity for joint visual attention in the infant. *Nature,* 253:265–266.

Freeman, D. (1981), Mythological portrayal of developmental processes major intrapsychic restructuralizations. *The Psychoanalytic Study of Society,* 9:326–340. New York: International Universities Press.

Freud, S. (1916), On transience. *Standard Edition,* 14:303–307. London: Hogarth Press, 1957.

——— (1920), Beyond the Pleasure Principle. *Standard Edition,* 18:1–64. London: Hogarth Press, 1955.

Kitayama, O. (1985), Pre-oedipal "taboo" in Japanese folk tragedies. *Internat. Rev. Psychoanal.,* 12:173–186.

——— (1991), The wounded caretaker and guilt. *Internat. Rev. Psychoanal.,* 18:229–240.

——— (1994), Japanese tragic legends and a maternal prohibition. *Res. Bull. Educat. Psychology* (Faculty of Education, Kyusyu University), 39:7–16.

——— (1995), Symbolic transitionality and maternal disillusionment. Presentation at 39th International Psychoanalytic Association Congress.

Kosawa, H. (1931), Two kinds of guilt feelings—The Ajase complex. *Japanese J. Psychoanal.,* 1:5–9, 1954.

Winnicott, D. (1953), Transitional objects and transitional phenomena. *Internat. J. Psycho-Anal.,* 34:89–97.

——— (1971), *Playing and Reality.* London: Tavistock.

Name Index

Abraham, K., 176
Acosta, F. X., 115
Alford, F., 201
Anderson, C., 129
Anthony, E., 218–219
Aristotle, 187, 189, 202, 203, 267

Bailey, J. M., 129, 131–132
Balint, A., 56
Balint, M., 56, 117
Bayer, R. V., 114
Bell, A. P., 131–132
Benedek, T., 218–219
Bergler, E., 86–87, 114
Bergman, A., 95, 151–152, 213
Bergmann, M., 221
Bion, W. R., xi, 19, 20, 31–34, 89
Birksted-Breen, D., 87–88
Blum, E., 226
Blum, H., xv, 144, 145, 212–213, 218, 222, 226
Bohlen, J., 129
Bouchard, J. R., 129
Bouchard, T. J., 129
Bouvet, M., 9
Braunschweig, D., 102–103
Britton, R., xiv, 30, 32, 176, 177, 178, 195–196, 230
Bruner, J., 256
Brunswick, R. M., 4, 4*n*, 173, 212
Burgner, M., 151–152
Byrne, W., 131

Cabaj, R. P., 122
Caretta, R. A., 129
Cave, T., 180
Chasseguet-Smirgel, J., 64, 72, 90, 147, 173–174, 220–221
Coates, S., 133
Courtney, K., 131

Dare, C., 80
D'Augelli, A. R., 122
Davis, R. H., 68
De Mijolla, A., 105
De Mijolla Mellor, S., 105
de Monchy, R., 89–90
Devereux, G., 69, 221
Diamond, M., 129
Diner, D., 91
Dorpat, T. L., 155
Dostoevsky, I., 214–215
Downey, J. I., xiii, 115, 117, 122, 124–125, 127, 131

Easterling, P. E., 246
Ebers, G., 129
Eckert, E. D., 129
Edgecumbe, R., 151–152
Ehrhardt, A. A., 121
Eickhoff, F.-W., xii
Eidelberg, L., 85, 141*n*
Eissler, K. R., 4, 90
Ellis, H., 115
Erickson, M., 121

Fain, M., 102–103
Fairbairn, W. R. D., 95
Feinleib, M. R., 141*n*
Feldman, F., 230

Fenichel, O., 150–151
Fliers, E., 131
Florance, E., 215
Freeman, D., 256, 262
Freidman, R., xiii, xvii
Freud, A., 147
Freud, S., ix, xi, xiii, xvi, 1–2, 3–9, 13, 17, 22, 37, 39–41, 44, 47–48, 49, 58–59, 65, 77–84, 84–85*n*, 86–90, 92, 95–96, 97–98, 100, 103, 116, 120, 121, 123–124, 128, 132, 133, 134, 140, 142–143, 148, 154, 156*n*, 162, 171–174, 175–176, 180, 181, 183, 192, 194–195, 197, 200, 201, 204, 209–212, 214, 217, 222, 223, 229–230, 242, 253, 256, 268
Friedman, R. C., 114, 115–116, 117, 122, 124–125, 127, 129, 130, 131
Frosch, J., 145
Furer, M., 95

Galaburda, A. J., 131
Galenson, E., 123, 151–152
Gammelgaard, J., xiv
Gardiner, M., 4
Gay, P., 120
Geschwind, N., 131
Gillespie, W. H., 146, 154
Gooren, L., 131
Gorski, R. A., 131
Goux, J.-J., 182
Goy, R. W., 119
Green, A., xi, xvi-xvii, 5, 8, 13, 14, 16, 96, 99, 107, 133, 183, 214
Greenacre, P., 152, 163*n*
Greenberg, J. R., 95–96
Greenson, R. R., 144*n*, 146–147
Grinberg, L., 89
Grunberger, B., xii, 57, 85–89, 189
Guntrip, H., 95

Haldeman, D. C., 115
Hammersmith, S. K., 131–132
Hanly, C., xiv, 191, 195, 197, 201, 202
Hanly, M. A. F., 85
Hart, B., 119
Hartocollis, P., xi, 267*n*
Hegel, G. W. F., 181, 182
Heraclitus, 192
Herdt, G., 120
Hershey, D., 162*n*
Heston, L., 129
Hippolitus, 203
Hirschfeld, M., 115
Hoffman, L., 155*n*
Holder, A., 80

Ikonen, P., xii
Isay, R., 115, 127

Jacobson, E., 95, 152
Johnson, J. E., 116
Jones, E., 21, 55–56

Kahn, M. M. R., 153–154
Kanzer, M., 215, 221–222
Kernberg, O., xii, xvii, 97, 102, 105, 106, 107, 108, 117, 145, 153, 213
Kestenberg, J. S., 64–65, 152
Kierkegaard, S., 177–178
Kitayama, O., xv, 256, 262, 264–265, 266
Klein, M., xi, xvi, 9, 21, 25–26, 31, 80–83, 89, 95, 98, 176, 195, 210, 213
Kohlberg, L., 121
Kohut, H., 96, 153, 213
Kosawa, H., 266*n*
Kösters, C., 91
Krause, R., 96
Kristeva, J., xi, 46

Lacan, J., xi, xvi, 6, 39, 41–42, 97
Lampl-de Groot, J., 152
Laplanche, J., xii, xvi, 96, 98, 100, 103, 104–105, 108

Leibniz, G. W. H., 199
Limentani, A., 83
Loewald, H., 181
Lothane, Z., 156*n*
Lower, R., 215
Lutolf, P., 96

MacLean, P. D., 133–134
Magee, M., 115
Mahler, M. S., 95, 103, 151–152, 213
Mahony, P., 5
Marinov, V., 215
Martin, J., 129
Masters, W. H., 116
McClintock, M., 120
McDougall, J., 9
Meissner, W., 145
Meltzer, D., 83
Meyer-Bahlberg, H. F. L., 131
Miller, J. C., 115
Millon, T., 121
Mitchell, S. A., 95–96
Money, J., 116, 121

Nietzsche, F., 77, 89, 182

Obholzer, K., 4
Odier, C. H., 85
Ogden, T., 176
O'Shaughnessy, E., 230
Ovesey, L., 145

Pankejeff, S., 5
Parsons, B., 131
Parsons, M., xv
Patterson, C. J., 122
Pillard, R. C., 129
Pine, F., 95, 151–152, 213
Plato, 192, 196*n*, 202, 203, 204
Poumadere, J., 129
Propping, P., 129

Rado, S., 145*n*
Rangell, L., 217
Rascovsky, A., 218
Rascovsky, M., 218
Reik, T., 90, 217, 219
Rice, G., 129
Ricoeur, P., 179, 183
Risch, N., 129
Riviere, J., 80–81, 85
Roiphe, H., 151–152
Rosenfeld, H., 106, 164–165
Rosner, H., 218
Ross, J., 221
Rudnytsky, P., 182

Sandler, J., 80, 155
Sartre, J.-P., 177, 178, 191–192
Schönberger, K., 91
Segal, C., 179
Segal, H., xi, xiv, 26
Shakespeare, W., 193, 201
Slimp, J. C., 119
Socarides, C. W., xiii, xvii, 83, 113–114, 142–143, 144–145, 147, 148–150, 151–152, 153, 155
Socrates, 192
Solms, W., 4
Sophocles, ix, xiv, 172, 176, 178–181, 182–184, 187–203, 218, 229–250, 266
Sor, D., 89
Spiegel, L. A., 90
Spinoza, B., 199
Stein, T. S., 122
Steiner, J., 84, 183
Stern, D., 103
Stoller, R. J., 9, 68, 103, 117, 121, 151
Sullivan, H. S., 95

Tabak de Bianchedi, E., 89

Van der Leeuw, P. J., 152
Vernant, J.-P., 179

Weil, A., 212–213
Weinberg, M. S., 131–132
Weinrich, J. D., 129
Whitam, F. L., 129

Wiedeman, G. H., 114
Wilson, E. O., 121
Winnicott, D. W., x, 6, 19, 21, 42, 95, 254
Wright, R., 121–122
Wurmser, L., 89

Yates, A., 123

Zucker, K. J., 131–132

Subject Index

Acting out, 18–19
in obligatory homosexuals, 153–154
Active ego-directed experimental play action, 153–157
Addictive sexuality, 9
Adult sexual fantasy, 125–126
Adult sexuality, 267
condensations from oedipal and preoedipal past in, 117–118
hormonal considerations in, 116–117
instinct mastery and, 202–206
resolution of Oedipus complex and, 182–184
Affect theory, 99–100
Affective messages, 108
mother's, 104–105
unconscious, 104
Affects
in object relations, 97
as primary motivators, 96
Agamemnon, fate of, 191–192
Agamemnon (Aeschylus), 181
Aggression, 70–71
in pathological organizations, 84
preoedipal, 213
superego and, 79
theme of, in *Trachiniae*, 235–237
toddler's projection of, 212
Aggressive-competitive behavior, 124–125
Aggressive object relations, 89
Aggressor, identification with, 71, 220
Aggressor-father, 216, 217
Alpha elements, 32, 34
Ambivalence, 21
Anagnorisis, 267
Anal eroticism, 8
Anal fixations, 14–15, 18
Anal masturbation, 26–27
Anality, 7, 8
primary, 14
secondary, 14–15
Analyst
self-reflection on countertransference of, 105
unconscious communication from, 108
Androgen
organizational effects of, 124–125
prenatal exposure to, 131
Androgyny, 49
Annihilation, threats of, in homosexuality, 163–164
Anxiety. *See also* Castration anxiety; Separation anxiety
protection from, 86
Aphanisis, 21
Apollo
forces of, 182
influence of, on Oedipus' fate, 189–191
Archaic sexuality, xi, 1–2, 9–10
Asceticism, 203
in instinct mastery, 205
limitation of, 204
Atheism, 52
Atonement, 181, 212
Autoerotic activity, 159, 162
Autoerotic fantasy, 159, 163

early infantile, 166
Autopotency, 67–68
Awareness, triangulation of, 196

Behavioral genetics, 128–130
Being and Nothingness (Sartre), 177
Belief, 178
Beta elements, 31–32, 34
Bisexual fantasies, 222–225
Bisexuality, 37, 49
denial of, 39
female, 38, 50–52
female psychical, 45–46
unconscious, 52
Blind seeing, 180–181, 183–184
Blindness
defensive, 183
understanding and, 180–181
Body representations, 152
Borderline personality disorder, 1
neurosis and, 12–13
preoedipal pathology of, xi
Wolf Man case and, 1–2, 3–9
Borderline Personality Disorder conference, xi
Borderline personality organization
in homosexuals in analysis, 114
symbiotic link with, 105–106
Brain, triune, 133–134
Brain-behavioral integrations, 119–120
Breast
equation of penis with, 114
erotic response to relationship to, 100–101
in need gratification, 254–256
The Brothers Karamazov (Dostoevski), 214–215

Castration
denial of, 7–8
female, 265–266
Castration anxiety, xii, 7–8, 12–13, 63–64, 122
in homosexual dread, 162
passive-phallic fulfillment and, 66
self-induced, 86–87
Castrator-castrated relationship, 72
Catharsis, 189, 203–204
Central nervous system, sex difference in structure and function of, 131
Child abuse, crippling effects of, 218–219
Child being beaten fantasy, 38–39
Child-mother relationship. *See* Mother-child relationship
Child-phallus, 48–49, 51, 70, 71–72
Childhood
erotic fantasy and orgasm during, 123
same-sex experimentation during, 141
sexual fantasy in, 125–126
sexual inadequacy in, 57–58
Childhood Gender Identity Disorder (GID), 133
Childhood sexuality
distortion of, xiii
retrospective distortion of, 119–120
variable intensity in, 126–127
Civilization
versus savagery, 235–237
as sublimated masochism, 90
Clitoris, support in, 43
Cognitive bridges, 125–126
Cognitive development, 195–196
Coitus, destructive, 73
Collective memory, restratification of, 91
Competitive-aggressive fantasies, oedipal, 124–125
Compromise formation, 139
Conflicts, genitalization of, 1
Consummatory behaviors, 97
Container-contained relationship, xi, 31–32, 34
Copulatory behavior, impaired, 119
Countertransference, 200
unconscious affective messages in, 104

The Crane Wife, 263–266
Crime and Punishment (Dostoevski), 214–215
Critical self-reflection, capacity for, 198
Curiosity, as oedipal wish, 66

Death, sexuality and, 21–22
Death drive, xii, xvi-xvii, 78–79, 98, 99
Death instinct, 204
Debt, toward benevolent mother, 267–268
Defense mechanisms, 1
  phallic organization as, 60–61
Defensive genitalization, 1
Defensive sexualization, 13
Defensiveness, 68
Deianira myth, 231–237
Delphic oracle, 220–221
Depressive position, xi, xvi, 21, 80
  creative aspects of, 82
  Oedipus complex and, 25–30, 176
Destiny, 191–192
Determinism, 201
Developmental process, Oedipus complex in, 229–250
Developmental psychoanalytic theory, 128–131
Differentia specifica, 68
Dionysian forces, 182
Discovery, 266–267
Disillusionment
  acute, 263
  transience and, 254–261
  transitional process of, 262
Dora case, 211
Dreams
  in Greek philosophy, 192
  in latent homosexual, 148–149
  manifest content of, 200
  pseudo-oedipal, 27–30
Drive-instinct theory, 116–117
Drive theory, 21–22
  contemporary, 95
  object relations theory and, 95–97
Drives
  classification of, 98
  contemporary psychoanalytic view of, 97–98
  versus instincts, 100
  renunciation of, 90
  traumatic experience in development of, 104–105
Dual drive theory, xii
  object relations and, 95–97
Dual relationships, 16
Dysenteria, 5

Ego
  boundaries of, 98–99
  preoedipal issues and fragility of, 212–213
Ego-dystonic homosexuality, 149–150
Ego-syntonicity, 149–150
Eleos, 176
Emotional reality, mutual, 56–57
Engulfing mother, fear of, 153
Envy
  in Kleinian theory, 82–83
  in Oedipus complex, 82
Erogenous gratification, 100–101
Erotic, sacred and, 22
Erotic desire, 116–117
Erotic fantasy
  preoedipal, 123
  primitive, 96–97
Erotic object, xiii
Erotic response, 102–103
Excluded third person, 105
Exhibitionism, xii, 18, 66–68

False good conscience, 91
Family triangle, tensions of, 241–242
Fantasy. *See* Autoerotic fantasy; Erotic fantasy; Homosexual fantasy; Matricidal fantasy; Phallic fantasies; Sexual fantasy; Unconscious fantasy
Fascination, 67
Fatalism, 202

Father
as excluded third person, 105
as homosexual ogre, 69
incorporating phallus of, 87–88, 165–166
murderous attitudes toward, 214–215
Father-son relationship, 245–246
competitive, 249–250
missing, 241
Fellatio, motivation for, 114
Female castration, 265–266
Female genitals, unraveling mystery of, 217–218
Female sexuality, controversy over, ix-x
Feminine masochism, 45–46
Feminine sadomasochism, 50
Femininity, castration consolidation with, 8
Fetishism, 5
Fixation, points of, 9–10
Folktales, Japanese, xv, 251–268
Foreclosure, 1, 6–7
Frames, 118
Free association process, 200
Free will, 201
Furies, 214

Gender dimorphism, 132–133
Gender identity
development of, 121–122
foundation for, 151–152
homosexual dread and, 166
perversion and, 151–154
problems with, 141*n*
Genetics, behavioral, 128–130
Genital Oedipus complex, mature, 35–36
Genitalization, defensive, 13
Girl-mother dyad, 44
Girl-phallus, 46
Gods, 188–189, 191–192
fear of, 202–203
Good enough mothering/parenting, 195
failure of need gratification in, 255–256
Grammar, inborn sense of, 31*n*
Grandiose self, pathological, 106–107
Guilt
depressive position and, 80
emergence of, xvi
of incest, 219–220
masochistic discharge of, 87–88
toward benevolent mother, 267–268
unconscious sense of, 79, 81

Hallucinations, 28–29
Hallucinatory wish-fulfillment, 163
Hatred, xii
affect of, 101
Heracles myth, 231–237
Heritability, 128–129
Homosexual desire
psychoanalytic explanation of, 139–167
sexual fantasy in, 142–144
Homosexual dread, xiii-xiv
clinical explanation of, 139
defensive function of, 165–166
description of, 140–141
gender identity and, 151–154
literature on, 144–148
with neurotic personality organization, 156–166
versus obsessional neurosis, 150–151
in personality organization, 156
in psychiatric patients, 146–147
psychoanalytic explanation of, 139–167
sexual fantasy and, 141–144, 164
Homosexual fantasy
homosexual dread and, 141–144, 164
in latent homosexual, 148–149
matricidal conflict in, 222–225
Homosexual feelings, 141–142
Homosexual ideation, formerly repressed, 147–148
Homosexual love, sublimation of, 203

Homosexual panic, 144–145
Homosexual transference, 12
Homosexuality, xvii. *See also* Male homosexuality
  ego-dystonic, 149–150
  factors in shift from latent to overt, 148
  fear of, 10–11
  function of behavior, 153–154
  latent, 148–149
  Oedipus complex and, 113–134
  primary, 43
  psychodynamic formulations regarding, xiii
  psychodynamic versus etiologic issues of, 130–131
  psychoneuroendocrinology and, 131–133
  superego role in, 154–156
  as unresolved conflicts, 113–114
Homosexuals
  higher functioning, 115
  obligatory, 142–143, 153–154, 166
  preoedipal type I, 153
Hormones
  in adult sexual experience, 116–117
  organizational and activational effects of, 124–125
  prenatal exposure to, 131–132
Hubris, 182, 188–189
  destruction of, 180–181
Human condition, 201–202
Human nature, 192–193
Hypochondriacal fantasies, 34

Identification, internalization processes of, 107
Illness, narcissistic gain from, 85–86
Illusion, female bisexuality and, 52
Imaginary playmates, 127
Incest
  guilt of, 219–220
  parricide and, 181
  prohibition of, 19
Incestuous seduction, 216–217
Incestuous wish, 158
  in Oedipus myth, 180, 181
  universality of, 121–122, 126–128
Infantile genital organization, 40–41
Infantile sexuality, 173, 267
  displaced manifestations of, 18
Instincts
  versus drives, 100
  mastery of, 202–206
Internal tormentor, 33
Internalized object relations, 81, 107–108
  all bad, 101
  basis of, 101
  pathological, xii-xiii, 153–154
Internalized soothing structures, 162
International Psychoanalytic Symposium at Delphi, Fourth, x-xi
Interpretation, 199–200
The Interpretation of Dreams (Freud), 175–176, 209, 210–211
Izanami myth, 262

Japanese cultural transience, 251–268
Japanese mythology, themes of, 262–263
Jealousy
  as oedipal wish, 66
  in Oedipus complex, 82

Kairos, 39–41
  in girls, 42
Kleinian theory, xvi
  negative therapeutic reaction and, 80–84
Knowledge
  versus belief, 178
  ignorance and, 180–181
  objectivity and, 193–194

Language
  cathected, 50–52
  function of, 41–42
  illusory nature of, 46
  in psychic life organization, 42–43

right hemisphere in, 43*n*
subjective experience in, 104
thought and, 37–38
Libidinal sympathetic excitation, 77–78
Libido, 2, 98
contemporary psychoanalytic theorizing and, 95–108
origin of, in erogenous zones, 100–101
Life drive, 98
Looking, breaking prohibition against, 262, 263, 264–267
Love
drive for, 22
object of, 173
sex and, 21

Male homosexuality
clinical considerations in, 126–128
Oedipus complex and, 113–134
reasons for revising paradigm of, 114–116
Male homosexuals, in analysis, 114–115
Male sexuality, 140
Manic position, 81
Marriage
between human and animal, 265*n*
in Japanese myths, 262
Masochism
cultural dimension of, 89–92
Grunberger's conception of, 85–89
moral, 77–80
Masochistic defense, 87–88
Masochistic position, 83
Masturbation
anal, 26–27
reinforcing focus on own pleasure, 62–63
Masturbatory behavior, 119
Maternal incestuous fantasy, 221
Matricidal fantasy
case illustration of, 222–225
in mold of parricidal fantasy, 214
Oedipus complex and, 225–226
in Rat-Man case, 211–212
universality of, 225–226
Matricidal transference relationship, 226
Matricide, xv
in Dostoevski novels, 215
internalized prohibition of, 226
in myth and literature, 213–222
preoedipal issues in, 212–213
symbolic, 182
traditional psychoanalysis and, 209–212
Meanness, phallic, 70–71
Mental apparatus, Oedipus complex and, 30–31
Mental space, elements of, 31–34
Minoan-Mycenaean civilization, 48
fusion of, 44
Mononoaware, 268
Moral masochism, xii
Freud's conception of, 77–80
Moral rationality, roots of, 202–203
Moses and Monotheism (Freud), 209–210
Mother
affective messages of, 105
all-good idealized, 99
castrated-castrating, 48
castrating and vengeful, 212
debt or guilt toward, 267–268
destructive, 218–219
disillusionment by, 254–261
dreams of death of, 210–211
engulfing, 153
erotic desire for, 121–122
hostile, enigmatic responses of, 99
hostility toward, 210
identification with, 69–70
incestuous feelings for, 158
injury of, 265–267
murderous rage toward, 224–225
murderous wishes of, 221–222
omniscient, 220–221
phallic, 212, 223–224
primary feminine identification with, 152

psychic image of, 173
rejection by, 262
relationship with, during depressive position, 25
separation from, 173
transitional, 262
unconscious fantasy of, 103–104
violent separation from, 182
Mother-child relationship
libidinal organizations of, 70
murderous rage displaced from, 224
preoedipal, 181
transience of, 254–261
Mother imago, seductive, 11
Mother-infant relationship
mother's unconscious fantasy in, 103–104
restored unity of, 212–213
Mother-son relationship, sexualization of, 242–244, 248
Murderous rage
from mother-child conflict, 224
object of, 213
toward mother, 224–225
Mutuality, 56–57
defense against incompetence for, 72–73
disappointment of wish for, 60
phallic relationship and, 72
in phallic universe, 73
rejection of, 67–68
Mystery, 38–42
of female bisexuality, 50–52
Mythology
Japanese, 262–263
matricide in, 213–222

Narcissism, xii, xvi-xvii
male homosexuality and, 164–165
malignant, 107
at metapsychological level, 106
pathological, 106–107
Narcissistic humiliation
inversion of, 65
phallic defense against, 61
Narcissistic impairment, 14–15
Narcissistic insult
with failure of mutuality, 57
with superiority of object, 58
Narcissistic libido, 205–206
Narcissistic neurosis, 17
Narcissistic transference, 155–156
Narcissus myth, xi
Natural sex, 21
Nature, transience in, 251–254
Need gratification
breast in, 254–256
failure of, 255–256
Needs, primary, 199
Negation, 147–148
Negative, work of, 21
Negative therapeutic reaction, 79–80
Kleinian perspective on, 80–84
Neoneeds, 9
Neuroendocrine determinants, prenatal, 132
Neuroendocrine system, 125
Neurosis
borderline personality disorder and, 12–13
etiology of, 121
obsessional, 150–151
perversion and, 17
sexuality and, 2–3
Neurotic personality organization, 156–166
Nonconformity, 131–132
Nonneurotic structures, sexuality in, 1–22
Nuclear complex, 171–172

Object relations, 19. *See also* Internalized object relations
affects in constructing, 97
poor, 15–16
theory of, x
dual drive theory and, xii, 95–97
Object seeking, 199
Objectivism, 198–201
Objectivity
about self, 197–198
in knowledge, 193–194

Obligatory homosexuality, 166
Obligatory homosexuals, 142–143
  acting out in, 153–154
Obsessional/anal fixation neurosis, 4–5
Obsessional neurosis, 150–151
Oedipal conflict
  inverted, 244–247
  unresolved, 113–114, 120–121
Oedipal seduction, xii
Oedipal-sexual wishes
  collapse of, 73–74
  expression of, 66–68
Oedipal situation, 195–196
Oedipal triangle, xv, 175–176
  in cognitive development, 195–196
  third position of, 177–179
Oedipus
  responsibility and, 201–202
  significance of, 73–74
  Trachiniae and, 231–232
  tragedy and history of, 187–188
Oedipus-1, 38–39, 42, 47, 50
Oedipus-2, 39, 42, 49, 50
  mechanism of, 47–48
Oedipus at Colonus, 172, 181, 184
Oedipus complex
  archaic matrix of, 90–91
  controversy over, ix-x
  before depressive position, 25–30
  elements of mental space and, 31–34
  end-point of, 229–231
  envy and jealousy in, 82
  Freudian theory of, 172–174
  instinct mastery and adult sexuality in, 202–206
  inverted, 244–247
  Japanese view of, xv
  Kleinian views of, 172, 230–231
  lifelong process of, 229–250
  male homosexuality and, 113–134
  matricidal fantasies and, 209–226
  mental apparatus and, 30–31
  new perspectives on, 25–36
  Oedipus myth and, xvi-xvii
  phallic sexuality and, 174–175
  phallicism and, 55–74
  positive, 113–114
  primitive, 35–36
  in psychoanalysis, 171–172
  rationality and, 193–197
  reconceptualized, 120–122
  regression from morality to, 78
  resolution of, 182–184
  self-awareness and, 34–36, 193
  third position and, 171–184
  triangulation of awareness in, 196
  as unitary entity, 122–124
  universality of, 188–191
  in women, 37–52
Oedipus complex fixation, negative, 3
Oedipus myth, x
  father in, 215–216
  mother figures in, 215
  in sexuality, xiv
  Sphinx in, 216–217
Oedipus Rex (Sophocles), ix, xiv-xv, 172, 176, 188–191, 202–203
  breaking prohibition in, 266–267
  interpreting tragedy of, 178–179
  self-recognition in, 180–181
"Oedipus Without the Complex" (Vernant), 179
Oral fixations, 18
  intense, 15–16
Oral phase, 9
Orality, theory of, 86–87
Orestes myth, 214
Organizing experiences, early sexual, 142–143
Orgasm, during early childhood, 123
Other, 2, 19, 49
  leaving, 52

Parallel looking, 256
Paranoid anxiety, 164–165
Paranoid-schizoid position, 26, 84, 89, 195
Parasitic double, 92
Parent. *See also* Father; Mother
  murderous wishes of, 221–222

as self-object, 195
sexual desire for, 123
Parent-child relationship, breakdown of, 57
Parental couple, hatred of, 30
Parental deprivation, early, 163–164
Parricidal wish, universality of, 121–122
Parricide, 87–88, 209–210
Dostoevski and, 214–215
in Oedipus myth, 180, 181
as substitute for matricide, 226
Part object relationship, 27–28, 35–36
Passive phallicism, 65–66
Pathological personality organizations, 84
Pathos, 180
Pederasty, of Laius, 215–216
Penetration anxiety, 12–13
Penis
cathexis of, 39–40
equation of, with breast, 114
Penis-as-link, 87–88
Penis envy, xi-xii
Personal destiny, 192
Personality disorders, serious, xii-xiii
Personality structure, 121
Perverse impulses
ego acceptance/nonacceptance of, 167
formation of, 163*n*
Perverse universe, 72–73
Perversion
function of, 151–154
neurosis and, 17
Pervert, absence of dread in, 147
Phaedrus (Plato), 203
Phallic defensive organization, 60
Phallic fantasies, 62–63, 173–174
Phallic fixation, 62–63
Phallic hegemony, 71–72
Phallic Kairos, 37–38, 39–41, 43
influence of, 43–44
Phallic meanness, 70–71
Phallic monism, 38, 39, 40–41, 50
unconscious, 52
Phallic mother, fantasies of, 223–224
Phallic-narcissistic satisfaction, 65
Phallic-oedipal sexual fantasies, 59
Phallic organization, 58–59
as defense, 60–61
Phallic phase, 39–40
Phallic primacy, 40–42
Phallic sadomasochistic defense, 65–66
Phallic sexuality, 174–175
Phallic signifying order, 51
Phallic universe, 72–73
Phallicism, x, xi-xii
as defensive organization, 55–56
encouragement of, 68–70
idealization of, 70
image of power and, 61–62
imaginary, 47–48
oedipal problems and, 55–74
passive, 65–66
sexuality and violence in, 73
Phallus
child as, 48–49, 51
detachable, 63
as extraneous, 37–52, 42–47
illusory nature of, 43–47
as signifier, 43
without incarnation, 39
Phallus-baby, 70, 71–72
Phobos, 176
Pleasure, forbidden and shameful, 56
Pleasure-giving object, 99
Pleasure principle, 204
Poetics (Plato), 202
Polymorphous perverse thoughts, 10, 162–163
Power
image of, 61–62
in phallus, 64–65
Predepressive oedipal constellation, 26
Pregenital fixations, 1, 6, 12–13, 20
development of, 13–16
genitalization of, 9
Pregenital phase, xi
emphasis on, xiv

Pregnant women, murderous rage against, 226
Preoedipal mother, separation from, 173
Preoedipal stage, xvi
ego fragility and issues of, 212–213
shifting emphasis on, 171–172
Preoptic-anterior-hypothalamus, 119
Primal horde, parricide by, 209–210
Primal scene, 59–60
fantasies of, xii, 31
Primitive projections, 31–32
Prohibition
breaking, 264–267
breaking of, 262, 263
Projective identification, 83
self lost through, 84
Projective identifications, 28
Pseudohallucinations, 14
Pseudoheterosexuality, 146
Pseudohomosexual anxiety, 145–146
Pseudopsychopathy, 10–12
Psychic life, intelligibility of, 199
Psychic reality
ancient Greek quest for, 191–193
universality of Oedipus complex in, 188–191
Psychoanalysis
asceticism and catharsis in, 204
centrality of Oedipus complex in, 171–172
matricide and, 209–212
in self-knowledge, 199–201
Psychoanalytic ego psychology, x
Psychoanalytic theory, 95–108
Psychobiology, 128–131
Psychoneuroendocrinology, 128
in homosexuality, 131–133
Psychoses, etiology of, 121
Psychosexual development, x
Oedipus complex in, 175–176
Puberty, sex steroids in, 125

Rage, repetitive activation of, 107
Rape fantasy, 15
Rat Man case, 4–5, 211–212
Rationality
emergence of, 197–198
Oedipus complex and, 193–197
Reality
external versus internal, 25–26
testing of, 98–99
Reality principle, 194
Regression, sexuality in, 20
Repression, 5–6
foreclosure and, 6–7
splitting mechanisms and, 103–104
Repressive fixations, 17–18
Republic (Plato), 202
Responsibility
agency and, 189
Oedipus and, 201–202
Reversals, 267

Sadomasochism, 17–18, 38–39
feminine, 50
phallic, 65–66
Sadomasochistic unconscious fantasy, primitive, 96–97
Satisfaction, memory versus experience of, 194–195
Savagery
versus civilization, 235–237
sexuality and, 237–240
Schizoid position, xvi
Schreber case, 156*n*
Screen experience, 88–89
Self
origin of, 177–179
as relation, 177–178
Self-awareness
development of, xi
Oedipus complex and, 34–36, 193
Self-blinding, 180–181, 183–184
Self-consciousness
emergence of, xiv
origin of, 177–179
third position of oedipal triangle and, 177–179
unreflecting, 178
Self-criticism, development of, 197–198

Self-destructive drive, 96, 98
Self-knowledge
  dialectic with self-ignorance, 180–181
  oedipal triangulation in, 195–197
Self-object
  differentiation of, in homosexuals, 152–153
  double splitting of, 107–108
  parent as, 195
Self-other differentiation, 194–195
Self psychology, 96
Self-recognition, 180–181
  process of, 184
Self representation/object representation, 101
Self-righteousness, 92
Sensible, versus signifier, 42–47
Sensuousness
  dissociation from signifier, 44–45
  of girl, 43
Separation anxiety, early childhood, 163–164
Separation-individuation process
  preoedipal aggression and, 213
  unresolved, 152
Sex role nonconformity, 131–132
Sex scripts, 117–118
Sex steroids, 124–125
Sexual arousal, childhood, 123
Sexual behavior, stimulation-ablation studies of, 119
Sexual excitement, xii
Sexual experience
  discontinuities between childhood and adulthood, 119–120
  hormonal considerations in, 116–117
  integrated patterned activity in, 118
  oedipal and preoedipal past in, 117–118
Sexual fantasy
  in adulthood and childhood, 125–126
  homosexual, 159
  homosexual desire and, 142–144
  homosexual dread and, 141–144
  patients' history of, 115
Sexual identity. *See* Gender identity
Sexual inadequacy, 57–58
Sexual organizing experiences, homosexual, 142–143
Sexual part objects, 11
Sexual perversion, 6–7
Sexual relationships, triangular, 247
Sexuality. *See also* Adult sexuality; Archaic sexuality; Childhood sexuality; Infantile sexuality; Male sexuality
  adult, 116–118, 182–184, 202–206, 267
  childhood, 119–120
  direct manifestations of, 17–18
  double orientation of, 20–21
  as evil, 61
  female, ix-x
  forbidden, 56
  infantile, 173, 267
  Japanese view of, xv
  meaning of, 19–22
  neuroses and, 2–3
  in nonneurotic structures, 1–22
  Oedipus complex in, x-xi
  Oedipus myth in, xiv
  phallic, 174–175
  in psychic life, 16–19
  resolution of Oedipus complex and, 182–184
  theme of, in *Trachiniae*, 237–240
  transience in, 251–254
Sexuality-thought copresence, 39–40
Shameful pleasure, 56
Shock, wish to, 67
"A Short Account of Psycho-Analysis" (Freud), 172–173
Signifier
  dissociation with sensuousness, 44–45
  illusion-disillusionment of, 50
  sensible versus, 42–47
Social responsibility, 195
Sociobiology, 121–122

Soma, 2
Speaking-being copresence, 41–42
Speaking-being expression, 37–38
Sphinx, 216–217
  as destructive mother, 218–219
  riddles of, 217–218
Spirituality, love and, 22
Splitting, 1, 8, 84
  double, 107–108
  in homosexual identity, 153, 154–156
  of maternal love object and murderous urges, 226
  preliminary intuition of, 5
  repression and, 103–104
  self-object, 98–99
  sexual perversion and, 6–7
Stimulation-ablation studies, 119
Subframes, 118
Subject-object differentiation, 194–195
Subjectivism, 198–201
Sublimated masochism, 90
Sublimation
  growth-promoting, 204–205
  spirituality of, 22
Suggestiveness, 67
Suicidal impulses, 211–212
Superego
  aggression as part of, 79
  formation of, 121
  in homosexuality, 154–156
Superwoman, 38–39
Symbiotic relationship, disrupted, 105
Symbolic-phallic order, deceptive, 43–44
Symbolization, 194
  in dreams, 29–30
Symposium (Plato), 203

Taboo, to be broken, 264–267
Teiresias, as blind seer, 180–181, 183–184
Tensions, discharge of, 2
Testosterone, prenatal exposure to, 123
Third position, xiv, 177–179
Thought-language
  copresence of, 41–42
  development of, 37–38
Three Essays on the Theory of Sexuality (Freud), 77–78, 173
Tool fixation, 62–65
Trachiniae (Sophocles)
  aggression and sexuality themes of, 237–240
  clinical material and, 248–250
  inverted Oedipus complex in, 245–247
  Oedipus and, 231–232
  structure and characters of, 234–237
  summary of, 232–234
  triangular relationships in, 240–245, 247
Tragedy, cathartic function of, 203–204
Transference, 199–200
  internalized object relations in, 107–108
  psychotic, 2
Transference-countertransference relationship, 105
Transference mirroring, 156
Transference psychoneuroses, 2–3
Transience
  maternal disillusioning and, 254–261
  in sexuality, 251–254
  value and, 267–268
Transition, 262
  to activity, 18–19
Transitional objects, 255–256, 256–261
Translinguistic experience, 43
Trauma
  in drive development, 104–105
  responsibility for consequences of, 202
Triangular relationships, 16, 249–250
  oedipal, 175–179
  in *Trachiniae*, 240–245, 247
Triangular situation, 26

Triangular space, xiv, 177
escape from, 182–183
Triangulation, 105
oedipal, in cognitive development, 195–196
Triune brain paradigm, 133–134
Two-body relationship, 32

Ukiyoe pictures, 251–254
sexuality in, 267
Unbearable, 38–42
Unconscious, 37–38
Unconscious desire, 101–102
Unconscious fantasy, 103–104
analysis of, 108

Vagina
dentata, 162
discovery of, 51
Valuable, transient and, 267–268
Violence
culture of, xii
as defense, 60–61
hidden, 62
overwhelming sexuality, 13
of phallic-oedipal sexual fantasies, 59
sexuality and, 73
Voyeurism, 18

Wife battering, 226
Witches, burning of, 213–214
Wolf Man case
analysis of, 1–2, 3–9
borderline personality disorder in, xi
fantasies in, 212
negative therapeutic reaction in, 79–80
Women
disillusioned, 44–45
twofold Oedipus complex of, 37–52
Working through, xvi

Zeus, as father, 245–246